THE DIARIES

MUSIC, LOVE AND IMPOSSIBILITIES

by

THE DIARIES

First printing 2025
Cover photo: Chalo Galura

Publisher: The Diaries Productions LTD
ISBN: 978-1-0683414-0-3

There are many more books to come in this series. To read the raw diary entries those books will be made of and to follow us in real time you can go to our website

www.thediaries.band

There you will also find studio releases, videos, our shop for all things Diaries and so much more

Hope to see you on the road

Mark and Maja
The Diaries

January, 2025

Maja:

This book is about some of the hardest times I have ever experienced. It greatly saddens me to admit that during this time, I was not as close to my core family as I've always been. As things got harder on a personal level I started to withdraw and isolate myself from the people that love me unconditionally and I was not able to see the support I had. Now as I've grown, I have learned a lot about myself and I can now realise what a strong family I've had standing by my side, all along.

I want to thank my mum. Who has always been my greatest support and has been standing by my side in everything. I am absolutely heartbroken how things got so wrong during this time, and how blind I was. I will always be so sorry. And now, I am absolutely overjoyed that we've managed to come through to the other side. I love you. Unconditionally. And I know you love me. Always.

And thank you for being the best dog mum to my amazing little Tommy.

I think about you every day.

I also want to thank my family and my friends. All of you. We might not speak that often and as I live all over it is hard to regularly meet. Everytime we meet it's like no time has gone at all! Thank you for being the best!

Camden Town, London, January 2025

PROLOGUE

Maja's Diaries
Stockholm, Thursday February 11, 2021

I feel devastated. Absolutely horrible. Life isn't easy right now. My chest is tight and it burns. I feel cornered with nowhere to go. I want to concentrate on something fun, like playing bass. Preparing for an audition maybe, but my brain simply will not let me focus.

Last Friday I made a couple of phone calls to friends to look for a place to stay in case my home situation became unbearable. Well, here we are. I have one possibility. My dear friend Alexander. Me and Alexander go deep, and have been hanging out regularly since we were about fifteen. So when I called him and told him about the situation last week he said he was going to check with his flatmate/landlord who I quite like. I wouldn't mind staying with them for a while. They have an extra little sleeping alcove which I could make a bit of a refuge home out of. But a couple of days later Alexander got back to me to say they'd turned the little alcove into a home office for the landlord. However, he said I could stay in his room, probably making a space for myself in a corner, but added I would be able to do that for a

1

maximum of two weeks. My heart dropped hearing this. He is the only one of my friends living independently enough to be able to casually have someone stay over. No matter who else I asked, I would only be a huge burden. And since I don't really feel comfortable telling my parents of my situation yet, I can't really stay there. Even if everything got worse and I told them what's been happening, staying there for too long isn't something I'd like to do if I can avoid it. Instinctively I know I'm welcome there if I need to, but it's really not an option I'd prefer right now.

I've also been looking around for rentals just for myself but that's almost impossible; Stockholm has a queuing system for apartments which you can pay to be on which you can enter when you turn 18. I've been on it for close to 10 years now. Even if I tried to take advantage of that, it would take months from now for anything to actually happen. There's always the second hand market, but that's dodgy and uncertain. And it'd probably be a no pets policy. I wouldn't want to get involved in that right now.

So, what are my options? Well, I could stay where I am and endure the terms that have been newly imposed upon me. I could decide to not put up with it anymore and take Alexander up on his offer. But for just two weeks? And after that move where? To nowhere? A hotel? The street? With a puppy? It simply isn't happening. No way I am able to pull that off. Not this suddenly, by myself.

I haven't been able to eat properly for two weeks. The

immense stress has made it impossible for me to eat any kind of proper meal. I've been trying to eat protein bars but have barely been able to stomach 500 calories a day. For reference, the recommended average is 2000 calories. The stress all this has caused has also made me sleep even worse than usual. Last night I managed to sleep a couple of hours, dropping off somewhere after 5 am, and then forcing myself up at 10. And that's pretty decent by any recent standards. The insomnia combined with the relationship based stress combined with the inability to eat is starting to show its effects. I've been able to hide it from anyone I know so far, but with what happened yesterday I am now itching to talk about it with someone.

I try to forget about it and do what I have to do next, as one of the demands I have upon me. I have to train. I don't want to, I want to sleep. I feel absolutely drained, lethargic. But I change into my training clothes and get started. Today I feel too tired to do anything too strenuous, so I am going for yoga. I bring out my book and mat and try to focus on the exercises. They're physically challenging, and it also takes quite a lot of a mental effort for me to both stay focused on it and on myself. I manage to get a little calmer, but I am seriously bothered.

My freedom has been taken away from me. Completely.

I hate it.

I. Absolutely. Loathe. It.

Even something as relatively simple as being in a band

is an unattainable dream right now.

At least I still have my phone on me. But I don't feel like I can really just call any of my friends and tell them about what's been happening to me. It's just too much to explain. How do you tell them that something is even wrong to begin with? No-one even really knows that I am feeling unhappy. Except one person. Mark. And he is not connected to any of my other friends, so word will not get around.

So I message him. I am not sure how to approach it. He was busy yesterday, so he doesn't know that anything bad has happened yet. The text-chat starts normal. Fun even, and goes into the night. It's a relief just to talk about normal things, even if I know it is all coming to an end. But I really want to tell someone what has happened to me. It is eating me up inside. So I start slowly with telling him about the situation I am in. I am startled when I see what comes back from him.

'Call me in two minutes.'

Mark's Diaries

London, Thursday February 11, 2021

Just another day helping Maja with her set, although we nudge things in a much more professional direction when we hit upon the concepts of articulation and consistency which she thinks will take her bass playing to the next level. I really think it will, especially when it comes to the job of holding down the solid end in a professional cover band. That and repertoire of course, which we're covering as quickly as possible.

We chat about a few other things, including her getting more into yoga which I'm delighted to hear. This is really cool and another thing I'm sure I can help with. A tip or two here and there.

We carry on for a while talking about fun stuff and I think we're getting ready to wind up and maybe I'll look at another song or two before going to bed. I'm really enjoying getting into this with her. It's giving me so much great stuff to practice myself in terms of so many basics and repertoire, as I'm learning the songs at the same time as well. But then Maja drops a message on me, saying that her husband has threatened to end their relationship again. But she also says that she's getting jaded with this now and that no matter what she does, she feels it isn't good enough.

She tells me that this happened yesterday but she didn't feel ready to tell me until now. All of a sudden, those nice little thoughts I had a little while ago about jolly yoga chats are gone. There would have been nothing jolly about those chats. Nothing at all.

We get serious in text now as she also says she feels controlled from all angles and trapped. I say this sounds like she's looking for an exit. Yes, yes she is. So what's stopping her? 'Not having the slightest idea how to do that. Simply put, I'm afraid.'

My reply is instant. 'Call me in two minutes.' She does. With that I step outside into the cold to go for a walk and take a phone call. It will be the most significant call I've ever had and it will change entire lives, including mine.

Mark's Introduction

It's 4am and we've been in Stockholm just short of a week. As has happened every night since the day we arrived, I'm already up and wide awake. I might go back to sleep later, I might not. At the time of writing I have no idea. Also at the time of writing, we are around three and a half months behind, by far the furthest I've ever been behind in Diaryworld. We? Yes, we're an item. In every way. Emotionally, musically, professionally, aspirationally. Might as well get that out there. It's kinda implied in the title, so it's hardly spoiler. As for this early, middle of the night bout of writing, you can thank the summer Stockholm sun for that. Right now it never really gets fully dark, and by around 3:30am the sun is shining bright. So yeah, almost a week in and I'm still rising with it. Sometimes I go back to sleep, sometimes I don't.

A little background incase you're coming to this cold. I started my writings back in July 2014 when I took off from Madrid to the Costa Blanca in Spain to see if I could make a living playing bass for the summer.

Around six years to the day later, Maja began her own Diary, choosing her starting date as the day she picked up the bass and started learning from scratch. So her Diary really does start on day zero. If you want more context for what's in here as you go forwards, going back and reading hers from day one would be a pretty good place to start because it contains the story of how we met through the SBL forum - Scotts Bass Lessons - and innocently began working on bass related projects together, just like so many people have in there. At the same time, we were also working on developing my own website to get myself more marketed as a professional bass player. That story begins somewhere in December 2020 when she first got in touch, having read the entirety of my Diary in a matter of two or three months. She just wanted to say hi through the thread, but also had an idea of how she might be able to use her professional internet experience to help out. Make a website for me maybe. In return, I'd become her bass mentor, maybe. Yes, both of those things happened.

If you want the full on experience, my own piece encompasses five actual Diaries, hence the title Mark's Diaries. It covers around six and a half years and comes in at just over a million words. Basically, it's around the same size as the original seven book Harry Potter series which itself stands at just over 6000 pages.

I always had a feeling that, as big as my thing was getting, it was really just prologue. And so it's proved to be. The real story starts now.

At first we didn't write about our more serious conversations or experiences; when we first started really communicating in a serious way beyond music, it all just seemed way too private to go in anyone's diary, and none of it seemed relevant to the kinds of diaries we were both writing at the time anyway. As a result, no notes were made and there were no attempts to mark or try to remember anything. Ditto for the early days after we first actually met. But then thoughts turned to music we could make together and we realised the Diaries were starting up all over again, but as a joint project this time. Cue frantic retroactive note making. What follows is the story of our music, and the story of our music will be the story of us.

Stockholm, Saturday June 5, 2021

Maja's introduction

I never imagined that my story would get told. At least not like this. And I certainly didn't imagine that my story would be a story of music. But the story needs to get told. As I've been living it, there have been things that are too important to be left forgotten in time. These stories have a life of their own, and I feel obliged to tell them. To let them breathe, to share them and let them live through you as well.

I never had taken any platform to express my stories, but now, carefully writing my diaries, and my music, I finally have a way to express myself. The means of expressing myself like this is new to me, but even when I stumble, weighted by inexperience, I want to tell my stories.

If the story is alive enough, it will find its way to you. It will suck you in and make you feel. It will be alive through you.

And that is what I want to give you, while sharing my life, my dreams and my stories with you.

I hope you want to follow me along. Through the ups and downs. Standing in the rain by the highway in the dark. Or just joining me for a nice sunny Saturday afternoon rehearsal. My dear friend and companion.

Stockholm, Saturday June 5, 2021

PRELUDE
The Stockholm/London Diary

Day minus eight
Thursday February 11, 2021

Part two
Mark:

It's 11 at night and I'm about to go outside to have a chat with a friend about a relationship issue she's having and that she wants to talk about. That's what I innocently think as I close the front door and confront the cold. But this is a marriage. And it becomes clear pretty quickly that I have a scared girl on the other end of the line. I'm not going to get through this one by just listening like I did the other night. But what to say? I have no idea. So I just listen. As I do, it becomes clear that Maja really does want a way out. That could be simple enough, I think. If you really, really want to. Just leave. Pack, go and sort out the details later. This is where we hit a bump in the road. She says she has nowhere to go.

I decide to push a little on this one. Get another apartment? I hear a bitter laugh through the icy phone. She's already looked into that, she says. Do I have any idea how hard it is to get an apartment in Stockholm? I'll assume that's a rhetorical question. OK. A friend's place somewhere? That's been looked into already. Nothing works. Surely you can stay with your mum? With this question I realise what it is I'm actually doing and it's so far beyond ridiculous I try to push the thought out of my mind. But it got there all by itself and it's deciding it isn't going anywhere. I'm seeing the whole situation and realising I actually have an exit to offer. But I'm not going to offer it until I know all options have been explored. She says that maybe, just maybe, the mum idea could work for a while, but she's very clear that it wouldn't be sustainable for any long period of time. So a mid term temporary solution at best. I start to see where we're at. From what I understand, it wouldn't really solve anything either; it would only be a matter of time before she was back where she started anyway.

I truly can't believe where my mind is going, but the facts are these. In my rented house share in Kentish Town, which borders Camden in north London, we have a room about to come available. From February 19 to be exact. So a week exactly from tomorrow. Someone was interested in it and we all thought that was a done deal. I even met the guy. In our kitchen. But then he unexpectedly pulled out a few days ago. So it's still free. With that, I realise I can offer Maja at least the possibility of an escape so that she might not feel so trapped. After she's finished talking to me about what a no-no living with her mum would be, I realise she's out of options and it's time to say what I'm thinking. But will I really? Can I really? Can I say those words? It's one of the most ridiculous ideas I've ever thought of and is sure to be met with hollow laughter and a reply along the lines of, 'I'm not just going to up and move to London.' But what I'm really thinking is that mentioning this as even the vaguest of possibilities will give Maja a new feeling of control because she'll know she can now change the situation if she wants to. I think the offer of somewhere else, no matter how implausible, could remove the feeling of being trapped. You see, I'm even procrastinating here writing it.

I must contemplate this longer than I realise because I get a prompt. 'Are you still there?' I am. I'm just thinking. With that, I realise I now have to say something. It's my turn to do the talking thing. But the words I'm about to do the talking thing with don't feel real. They're there, but until I say them they won't actually exist. Is that true? It's like nothing else could possibly come out of my mouth right now, but at the same time I can't bring myself to say it. The silence hovers for an uncomfortable few more moments. Moments which will be the last of the before before the after. Moments in both of our lives which will never be the same again. Like someone about to dive into an icy lake, I take a mental run and jump and just do it. The words happen, almost independent of any thought, tumbling impatiently out of my mouth in a mini torrent of absurdity.

'You could come here.'

It's her turn to stop, to pause, to feel the same disbelief I'm feeling as the words are now suddenly out in the open. Newly born yet already fully formed and stumbling around on uncertain legs. My saying them hasn't changed anything. They were always going to happen once they'd assembled themselves, foetal like, at the front of my mind. It doesn't even really feel like I'm the one who said them. In fact, I'm sure I didn't. They just saw the gap and jumped out. All on their own. Now it's for Maja to see if they can be harnessed, controlled, or led in any way. She does her best.

Maja:

I kinda expected it. I'm still shocked but I kiiiiiinda figured it could come to this. I was looking at Mark's Facebook a couple of days ago and I saw an ad for a room that he was trying to find a new tenant for. I also saw it had been posted months before, so this couldn't be the room he was talking about. But that didn't matter. This got me starting to dream about being able to go there because I was thinking I just didn't want to be in my situation any longer. I even looked at the car route to the UK. But I really didn't quite expect anything to happen. How could it? Ever? Just not possible. A total impossibility. Inconceivable. Now an offer has actually been made, it feels unbelievable. Hearing the hesitation and tone of Mark's voice while he was talking me through my options I realised how inappropriate he must think it would be for him to offer that room to me. So when I think of how to answer, I'm very careful to be sure I respond in a way that he won't know I've looked at and considered this before. I make sure not to say yes right away but instead give the impression I'm only thinking about it, that maybe going to sleep on it. My idea is that I could give a more concrete answer tomorrow.

Mark:

'What do you mean?' Maja asks, sounding stunned. 'All the rooms in your house are taken.'

I'm a bit perplexed at this reaction. Surely she knows I wouldn't say something like this if it wasn't possible. I take a breath to keep my tone on an even keel and begin to explain. 'One of the guys is moving out next week. It becomes available on Friday. The 19th.' This is where I tell Maja what I told you above; that this offer is really just a conceptual thing. I'm not at all expecting her to take it up and move here. That would be an absurd idea. What it does do, I think, is give her the possibility of knowing she could have the freedom to change things if she wants. It might just prevent her from feeling as trapped as she has been feeling recently. Now she takes me by surprise, saying she's already considered this as far as even looking at the route she might take from Sweden, through Europe, to France by car to catch a ferry to the UK. Damn. She even knows how long the drive will take. I'm stunned by this little turn. 'So you've already been thinking about this?' Well, that was a silly question. But what else do you say to something like that?

I'm close to home and we agree there is a lot to think about and maybe talk about seriously tomorrow. We finish the call and I get home just around 12:30am. The calendar has just crept into Friday 12th, exactly one week from the 19th. As I take off my jacket, a new disbelief takes hold of me. I don't expect anything to come of what we've been talking about. I really truly don't. But a huge question hits me, the words coming all at once, crashing down instantaneously on top of each other. What the hell have I just done?

Day minus seven
Friday February 12

Mark:

Damn. I can't believe it. Ten thirty in the morning and Maja's been on this already. A little hello chat and then she says, 'I think my driver's licence should work.' What now? That's all she says about it as an introduction. Not, 'I've been thinking about it,' not, 'Were you serious about what you said last night?' No. 'I think my driver's licence might work.' 'That tells me someone's been thinking,' I say. 'Of course,' she shoots back.' Alright. I'll leave it alone. Someone's in the serious tree. I climb up and join her. It's begun. This is her plan. She's going to move here in her car, crossing a whole bunch of countries in a 22 hour drive. And I'm about to discover she isn't planning a quick visit either. I'm massively surprised when I get her next message which suggests, pretty much states really, that this is a full on move she's contemplating. She sends me the link to the government website for applying for a Global Talent Visa. OK. I'm going to have to go there. Here's the thing that's going to underpin so much of what is to follow. And for the first time, on just day two of this new diary, we're going to have to go full on political. There's just no avoiding it anymore. In all previous writings I've tried, at every turn, to keep things totally out of that sphere. When I've absolutely absolutely had to, I've dipped the tippiest of tippy tip toes, no, of a little toenail, into the freezing cold and stormy waters and then got the hell out of there. But I'm afraid through quite a bit of this we're gonna have to just take a deep breath and dive in and swim. I'll keep us up for air as much as possible.

The reason? Brexit. Sorry, but it's out. I've said it. If Maja has any aspirations at all about living and working in the UK, and it seems she is suddenly at least considering to have such aspirations, proper accesses and documentations are going to have to be followed because UK and European citizens no longer enjoy freedom of work and movement between each other's' territories. Oh. OK. It's apostrophe, 's' apostrophe again apparently. Not seen that one before.

So if Maja wants to come here and then later decide maybe to attempt any kind of working relationship with the UK, she'll have to jump through all the hoops previously associated with going to live on other continents. The UK is out of the European loop now.

So yes, she's been looking at how to get a visa and, as far as she can see, this Global Talent thing seems the most likely. I revisit my doubt and say it now. 'Wow. I'm really getting the impression your mind's made up. Is that right?' I get the reply in three messages.

'Pretty much.'

'I dunno'

'But yeah.'

We have a little delve into it and it very quickly becomes clear this will not be a quick fix. Everything is just so complicated and involved and there are a lot of steps to go through which can take weeks at a time. It looks like she won't be coming anytime soon afterall. But that's not how Maja rolls. 'Dammit,' she says. 'Can't I just come as a tourist and do this later?' You know what? I think that might just work. And as she says right now, she can be here legally as a tourist for six months. And let the after that take care of itself for now. I think taking care of the now is just enough for now.

Maja is in no doubt anyway. 'When I get a job, they'll fix that for me.'

Let's get something up front and out there now. Maja will not be coming here to work in the back of a coffee shop, or pour pints next to me in the bar job I most assuredly would be able to get her, at my place or someone else's. No. Maja's fish are somewhat bigger. Somewhat huger. Among other things she's a cloud engineer. Which basically means she designs, maintains and manipulates the infrastructure that makes the internet work. That computer game you're playing with your buddies who live all over the world? Chances are she developed and then maintained the software that allowed the game to even exist in that format. She's done similar jobs for governments and corporations across nations in aspects of projects even the managers knew nothing about. So yeah. It's fair to imagine that a company would take an extra step or two to bring her on board.

With this, we start looking at it in full earnest, researching how to come here and what the legals are. Oh. We've covered Brexit as one obstacle, but I'm afraid we have to look at another one now. Coronavirus. You see, this is early 2021 and we're still very much in pandemic territory.

London is in lockdown and travel restrictions of varying levels are in place all over the world, including a lot of outright travel bans. Once more we delve into the official websites and come up with the little gem that there's no travel ban for Swedish citizens thinking of coming into the UK, but there is a 10 day quarantine required. And they're really not messing about with this; failure to comply could actually result in jail time. 'Well, if you help me out with groceries I'll be fine,' she says. Yep. Done. And a Covid test has to be taken and proved negative before beginning the journey here. OK. That will be something to have a look at in a little more detail later. So it seems that's the two biggies out of the way. She's looking at flights now, as a possible alternative to driving over. It's way cheaper, she says. OK. It seems she's just taken a breath to think about all this because she comes back with, 'I'm just mildly surprised by the reality. My head is just spinning with all the ifs right now.' Yep. This is starting to feel pretty real and it's only midday. It's less than 12 hours ago that I spoke those four little words. You Could Come Here.

So yes, we're really doing this. Basic practicalities get discussed now, including the fact that she could soon have a place to call her own in London. And a place that is now going at 20 per cent its pre pandemic price with no deposit required. However, I'm very keen to stress that it's part of a five person house share, and is a tiny, tiny room. That doesn't cool the waters one bit. 'It's huge to think that I could have a place to call my own,' she says. 'Just enormous for me.' It's also handy that all bars are closed in the UK right now meaning I'm currently on very decently paid furlough from my bar job. So I'm available any time day or night right now, and will be available to take care of anything Maja might need once she gets here. Perhaps most importantly, I can do the shopping.

Maja then asks about Jenn. Does she know about this as a possibility? Yes, we've had that chat and she's cool with it. And I've made sure Elvin, the guy currently in the room, is definitely leaving on the 19th. But I tell her there's no need to actually aim for that date as I can totally hold the room. I have a great relationship with the landlord and he pretty much lets me organise things around here, even to the extent of finding and bringing in new tenants. With that, she tells me that once he's left she'll pay for it even if she's not arrived yet. She'll even pay before he leaves if necessary, just to be absolutely sure it's held. She says she just doesn't want it to disappear from under her. 'Of course it will be held,' I say. "Don't have this on your worry list. Once it's paid for, it's yours whether you're here or not.' And I add that the rent can be paid through me and I can deal with things this end, which means she knows she's dealing with the de facto decision maker. 'You're like a mini landlord,' she says. Not quite, but I can see how it might look.

Yes. This really is happening now. I get straight on the phone to the landlord to tell him of the new incoming tenant. He says he'll make the contract up right away and date it from the 19th. I get back to Maja with this news and I think I make her head spin. 'It's really getting sorted now,' she says. 'That's crazy. I haven't even told anyone about this and I suddenly have a place in London. Amazing.'

Now she goes full on practicalities. What to bring, what not to bring, how and when to tell people. Oh, everything's spinning everywhere now. And more Covid stuff keeps coming; as well as a negative test to be able to get on a plane, she's now discovered that two tests have to be taken during quarantine. We have no idea how this gets organised or anything, but this is happening now so we put that on the later pile, although it really can't be too much later. The 19th looks like a date around which this will all revolve although I expect things to really happen quite a bit after that. But hey, she already has a room sorted out in London and that's just about the biggest thing to get in place for any move anywhere.

As covered in the later parts of Mark's Diaries, I recently started working on a music project with my friend Kylie who lives just a short walk away. I was going to have to leave this online chat with Maja soon for a rehearsal, but Kylie now messages to see if we can move it to Sunday. No problem. Almost immediately after that message comes in, Maja asks if I can talk. Well, I can now. Five minutes later she's on the phone. But there's no excitement in her voice. As much as it might seem to be, this is no time for excitement. For a start, there are still so many things to organise. But second, right now it's too cold to go out where she is so she's calling me from the apartment while her husband is still there. It's a whispered conversation while she stays in the bedroom, carefully monitoring the doorknob so that she won't be caught talking about, well, all the stuff we're talking about. We're on the phone for about two hours but as soon as we hang up, my messenger pings again. 'I'm alone?' she writes. 'And it's dark in the apartment. I knew it was gonna burn soon.' This is just as we're coming to 7pm.

Maja:

I put the phone down and brace myself to open the bedroom door, mentally preparing myself to handle whatever comes next. What's going to happen now? I have no choice but to leave. My puppy Tommy clearly needs to go pee. Trembling, I hold my hand on the handle and slowly push the door. As it opens, I see the apartment is dark. It's just totally dark. There's no-one there. I go through to the living room just looking around. Then I open the bathroom and kitchen doors. 'Hello. Are you there?' I shout. I even check in the closet. Crazy, I know, but this is a crazy situation. He's gone. Where the hell did he go? He was supposed to be working. Working at his desk in the living room as he does everyday. It's minus 10 degrees outside. You don't go for a walk in that kind of temperature. You just don't. Not if you don't have to. And he doesn't have anywhere to go. What am I supposed to do now? First, I do what needs to be done, which is taking Tommy for a little walk so he can pee. 'm absolutely sure something bad has happened. I don't know where he is. I don't know what's going to happen when he gets back and I have no idea how to prepare myself for that. All I can think of is to call Mark back and tell him about this. I do that while frantically walking in circles around the little stone garden close to my home. 'Mark. He's gone. He's gone. He's gone. What am I supposed to do now?' We talk for a little bit, I calm down and then it comes to me. I'm not really sure how to do it but I realise I need to leave. Now. I go back inside, keeping Mark on the line while I try to find something I can eat this instant. I haven't had anything to eat today at all. I find some cold cooked rice in the fridge and force myself to eat a couple of spoonfuls. It tastes horrible but that's irrelevant. It's food and food equals energy, which is all I need right now.

What I'm going to do when he gets back doesn't matter anymore. I'm not going to be here when he gets back. I say to Mark, 'I'm leaving for my mum's now. I can stay there at least until I'm ready to leave for the UK.' I keep him on the phone while I take a suitcase and just start shoving clothes into it, grabbing whatever I see nearest to me each time I look up. All through this, Tommy is by my side. The suitcase is almost full and I'm just a minute or so away from walking out when I hear the door open. Into the phone, I kind of shout-whisper, 'I gotta go,' and hang up.

In the same second, he comes back home. I cram the suitcase into the closet and force the door shut on it. Then I walk out into the living room and see him walking towards the sofa. He doesn't look up, doesn't say a word. Just reaches the sofa where he sits down and turns the TV on. I try to speak to him. Nothing. I ask where he's been. I ask him a lot of things. I get no answer to any of it. He's just silent, ignoring me, looking at the TV. Nothing's on. It's just the homescreen of Netflix with the movies you can choose. He looks at that, ignoring me, just blindly looking for something to put on. I'm kinda used to being treated like this, completely ignored. So I know that there's only one way for me to really break the cycle. I need to say it. I need to. I don't wanna. I'm fearing the words but they need to be said. So I sit down close to him, just in front of him. I pull up a chair so I can sit just in front of him, my face a couple of centimetres away from his. I look into his eyes and say it. 'I want a divorce.'

We have a long talk about this, and feelings become heated as the full gravity of the situation really starts to hit us. Seeing his remorse, I back down on my demand for a divorce and we settle on the reality that I will be going to London at least for a little while. I can't handle living like this anymore, and if we're ever going to get to a place where we can be decent with each other again we need to part ways right now. We talk for hours. When our words finally die out I excuse myself by telling him I have to go out and repark the car. With our severe winter weather, that's just something we regularly need to do around here so the council can clear the road of snow in the morning. I take the opportunity of being alone again to call Mark to tell him what's just happened.

Mark:

Around three hours after we speak she messages to say that she's told him she's leaving. For now at least. 'Long conversation,' she says. Now she wants to talk to me. I go out and wander the silent residential streets of Kentish Town, avoiding the busy roads as much as I can. Each time I come to one I go straight across and into side streets again. It's strange, this way of walking and talking late at night on deserted roads. This is lockdown London and no bars are open so no-one is on the streets. We basically cover what we've been writing about today in our chats, while she also tells me about what it's like at home right now. She says she's being treated kindly enough so it's manageable, and she feels good now that the news is out. We chat for about an hour and then we're both close to home so call it for the day. But there's one more thing. Just after I've settled back in at home I get a ping. It's a screengrab accompanied by the message, 'This is the flight I'm thinking of.' Then, in reference to all we've been talking about, 'I can't believe this is what it had to take to make it feel good again. Goodnight friend. I'm exhausted now.' That makes two of us.

Now I have a closer look at the details of the possible flight she's sent me. Damn. It's this coming Friday. The 19th.

Day minus six
Saturday February 13

Mark:

After the initial rush, it's onto details today, mostly getting the Covid nitty gritty stuff sorted out. Which means knowing exactly how to go about everything, especially as we're looking at, bizarrely, this Friday probably being the day this will all happen.

I just want to make sure she knows the room might not be ready if she arrives on that day as Elvin has frustratingly started prevaricating; his plans are now changing almost by the minute. I'm even starting to get worried that he might actually not leave on the 19th like he said so I gently make it clear to him that he's given us his intentions and, based on that, someone has now already made plans to be here on that day. He says he understands and he'll make sure to move out on that day even if he has to stay somewhere else before leaving the country like he's intending. OK. But I still tell Maja that she might want to postpone until at least Saturday to give me a chance to clear the room out and have it ready for her. She's not phased by that in the slightest. No need to have the room ready, she insists. She'll help clear it out and clean it if needed. And if he's still there when she arrives, she's cool to chill until he's disappeared. OK. As long as she knows and is fine with it. Her reasoning is that if she comes almost any other day after Friday next week, she'll be looking at two flights, meaning possible Covid planning for any transit country as well. Basically, if it's not this Friday it could all start to get messy and complicated, not to mention more expensive. As if things like this aren't already messy, complicated and expensive. OK, so Friday it still most likely is then.

Now to book the Covid travel test, which will happen on Tuesday with the plan to have a negative result returned from a test time no more than 72 hours before flying. Which means Wednesday and Thursday could well be spent worrying about a possible positive result. Nothing to be done about that. Take the test and wait and see is all you can do.

Ten PM and she tells me the flight is booked, and the corona test is also in for Tuesday. This really is motoring now. Next up is the passenger locator form and ordering the test kits which she now knows are to be used and posted for analysis on the second and eighth days after arrival. Unless subsequently told otherwise, you are then free to go out and about on day 11.

Now we start to look forwards and Maja asks if she can send me a shopping list for things she would like me to get from here. So I'm now acting as a sort of a one man advance party, making sure everything is ready on the ground for a new arrival. We're talking toiletries and bedding stuff. Nothing major, but still very preferable to have available from minute dot.

Now, beyond actual practicalities, we get to talk about fun stuff. First item on the agenda: She begins to wonder what bass she should buy when she gets here. She'll be travelling without any of the three that she currently owns, which will all be left in Sweden, along with amps and anything else bulky. So I get to help her shop online, which means I am now vicariously buying a bass. Cool. I guess that's a level or two above window shopping. It's fair to say we spend a lot of time on this and a lot of basses get chosen and then rejected. The main issue is doubt over really committing to making a purchase this big for something you can't even try out. I know you can return it within a reasonable period if you don't like it for any reason, but it's bad enough to have to think about this with buying clothes online, let alone a new bass. But really, this is a very nice problem to have after some of the other stuff we've covered so far.

The bottom line for today is that tickets have been

booked and practicalities, as far as they can be, have been sorted. Now she has the wonderful prospect of Friday to look forward to when she can leave the stresses of Sweden behind and head off to a new adventure in London, which of course starts with the mandatory 10 day period of quarantine or, perhaps more accurately in her case, a kind of legally enforced rest. I get the feeling it is being very highly anticipated as she says, during one exchange of a three hour skype chat that goes way past midnight, 'I feel I could sleep for a week.' But maybe just a thought or two of being active as well as she says, 'I'm not usually a runner, but when I get there I wanna run just a little bit. Just from the joy of freedom.'

Maja:

Today is about preparation. And about getting along. Me and my husband have a chat and he acts supportively towards the idea of me going to London. He knows that I've been serious about music lately and it makes sense that I want to do something that breaks the depressiveness we've been feeling at home lately. He really isn't happy about it, but accepts it, which is a relief for me. So for today, we decide to go on a date. I prepare some details regarding travel with Mark, and pack up a bag with Tommy's necessities. We decided to go on an outing to the forest with Tommy. It is sunny and it is beautiful outside. Minus 10 degrees C, so we need to have warm clothing on. All three of us. We have two layers of trousers, winter jackets, and of course Tommy is dressed in his winter jacket as well. Tommy is a Chinese Crested Hairy Hairless Puppy, around five months old. This breed is known for being very cold sensitive, which is why it is important that we dress him appropriately. And since it is so cold, I usually let him sit in my jacket as well. He is tiny, so it is OK. He fits nice and snugly under my big winter jacket.

We drive to McDonalds to have a little lunch in the drive through before our outing. We order food and park in a place with a beautiful view over a snowclad highway, where we eat our hamburgers and talk. We talk about my trip to London. About what I am going to do there. He is of the belief that if you're going to do something a bit crazy, you might as well get it over with while you're still young. I couldn't agree more, but that's not really what this is about. I keep that thought to myself. But I am hugely appreciative that he is supportive of my decision to do this. Even though I know he doesn't want me to go. He is acting tough handling the reality he doesn't want to accept. I'm having a hard time being cheerful. I feel like a traitor. But I do my best, as always. We finish up, and I am embarrassed by the amount I have to throw away. I can't possibly stomach a whole burger. I somewhat manage a third. I drive us to the national park 30 minutes from where we live. We've been there once before. Where we're planning to go is a beautiful place with cows, pigs, ducks and other farm animals. But we seem to have put a different part of the enormous park into our GPS, so we end up at a place we've never been before instead. The forest we're driving through is absolutely stunning, with about 10 centimetres of snow on the tree branches. The branches of the oak trees are heavily weighed down by the snow, and it glistens in the sun. When the wind blows we can see huge amounts of snow fall down from some of the branches, which then shoot back up from the released tension, spraying more snow in the air which again spectacularly catches the sun. The ground is covered by about 50 centimetres to a metre of untouched snow, painting the landscapes in white. It is probably the most stunningly beautiful winter landscape I've seen in my entire life.

We park in a little parking lot in the forest, get out of the car and take a walk on a hiking trail in the forest. The trail goes over a little stream that amazingly is not frozen yet. The little stream trickles as we walk on a bridge a couple of metres over it. It feels a little scary to look down, I think as I lean closer to the edge to take some photographs. The sun is shining, and everywhere I look it sparkles and glistens. The wind is coldly kissing my cheeks, that get red and a little bit sore. We walk onto a little frozen lake, talking about the forest and how amazing it is that we can actually walk on top of a frozen lake without the slightest fear of the ice breaking. The ice is too thick to break, it's been minus degrees for weeks by now. After a while I take Tommy up in my jacket and carry him so he can warm up.

It is the ideal winter date, of a seemingly happy young family with a dog and a bright future. Our last date.

Day minus five
Sunday February 14

Maja:

I am having a hard time realising that I am about to move to London. It is post Brexit, and during complete Covid lockdown, so I don't really have anything of the usual London to look forward to, but that is really not what this move is about. This move is about me getting some space for myself to actually relax and find myself. Anyone who's been through a rough part of a relationship knows the importance of just getting away for a bit if you're not getting along. When a relationship becomes stressful, even during the times no arguments are happening it can be stressful just being close to each other.

I've really started to feel the need to be somewhere else for a while, and I am absolutely delighted with having found a place to go to. I'm happy with the friendship that has developed between me and Mark, and it feels like a good place for me to go to. I could just be there for a while, chill and let myself think about where to go next in life.

Since I've now decided to go ahead and move, there are preparations to make. I've spoken with my husband about it, and we've gotten to an OK place about it, so the next stage is to tell my family about it. We go there and I do that. They're shocked and saddened. So much so that over the next few days they will try more and more to persuade me not to go ahead with my plans, to just keep things as they are in Sweden. At times I will feel as though I'm being demanded to justify my decisions and motivations, as though this was a negotiation. It is not. I am going. For my own sake. For no one else but me. But the discussions wear me down and I feel like I'm having to fight for the right to do things my way. As the longest week of my life drags on, I start to feel more and more alone.

Even though I love my parents so very much, I need to be by myself right now. I am not confident enough in myself to handle input from other people; I'm not sure I'd have the strength to disagree. I fear I would be too easily persuaded that they were right and I was wrong.

Mark:

In a chat today, as we're going through the practicalities, which has become something of a watchword, Maja suddenly remembers my experiences and says, 'Oh yeah, I forgot. You also did the sudden London move thing. You're like the ultimate Londoner for me.' Not entirely sure about that, but yes, I see where she's coming from. Now she mentions it, yes, I did do it in similar fashion in my dash from Madrid, but also in a much less secure way and with a pretty damn nasty landing too once the whole thing had crashed and burned and totally fallen apart on me. That whole homeless period with nothing but a corner of a friend's room to call (extremely loosely) my own, no job, dwindling savings. If you can even call what I had savings. So yeah. I guess I do know what I'm talking about. But then, as she rightly points out, as much as she's coming into a little more of a secure situation than I, ahem, enjoyed, I didn't have Covid and lockdown London to contend with, so different challenges for different times. But security? She has the whole Brexit thing going on too because it's not like she can come over here and start looking for a job if needed, but that's a later issue if she even decides she wants to consider anything like that. She has far greater priorities to think about. Like now when she says, 'I'm not usually a runner but when I get there I wanna run a little bit. Just from the joy of freedom.' Yep. I think that's about where it is right now.

Oh, but London walks. That's really something to think about once she's able to get out and about again. We talk about my own experience of that in the early days of Lockdown when I took my daily exercise allowance to go and see an iconically empty central London. Seriously. I was in Trafalgar Square with maybe two or three other people tops dotted about the place in the distance. So enough for me to feel like I had it all to myself. And with just a little judicious angling, I was able to get photographs of Trafalgar Square with no-one in it. I mean, impossible to ridiculous to think you could ever have got that photograph before, no matter what time day or night. I had similar experiences and took similar photographs of Leicester Square, Piccadilly Circus and Regent Street. Lockdown ghost town London. Iconic, historic images.

And I took them and have them, and the experience is the memory of a lifetime. Maja might yet be able to share it. Things have loosened up just a little so it's not quite as extreme anymore, but it is still a little bit like that. So that's definitely something we can get out and see when the time comes.

So yes, we also have quite a bit to talk about, or rather she does, and I listen and pass a comment now and then. I was supposed to have that put-off rehearsal with Sarah today but that's been put off again so when Maja asks, I say that yes, I am free. The conclusion of today, at least on her domestic front, is that things have started to calm down. Because of this, she's also now starting to think in terms of a shorter visit. Maybe a timeframe of something like two months.

Day minus four
Monday February 15

Maja:

I am spending the days talking to my family and packing.

Mark:

I'm damn sure I had corona back in February, but things have been feeling a little strange again lately healthwise. Nothing major, but you never know. And corona tests are apparently a little easier to get than they have generally been. I checked that out last night and it worked as I was able to book myself in for one today. It's a bit of a walk away, 30 minutes or so to Islington. Not ideal if you really are full on symptomatic. How is someone supposed to be able to do that? But I can do it and I arrive at the place and I'm expecting at least some kind of gym hall. Maybe something that at least resembles some kind of medical centre. Nope. What I find looks more like a field hospital. It's a large tent, but it isn't even enclosed. Those poor people working in there, fully exposed to any kind of cold and wind that might happen. Which is a lot right now, as we're in February. Besides the small administration areas, there are ten rooms inside the tent. Five on either side, each one separated by canvas. In each of those 'rooms' are what look like rough, hastily constructed chairs and desks made of bare wood. I'm also expecting some kind of professional on hand to perform the test on me, but no to that too. Instead, when I'm indicated to enter, I'm given a little bag containing a test kit. I do what with this now? Go to the empty room over there, the one that someone's just finishing sanitising, sit down and follow the instructions on the wall. So yep. I've come to a testing centre to take a self test I have no idea how to do. Well, I guess millions of people have already done these so how hard can it be? Just follow the instructions on the wall step by step. OK. Sample tube goes here, stick goes there, bag goes there, and I have my bits and pieces arrayed out in front of me. It looks mildly complicated and quite medical and technical but again like I said, millions have done this before me and I must be more or as intelligent as at least a few of them so surely I can do this too. Step one, take stick and stick down the back of throat. Simple. Apparently after this you take same stick and stick up nose. Ah. I'm starting to get it now. Then stick is sticked, sorry, stuck, in bag. Then all done. OK, so not quite as intimidating as it seemed when I was first given a bag full of medical bits and told to get on with it and come back when I was done. But stick down throat. This doesn't go so well as the stick sticks my sick trigger. Oh dear. I try desperately to hold it back and, well, you can imagine the rest. Let's say I just about manage to not make a mess of the table. I now have to call out for someone to come and give me another bag of corona sticks so I can go again. I'm seriously apprehensive this time and really have to hold on so as not to have to repeat it yet again. Ten seconds you've got to hold that thing back there, right in the gag reflex zone. I reckon whoever designed this was having a bit of a laugh, imagining all the self induced projectile vomiting going on in test centres all over the country. But I just about manage it this time. All that's left now is to ram this thing up my nose to complete the sticky process. Done, all safely deposited in aforementioned tube, and now in self sealing bag. Drop that off at whatever you call the outgoing reception, and test experience concluded until the next bit which is to see whether I'm positive or not. I guess if I am I'll already be well aware by the time the results come but this is how the system works. Spoiler alert: it comes back negative.

Buying a bass in the time of Corona. Been looking into it, and yes they can be returned within a week if you're not happy. Still not ideal given the number of attractive basses you might try in a shop before buying but at least it's not a commitment to something you've only seen a pretty picture of.

I have a few things I have to do here to make sure things are prepared for when Maja arrives. Yes, we're working on the assumption that her Covid test will be negative. One of my little tasks is to make sure she has all the bed sheets and towels she needs. Jenn, being a girl herself, knows how important it is to get these things right and is happy to come out with me to make sure I pick up the right things. So that's one little fun excursion this end. We head out into Ktown and go Maja shopping. I return home with quite a decent haul and lay it out on our floor. All the necessary bedding stuff, towel, other toiletry bits and pieces, extension lead, coathangers, and a Europe to UK plug adaptor. I'll be adding at least another one of those.

I take a picture and send it to Maja so she can see that things really are coming along here and that things will be set up as well as they can be so that she can have as seamless a landing and arrival as possible. As well as my preparations here, our phone calls are starting to become more and more regular as she needs a little support. It seems like some of the conversations in Sweden are getting really quite intense.

This is making Friday become a more and more

anticipated date and we're starting to talk about English things to do and see, and just a few more fun things in general. Dr Who is a favourite show of hers, she says, and she's looking forward to maybe catching up on some episodes here that haven't been available in Sweden. I decide not to say it just yet, but star of the show Matt Smith is a regular at my bar The Lord Palmerston, and lives right here in the area. That's a fun little fact to keep to myself for now. We're also anticipating conversations without internet lag. You know, Skype freezes and the like. Very frustrating, especially when you talk a whole bunch about something then realise the connection dropped out sometime just after you started talking. Also, not always an optimal way to teach bass. When our conversations were all purely music related and very much at a professional level of chat, I'd get through a whole song she'd asked me to play so that she could film it, only to then discover her screen had frozen somewhere near the beginning and we'd have to go again. That happened quite a few times. But here's another thing now I mention Skype. Since Thursday when the possibility of her coming to London was mentioned we've only spoken on the phone. We haven't actually seen each other at all. I don't know about her, but I kinda feel like I want to keep it that way until Friday. Those Skype calls feel like they happened a long time ago.

Day minus three
Tuesday February 16

Maja:

Today I am going to take the corona test for travel. In this time of Corona, travel is hard and there are a lot of things that just need to be done correctly in the right order to avoid breaking any of the new corona laws. These laws have just appeared in several countries and are subject to change without any notice, so it is really hard to know if you will be able to actually go through with any of your plans. So right now I have to take several new things into consideration. First is the new demand to have a travel certificate that shows that you're fit for travel with no sign of Covid. To travel from Sweden to the UK, you need something called a RT-PCR test which must be taken less than 72 hours from arrival in the UK. My flight will arrive at 5 PM UK time on friday. So that means that I need to take it later than 6 PM Swedish time today. I book a time for 6:50 PM just before that centre closes for the day and hope I'll get the certificate in time before takeoff. These tests are surprisingly expensive. A trip to London in itself isn't that cheap, but if you account for these tests as well, any trip abroad suddenly becomes noticeably more expensive. The price is around 1300 SEK, which is about 130 euro.

I arrive at the centre in time, after getting lost all over the mall it is in. It's a little hole in the wall kind of store, with no visible personnel. It's really hard to see that the place really exists, but after walking past it about four times I finally notice it. I have to call a button and then a man in a lab coat comes out. He greets me and says that today's delivery to the lab has already gone, do you want to take the test anyway? This means that I won't get the results until the next night, but the taken test time will remain the same. I'm OK with that, I don't want to come back here and it'll be in time for my flight anyway so I go in to take the test. He checks my passport and we walk into the inner room which looks like a mix between a laboratory and an examination room. There are steel countertops with lab-like objects on them. He brings the testing kit which contains a test tube and a little object that looks like a small pipe cleaner. It's made of steel and has a small brush at the end of the stick. I'm asked to tilt my head slightly backwards and he slowly sticks that horrifying object into my nose. It hurts so bad that I jolt and he drags it out. Ouch! Are you done, I ask. No, I didn't get in quite far enough, he answers. Oh no. This really hurts. I tilt my head backwards once again and he goes in the other nostril. And he just continues. Deeper and deeper. Until he reaches what feels like the place where the nostril connects to the mouth. There he stops, turns the object around and takes it out. Finally. My nose runs, and it hurts in both nostrils. I take a tissue and blow it out. This really wasn't very pleasant at all but it is done now. I walk back to my car, and I can feel that that object has been in my nose for at least an hour afterwards.

Mark:

Damn. I've just realised I really really want Maja to come. What prompted this? She takes the corona test today and if it comes out positive, no trip. OK. I hear you, and I'm telling myself the same thing: This is all purely about helping someone out and offering a friend a safe space in a difficult time. But the test thing and the prospect of a positive result and a consequent cancellation has suddenly made me feel very different about the situation. I really really want this to happen much more than I thought I did. I have no idea what to make of that. And results won't be known until sometime Thursday. Of course a negative result is totally expected but you really just never know. It doesn't help when Maja writes things like, 'I don't think I have corona.' That's like saying I'm sure I did, in an attempt to persuade someone you really did do that important thing. But I know she has already had corona so it won't come back again will it? These are the kinds of things that are swirling in my mind all the time right now. I'm sure she's thinking the same.

We also start checking official travel guidance and the like and Maja comes up with the line that Sweden is advising against travel to the UK right now. Oh dear. The elements really are quite against this.

Me and Kylie manage a rehearsal today, and we really make good progress on putting together our little show. It looks like it will be something of a five song medley with me coming in and out on bass with backing tracks used for one of the songs, and also a little a capella going on. There's a nice little moment she's given me where I take a solo in between one of the pieces. When I finish my solo today she loves it so much that she says, 'That is no interlude. We're starting the whole thing with that.' Wow.

It's a seriously fun project to be working on and great to have a real musical focus especially now while my focus is being pulled all over the place, but mainly in the direction of Sweden. The goal for rehearsal right now is to have a tight 15 minute show to take out on this London road when it finally reopens for business. We're also planning to record it for Kylie to send off to some of her contacts. Apparently she can get some funding that way if it all works out. I have no idea what funding means and I'm not asking, but Kylie's contacts go deep into the A list of society and entertainment so whatever she shakes out of this could be quite interesting. Today we manage a full run through of what it could look like which is really cool. Still quite rough in parts, but we have something that feels like one complete piece. On Thursday we're going to tighten up a few more details and then start trying to get this thing recorded.

It also helps take my mind off how slowly the minutes have been ticking by since Friday. This isn't at all being helped by waiting for the results of the corona test. Thursday feels a hell of a lot of time away right now.

Well, it almost takes my mind off things. When we come to a close and settle down for our post rehearsal hang, Kylie says that as well as things have gone today, she can't help notice that I seem a little bit distracted and maybe a touch hyper. She says she can see a light in my eyes shining even brighter than usual. This is unfortunate because I'm not supposed to be feeling anything, let alone showing it. I decide to open up, although it feels really strange to be actually articulating things. OK, I say. There is a girl thing going on. 'I knew it,' she half shrieks. 'No no no. It's not like that,' I'm very quick to point out. I tell her about the helping out thing and the Maja coming thing, and the online chats and how they've led her to confide in me, which has led me to offer a way out, which has led us to getting really deep into, well, just about everything really. And feelings come out of that and I have no idea what to do with them. I don't know if she feels the same way and I don't know if I really feel anything anyway. And even if I do, I really don't want to. I tell her that this is not an excited boy is going to meet girl thing. This is a serious situation that I'm supposed to be helping out in, not getting all, you know. Kylie just looks all coy and gigglish. Excited even. But I can think of few less appropriate words or emotions right now than excited. I just want to be calm about all this, welcome Maja in and hope that whatever I think I'm feeling just dies down. There's a time and place for stuff like that. This isn't either. At. All.

Kylie suggests bringing her along to the next rehearsal and maybe even letting her jam with us, possibly even becoming a part of what we're doing. I drop cold water all over that idea saying, 'For a start, her playing is just nowhere up to any kind of level ready for us.' With that

Kylie seems to let go of the thought, but is still keen for me to bring her to rehearsal for a hang out. Me and Kylie are clearly in social mode now so I check my phone for a few messages that I saw come in during rehearsal, and yep, there are one or two from Maja. I tell her we've just finished, and she says a hi to Kylie which Kylie just absolutely loves, saying she now feels connected to the story. Whatever that could mean. Kylie, there's no story. I'm meeting this girl at the airport in a few days. We may hug, we may not. Then she's going to come to my house and have a chill and a safe space and I'm going to carry on with my things while doing some shopping for her and maybe listen to and share a few thoughts. That's it. There is no story.

Later when I get to message/chat to Maja a little more, she says she's thrilled at the idea of coming along to a rehearsal or two and having an opportunity to listen and see how the pros do it. Yeah, that will be kinda cool. I really have a thing about not having non band members at rehearsals. If it's ever in my control this is something I just do not allow. But I get the feeling Maja will be just fine and if Kylie's cool with having her around then so am I.

Yeah, I think I'll talk about that here. In my very first band, once we felt we'd got ourselves to a decent together sounding place, it was suggested that some friends come along one night. I have absolutely no recollection of where this suggestion came from; a band member, or one of those friends. But they were very good friends, very into music, so yeah. Great. Not great. Not only did it turn into them trying to treat us as a personal live juke box, but they got quickly and visibly - even vocally - bored and frustrated when we started repeating sections of a song again and again. Or, heaven forbid in a rehearsal, repeating a song again, then maybe again. No-one fell out with anyone at all, but after that night my mind was made up. Nobody from outside the band comes to a rehearsal. Ever. Maybe a music professional such as a manager or prospective manager, or the same relating to a producer. But that was it. So yeah. It's something I feel quite strongly about.

Day minus two
Wednesday February 17

Mark:

This is very strange. Me and Maja are starting to have longer and longer silences on the phone. Sometimes we kind of stay there simply hanging out saying nothing at all, waiting to see if one of us will break the silence. If no-one does, all cool. We just keep on hanging on. I really should watch myself with this. I must admit I'm really not best pleased with it. We're kinda starting to act like two people at the start of a relationship. Anything either of us is feeling here, if that's even a thing that's happening, has to be an illusion. I mean, our conversations are covering all kinds of really deeply emotional stuff as I'm helping her through this week while she prepares to fly away from her marriage for what could be just a month or two. Yeah. There you go. She's married. What the hell am I thinking about? Got to let this go. Having thoughts stray into that kind of territory when someone's coming to stay in your home to get away from a difficult emotional situation really is not cool. Seriously not cool. And acting on this could not possibly lead to any kind of good place so just forget it. Really. Please. I think we're just going through some really intense conversations that neither of us have shared too much in here, but just yeah, they are intense. And deeply personal. I can't help thinking that stuff like that is going to play with your head a bit. I've just got to not play back.

Today Maja gets a realistion that flying in the time of corona will create the possibility of iconically empty airport scenes. Much like my empty London. Yeah, we agree. It probably will be like that. This is a moment in history, and something people will ask about in years to come. I'm very curious about what it will be like too and we speculate a little. But then, there are also stories around of people being on packed planes, so who really knows? An interesting little item to play around with for a bit anyway.

Since Maja took the test yesterday, time has almost stopped moving. It feels like an interminable wait and thoughts do turn to what she'll do if it comes out positive. I'll let her discuss that small issue. For my part, I admit that I'll be very disappointed if it does come out positive and she seems very pleased to hear that. Like, 'You really do want me to come?' Yes, I really really do. We're on another long chat and walk into the evening when she asks me to wait. A message just came through on her phone. Oh, she says. It's from the test centre. I have to go and open this. It's no fun at all as we hang up and I wait to see what kind of Maja comes back on the phone. It rings about a minute later and I stare at it, knowing that there will be a before and an after of this very phone call. This is where I find out what the after will be. I answer and immediately hear laughter on the line. Oh wow. It's come back negative. That's it. Game on. She's coming. This has been the last thing on the list to check off. I stop and sit on a wall. The relief is immense. Far greater than I ever thought it would be. After the initial reaction, we just both hang on the line, neither of us saying anything, almost not able to take it in. Oh, this has felt like a long long wait, with so much resting on the outcome. I think we can tell from the reaction now that neither of us was taking this for granted. This is total relief and release territory. Weight lifted. And now I feel it come off, I realise it was sitting far heavier on me than I ever imagined. I walk now and still neither of us is hardly saying a thing. Just being together in this moment of magnitude. Finally we can say it. See you on Friday. Wow yes. It only occurs to me now that there's been a huge unspoken 'if' in the air. So much so that now I realise we haven't actually said it once until now. Now it's actually a when. See you on Friday. It doesn't seem real.

And of course I can and will go to the airport. This whole furlough thing has been a massive advantage in this highly unusual situation as it's meant I've been more or less available to take every phonecall, almost immediately reply to every message or jump on every chat as it began. And now to go to an airport on any day no matter what time a flight is scheduled to come in.

We talk about the arrival a little on chat as midnight ticks over and we roll into the 18th, realising that we will meet tomorrow. The thought that we've never actually met is just the strangest concept to both of us and we wonder how it will be in an airport in these times of Covid. The travel restrictions dictating home or hotel isolation for 10 days only came into effect a few days ago - February 15 to be exact - and how you're supposed to behave in all this is all so new and unknown. And I have a really shocking thought. This is a really big news story in the UK. Pretty much the biggest one right now, so of course the media and attendant photographers are all over the airports, mostly Heathrow. We will have no idea what it will be like until we actually both get there. A few questions. Will hugging be allowed and if not, how strictly will that be enforced`? Are you even allowed to meet someone off a plane and then walk through the airport with them. No idea about anything really. Especially if we do find ourselves right in the middle of a media spectacle in arrivals. It really is possible. So we formulate a plan which seems ridiculous, absurd, surreal. But these are surreal times. If it does all look like being a bit of a circus, I'll hang back away from the main arrivals section. Then, when Maja comes out, we'll make sure to have made eye contact. If she sees me stay where I am she'll know what to do. And that is to follow me as I turn around and walk directly to the airport bus station and to the stop for the shuttlebus. If there's a quiet place somewhere on the way we can then say hello in the more traditional manner. But really, a lot of this will have to be played by ear if there is something of a situation. This really is CIA stuff and to really take us to the right level of CIA clearance, I'll have to make sure to have walked the route to the bus stop from the arrival gate before Maja arrives so that I'll know exactly where to go. Otherwise we could have the ridiculous situation of someone following someone who's lost and is going round in circles or worse, doubling back on themselves. No. If it comes to this, I want to be able to see Maja, make eye contact, turn round and walk straight to where we have to go. Confidently, no messing. Yes we see the absolute absurdity of it all. And now, with this conversation having taken us into the small hours we have arrived at Thursday. Which means we can actually say it so we do. 'See you tomorrow.' But we're not quite finished there as we start to explore how this is making us feel after this long week that's felt more like a month. I let slip here that I've been really tired during the days just like Maja has. But my excuse is that I've been staying up all hours watching the Tennis Australian Open. She suggests this is a convenient excuse and she might just have a point. The truth is that yes, I have been a bit on edge about all this as well but I really don't want to go there in any kind of discussion. But we do start to go there now as I admit this is all hitting me a little. Hard? Maja asks. Just little tickles, I say. Like rabbit punches. But friendly rabbits. Oh dear. Line crossed there? But she says she feels it too and puts it into real words. Belly rabbit punches. Yeah. I feel you. And like that a phrase is born. Belly rabbits. Invented by us, I say. It really is time for goodnights and I sign off saying, Goodnight and hold those rabbits in. Oh, what the hell am I writing in these chats and what the hell are we doing?

Day minus one
Thursday February 18

Maja:

I'm excited about leaving tomorrow. But my body is filled with a myriad of emotions and self doubt. Am I doing the right thing? I am going to miss everything I have here, and it also feels absolutely horrible that I know that I need to leave my puppy Tommy as well. Pets are really hard. I've bonded so strongly with him, he even sleeps with his head on my upper arm, using it as a pillow. I used to toss and turn quite a lot before I got a dog, but now every time I need to move during the night, I wake up and make sure I'm not crushing him or disturbing his sleep. It's a beautiful bond we have, and I never want to leave his side. Never. Ever. He is still tiny. And he is so innocent. He has never done anything wrong and he has no idea of what is about to happen. That the only person he trusts in the world has to leave him. I know that my husband and my mum are going to take great care of him while I'm gone, but I'm his world. He doesn't really know anything or anyone else. He is only five months old.

It breaks my heart. I love him so much.

Mark:

Today seems to stretch out into an eternity. One more day in what has been one of the longest weeks of my life and, I'm beginning to suspect, the actual longest of Maja's. It feels like every day since the 11th has been a constant run of battles, justifications and fears of everything becoming derailed at any moment for any number of reasons.

Maja says she would like to walk a little when she gets to London. The Corona thing means self isolation for ten days meaning she will have to stay in the house during that time, but transport from the airport is, by definition, allowed. That includes having to be among people in enclosed spaces. Surely it would be better to walk some of the way. Makes sense to me. But her reasoning is more the fact that once she's arrived at the house she won't be able to see London at all for 10 days and I'm only just learning now that, as good as her English is, she's never been to an actual English speaking country. So this will be her first time in London and she won't be able to see any of it for the first 10 days. Unless she goes for at least something of a walk before getting to the house. I've also discovered in the past week that she knows nothing of London. Nothing. Never even heard of Leicester Square. Oxford

Street and Hyde Park could be little quiet backwaters for all she cares. And Big Ben? If I told her that was the name of the guy on top of the big column in Trafalgar Square, well she'd believe me. She's heard of all the places I've written about in the Diaries. The Blues Kitchen, Ain't Nothin But, and various other venues and such. But mainstream tourist places? Not a notion. So we'll start from the beginning then. I'd already decided it would be a good idea to get the London shuttle bus from Heathrow to Victoria rather than the tube so that we spend more time above ground and she can get to see London that way at least before disappearing indoors for 10 days. I want to give her the best view of London possible when she arrives so I decide I should go and check out the route from Victoria to somewhere near our place. I can kinda see it on a route map but I really want to see for myself. I also want to know exactly where we'll have to go to catch the next bus after getting off the shuttle bus. So I take a trip to Victoria, find the drop off point for the shuttle bus and then try to find the bus stop to bring us home. It's a lot harder than I thought and nowhere near the coach station so I already feel glad that I've taken the time to come and see the actual view from the ground. So yep, I've found the right bus stop and now I'm going to ride that bus all the way home to see how much through the sights it actually goes. It doesn't disappoint as it winds its way all through central London before taking me somewhere close to Kentish Town. I could take it a lot closer but I'm mindful of Maja's request to have a bit of a walk so I get off at a stop I consider to be a reasonable distance away for a 10 minute walk through north west London suburbia, emerging at the far end of Kentish Town. From there it's a full look at what will be her local high street and a straight shoot home. Which is where I find myself right now after completing all this.

When I arrive, Maja's there, on the computer, telling me she's just putting the finishing touches to her packing and asking if I'm ready for her my end. I am. 'Great, it's really happening,' she says. Yep. She asks if I'm going to be nervous about this first meeting but I don't think so. She says she is, but in an excited way. That's about natural. We look at buses and conclude she'll be leaving the apartment a little after 10 tomorrow morning. She goes on to talk about the wonderful day she has planned for tomorrow. The books she'll read, the music she'll listen to, the casual, meandering journey now the 10am leaving time has been decided on. And of course whatever is waiting at the other end, mostly the fact that she'll be in London and far from this situation she's been wanting to get away from for so long. The time is very much almost here. She still wants to pass a little more time tonight. Hell, we both do. So we get off chat and I go out into the street for a bit of a talk on the phone where we don't really cover much more than what we've already been talking about but it's cool to hang like this, although in not more than a few daylight hours we won't be needing the phone anymore. We don't sign off with a goodbye. Instead, it's what feels like a surreal, 'See you tomorrow.'

THE LONDON DIARY
MAJA'S LONDON

Day zero
Friday February 19, 2021

Maja:

I wake up early to finish up the last touches of my preparations. Bag is packed, I take a shower, then decide that I will bring that raincoat afterall that me and Mark have been discussing since yesterday if I'll need or not. It's always nice to have a raincoat so in the bag it goes. I can only take one suitcase so it has been really hard to choose what to pack. With Corona, it's not like I'm not really going to be able to browse in any stores once I'm there, so it's been important for me to choose wisely what to take. Mark's been helping by buying me the bulky necessities over in London, so I'm going to be set when I get there and that's a load of stuff I don't have to pack. I have what I need, and I'm ready to leave. With my heart as heavy as lead I say goodbye to my husband and Tommy, my dog. It's really hard to leave. But I can't stay. We wave and I take a last look at them and then turn around and walk away. With tears running down my cheeks. I look at the scenery around me, and it hurts so much seeing the place I had to fight so hard to get to slipping away from my reach. It's cold and sunny outside. The tired rays of light glisten on the snow that lies undisturbed foot-deep on the side of the footpath. I walk the same path to the underground station that I've walked so many times before, and everything is so familiar to me. I pass the hairdresser where I got my ear pierced when I was a little kid. The swimming pool me and my family would go to when I was still in kindergarten. I have so many memories of this place, and it is with a heavy heart and tear stained cheeks that I message Mark that I've arrived at the station.

The trip to the airport goes without much trouble. My suitcase isn't that heavy, and I'm only bringing one bag and a small backpack, so it isn't hard to carry. I arrive at the airport way before necessary to have plenty of time checking in and it goes smoothly. When I reach the check-in counter the lady sitting there seems very surprised to hear that I am going to London. She checks my documents to make sure that I've completed all of the required formalities such as the passenger locator form, ordered the Covid tests for after arrival and of course that I have a certificate telling me that I have tested negative for Covid. Everything is in order and I get to continue along. Once I've passed security and found the gate I finally start to relax a little bit. I call Mark up to see how things are going his end. Everything seems fine. He says he will soon be on his way to the airport to meet me. We talk for a while, and I feel kind of awkward not really wanting to call anyone else, so we stay on the line. Just hanging on. Hanging out. Not saying much or anything at all, feeling relieved to know that we're going to meet soon.

We hang up after a while and I have to wait a bit on my own. There's a lady walking around close to the gate with a survey and I decide to take part. It's about why are you travelling to London. In normal times this would have been a completely unnecessary survey to do, but with recent events it is very much a valid question. Who in their right mind would want to go from a country where everything is nice and open like it is in Sweden, to a country which is in lockdown and pretty much still totally closed? To one of the hardest hit countries of this pandemic? Well, someone like me. I answer something along the lines of: to meet family/ friends. That's a fitting survey answer for a question like that. I don't think too much of it until she expresses surprise and delight that she's found someone who is going to London as an actual destination rather than using it as a transit point like, apparently, just about everyone else who's going there.

It's finally boarding time and I reach my seat. There's not really anyone sitting closeby, which is greatly fitting for a day like today. But the plane isn't completely empty either. I would say, maybe about 20 per cent of the seats are taken, but I'm not really looking that carefully. There is about a flight every third day, so that's probably why they're able to fill it up as much as they had. I sit down next to the window, wearing my compulsory face mask. The plane soon takes off and I have this immense feeling of relief. I'm on my way. I lean back and let myself drift away, listening to the album In between dreams by Jack Johnson. At my request of something to listen to, Mark recommended it just before I left. It's a wonderful record, and I let it go on repeat as I allow myself to be transported to that wonderful state in between dreams. Dreams of a brighter, unknown future. I just sleep.

Time flies, and after I don't know how long, we start to approach London. I sluggishly look out of the window, seeing the city that I'm going to live in. The city called London. I feel excitement starting to bubble up in my chest as, more and more, I see the details of the endless rows of brown buildings beneath the clouds. They look like gingerbread houses. London, the city of endless gingerbread houses in their neat little rows. We get closer and closer to the ground and I feel the impact as the wheels of the plane touch the ground. I'm here now!

I can't help myself, and I text Mark, I'm here now! The first thing I do is tell him about the gingerbread houses.

Mark:

It's with some relief that I chat with Maja this morning. All seems to be going smoothly and she's out of the door by 9am my time. She's on her way now. However, by the time I'm on my way and leaving for the airport, she still doesn't have a room in London. I was really hoping Elvin would have left by then so that I would be able to get in there and have at least something of a once over but timings just haven't worked out so I'll have to leave with him still occupying the place. Which means Maja will see it for the first time in whatever state he's left it. I just have to trust he'll do at least something of a decent job before he leaves. He's been a good housemate and friendly enough, but he's been pretty much a keep himself to himself kind of guy so there are no tearful goodbyes. Or goodbyes of any kind as he's out at work early and will be leaving while I'm out. So that's that for Elvin. Good luck on your travels mate. On a scale of depth of feeling, it's the equivalent of one of your goldfish dying. Probably your least favourite one.

The flight's due in at 6pm but it can be a bit of a trek to Heathrow. And I have a few things to check out once I get there. I've also got one or two errands left to run to cross and dot the final i's and t's before Maja's arrival, including a trip to Ktown to pick up some essentials for her that she's asked if I could sort out. Coffee, orange juice, fresh fruit and the like. Nothing major because as I've heard, she's barely been eating in Sweden over the past few weeks. All that done and I'm on my way to the airport by around 2pm quite confident of getting there in plenty of time to find the arrivals gate, and then to make sure I know the route from there to the coach station. But oh dear. I get down into Ktown tube and it takes a while for me to discover that the train I want has got issues today and there's a substantial waiting time for it, rather than the usual zero to four minutes you can normally expect. Not cool. That almost never happens, but it's happened on this particular day. Balls. Very reluctantly I leave the tube station and go back up to the street to catch a bus to Kings Cross, where I will catch the train to Heathrow. Disaster up here too as a whole bunch of buses aren't running for some reason and I have another wait of 15 to 20 minutes when again, a maximum of four is to be expected. So, having given myself an extra hour for the journey, I've already lost most of the grace of that time. Then, when the bus does finally get here and we set off, I discover that Ktown is undergoing a whole bunch of roadworks down the far end and these cause even more delays. This really isn't going very well at all. If I'd left in what I thought would have been optimal time and had this lot happen I'd probably be looking at arriving late by now, and Maja walking out into London with no-one to meet her. That just would not be an option. As it is, by the time I finally get on the Kings Cross to Heathrow train the timing is looking at least half respectable and I arrive at the airport a little before 5pm.

Then I discover I'm already very close to the arrivals gate, and then that the coach station is also very nearby to that. Cool. I think I deserve those two mini breaks. All I have to do now is buy a couple of coach tickets and I'll be at the gate ready and waiting by 5:30. Perfect. No. Balls. There was nothing about this on any website I saw but the Heathrow coach isn't running due to Covid. Balls again. OK. Let's just get to the gate to be ready in situ and make a new plan from there. I park myself in sight of where the people come out and have a look at the tube plan I keep in my bag. Yep. This will do nicely. We can get a tube to Piccadilly Circus where Maja will be able to get her first look at central London. Then it's a really cool but not too long walk from there to the bus stop by Oxford Circus station to catch the 88 that will go all the way to our house, or we can get off it a little earlier if Maja still wants to have that walk she was talking about before having to start that 10 day quarantine thing.

Now I've done this and I really am ready, I have a chance to fully take in my surroundings and to see how people are behaving. First, the good news is that there is no sign of any TV cameras. And people are allowed to come and meet friends and relatives; a sign says that only one person is allowed to greet arrivals. That's fine. I counted myself on the way here and confirmed that I am indeed one person. The place is weirdly empty though. You'd normally expect to see whole families all milling around arrivals. But no. Just a few individuals dotted around, possibly also reflecting the fact that there will not be many people arriving at arrivals. This should be quite quick. I wonder how Maja's flight is getting on. We're very much edging towards 6pm now. It should be just about landing. And yep. There it is on the screen. Landed and on its way in. My phone pings. 'Just landed. Waiting to get out. Wooooooooooooooooooooooo!!' 'Welcome to London,' I shoot back. This really is it now and she asks what our strategy for meeting is. She's very pleased that I'm able to report we can just behave normally. With masks on, of course. She should be coming through soon, but no-one emerges from the gates at all and time starts to drag on. And on. And on. Then I start to hear people coming through the gates furiously complaining of waits of up to three hours. Oh dear. That's not good. Neither is the fact that they seem to be coming out in very intermittent groups of three. And Maja's talking of hundreds of people out there waiting to come through. I think I should settle in here. But after an hour she messages to say she's near the front of the queue. Great. Then a message a few minutes later. 'After this queue, do you know what they got?' 'Don't know.' 'Another queue.' Oh that's a good one.

I'm clearly not the only one waiting far beyond what I expected but I think I can see the most uncomfortable person in the room. Someone thought it would be a really good idea to turn up at arrivals wearing a dinosaur costume. Yep. Full on tyrannosaurus rex thing. I'm sure it was such a laugh to arrive and anticipate the delighted shock of their friend. I wonder how that's all working out now. I can see the costume over there this whole time. The poor guy, or girl, in there, has been waiting at least an hour and a half over the odds. And I'm sure that when whoever it is they're meeting comes out, their mood will be quite different to what it was when the plane landed. And who knows what mood poor stuck in dinosaur suit person will be in by then as well? How did that play out anyway? 'You'll have my name on a board so I can see where to go?' 'No. Not at all. I'll be the one in a dinosaur suit.' 'Oh. Er...OK. Didn't see that coming. But what if loads of other people decide to come dressed as dinosaurs?' And on it would have gone I guess, and they took their chances.

Unfortunately I don't see how that little drama plays out because I get a message. Only eight people in front of her now. Then two. Then.

I see her walking through arrivals all on her own, pink jacket on just like she said she would have, as though we wouldn't have recognised each other. But then, maybe we wouldn't have done with the whole mask thing going on. I'm looking straight at her but she hasn't seen me as her eyes dart from side to side looking for at least a semi familiar face in this country she's never seen before. I take a step forward and our eyes lock. Oh yes. Here we are now and we both walk to close the distance between us. All I want to do is hug her hard and let her know she's OK now. And that's exactly what happens as we say hello and pull each other tight as we finally find ourselves on the same little patch of ground. Then I tell her the bus is out but we have a new route. First, the lift, and arriving there we're on our own. So our masks come off and we see each other fully and up close for the first time. Cool. Another hug, without talking, then the doors open again and a few people walk in so the masks go back on. After the lift I take the lead as we head into the tube and it's really bizarre that there are hardly any people here. She asks where we're going and I say it's a surprise but that she'll like it. She accepts that and on we go. When the train arrives and we find a carriage, we're the only people in it. So once seated, we take the opportunity to remove the masks again but still neither of us speaks. Instead, she removes her left hand from her pocket and shows it to me, holding all the fingers up to give me a clear look. Oh wow. Am I seeing what I think I'm seeing? I don't actually ask the question but it's clear in my eyes. She totally receives the unspoken, incredulous words and nods slowly. With that she takes my hand in hers and leans against me like the weary traveller she is. As she does so I get a much closer look at her ring finger with that white band of skin circling it where a wedding ring used to be. I put an arm around her and we both snuggle in, hands still holding. But really, it feels very innocent. She's tired and I'm just comforting a friend who's had a really tough few weeks and more, and a bit of a journey today followed by an uncomfortably long wait in arrivals, all while travelling in the time of Covid. It just so happens that we only met for the first time a few minutes ago. It's often too loud on the tube to talk comfortably so she waits patiently and trustfully until I announce that it's time to get off. We've arrived at Piccadilly Circus and, with me carrying her suitcase, we walk up the steps and into the famous plaza with its overlooking motion and colour-filled advertising screens. Here, I get her to stand in front of them as I step back with my phone. Snap. Maja's first photograph in London and we are right in the heart of it, and again, it's eerily empty but that really adds to the drama of the moment. She has truly arrived. Phone back in pocket and I lead the way again, heading off to Regent Street. In my left hand I have the handle of Maja's wheeled suitcase. And now, in my right hand, I have Maja's hand. We look at each other and smile. She isn't letting go. And just for the record, neither am I.

We walk down Regent Street then I direct us down a side street to the right, then left to continue walking in the same direction. We're now on Kingly Street and I ask if she has any idea where she is. She doesn't. We continue a little way, and then she lets out a little oh wow, of recognition as we arrive in front of Ain't Nothin But.... London's world famous blues bar and a major venue character in the world of Mark's Diaries. We stop here for a selfie, chat for a little while, and then we're back off on our way, talking about everything, nothing, and just generally laughing a lot. And in this lockdown London world, it's still unpopulated enough that there are times when it feels like we have the city to ourselves. At the very least we are totally alone in these side streets. Yes. Right now, London is ours so much that it feels as though we're wearing it. We walk past the famous Carnaby Street and its imposing sign and back onto Regent Street where we cross the road at Oxford Circus and go on over to the bus stop for the 88 which, as I said, goes all the way to my house in Kentish Town. We wait there, still holding hands and talking for five minutes or so and then Maja asks if it's possible to walk back to my house from here. It is. 'Can we do that?' she asks quickly and excitedly. Yep. We can. And so we walk. Hand in hand all the way. She sets a fast pace, I'm happy to say. I'm a fast walker myself and I'm more than happy to keep up. As a result we heat up quite quickly and jumpers come off somewhere halfway between here and Camden town. All the way she's marvelling at how old so much of the architecture seems to be and I delight in pointing out buildings that are hundreds of years old, yet sit perfectly comfortably wedged in between their modern cousins. Through Camden and Maja doesn't know it yet, but we're on the final strait as the road merges seamlessly with that of Kentish Town's high street. We're still holding hands and are just past the main shops of KTown when a woman remarks on our T-shirted appearances. 'Are you guys not cold at all?' she asks as she approaches, walking in the opposite direction. 'Not at all,' I answer honestly. 'You should try it. It feels lovely.' 'I think I'll leave it to younger people like yourselves,' she says. 'I'm freezing.' 'Walk a bit faster, it works for us,' I call good naturedly to her as she starts to disappear into the night. She laughs and politely declines again. Next to me, Maja is almost in shock. 'You talk to strangers over here?' 'All the time,' I say laughing at the clear awe in her face. 'You should try it.' 'No thanks.' Give it time.

We've arrived and we take a left turn into the Carrol Close estate. For the past 10 minutes or so she's been asking if some of the houses we've been seeing look like ours and I've been saying no, and she's also been asking if our house looks like the gingerbread houses she saw from the air on her London approach. Again, no. Then we're in the estate itself and she sees the row of houses we're heading towards. 'Oh, they're totally like the gingerbread houses I saw from the air,' she says emphatically. OK. I guess we do live in a gingerbread house then.

I open the front gate and go to open the door to the house but Maja stops me. 'Not yet,' she says. 'Can't we wait outside for a while? I'm not ready to go in and meet a load of new people yet.' Fair enough. I suggest leaving the suitcase right inside the door and going for a walk but she doesn't want to walk anymore either. So we sit down on the small front garden step. There, still holding hands, we talk quietly about nothing in particular.

I'm sure you're wondering if I'm feeling the slight stirring of something here and the answer is very much yes. And for the Jenn situation, it's about time I say here that we're just friends, just very close friends who happen to have lived together for quite a long time. Going on 12 years in fact. I might as well get this bit out now as well. We did start out as a relationship, and that lasted a year give or take. The joke back then among our Madrid friends was that we split up and then started dating, which is actually a pretty fair take on what happened. So yeah, we still got on very well and just seamlessly carried on living comfortably together. It probably helped that the Hamburg jaunt with Drunken Monkees straddled the two realities of couple Mark and Jenn and friend Mark and Jenn. Drunken Monkees was my pop punk band in Madrid, and Hamburg was the German adventure we went on after recording our debut album to try to emulate some foursome from Liverpool and set ourselves up there as a band that could really have a chance of doing something.

I'd joined them not long after moving to Madrid when I met band leader and singer Rick in a bar after overhearing him talking about his band needing a bass player. Talk about time and place. I just walked up to him, introduced myself and said I was a bass player. This led to us hanging out all night and then going back to Bachus, the bar he owned, where he introduced me to the guys in his band who worked there with him - guitarist Rob and drummer Joey. We arranged that I would audition the next day. That went great and just like that I was the bass player in Drunken Monkees.

Fast forward to the Hamburg thing and it didn't work out. I returned to live in Madrid with Jenn, who I'd broken up with on the phone while in Germany. It was pretty much mutual to be fair and we made it quite clear in the subsequent years, through a few more moves together as well, that we were both free to pursue other avenues if something came along. She even once said the words, 'Don't think we're going to grow old together.' However, nothing really did come along for either of us, so we settled into a quite comfortable pattern around each other which included living in the same room in this house in Kentish Town where we've been for the better part of five or six years now. I don't really know about her, I don't think she has, but I haven't really been properly looking for anything to replace this. Not seriously, except for the odd mild dalliance here and there which I've always been open about and all of which have very quickly gone nowhere. Over the years I've quite got to like our cosy friendly, companionable-but-apart comfortzone and I think she has too. So much so that, without any ceremony and without saying the words out loud at all, I eventually decided quite a few years ago, why look for anything else? This works. And so it has. And through this whole thing I've been thinking there's nothing going on to change this despite some of the things we said to each other in little veiled hinting moments.

Well now Maja's sitting next to me and our chat has subsided to a very comfortable silence with her looking the other way to me and out towards the far end of the close. I start to let in whatever it is I've been feeling and holding back over the past few days as I realise this could actually be something and I suddenly realise I'm in one of those moments in life you just can't let pass you by. You think you'll get another chance some other time but you really don't. You have to take this one. This one or nothing at all. This one that I've arrived at completely by accident. Alright, I deliberately said the words, 'You could come here,' but they were just words to help out. Nothing more. But then the seriousness began and I became a very virtual shoulder to lean on. Now I'm a very literal shoulder to lean on. If she chooses to, which she isn't right now. Yes. I've opened the gates to my thoughts and feelings. I had them locked so tight, I thought, but they've suddenly turned into floodgates and become overwhelmed. With that, I know I really do have to do something right now or regret it and forever wish I had. But she's suddenly so physically far away. She starts to say something, I think. But I cut her off. With my left arm already over her shoulder, I gently but firmly and quite quickly direct her head so that she now faces me. I can't allow for hesitation now. I just can't. To hesitate would be to stop. To stop would be...I don't want to think what it would be. I just follow on through with the movement, but then suddenly realise that she's completely going with it. We meet in the middle and kiss. It goes on for quite a long time. With that, everything comes together. We part and I realise all my mental energy just went into making that moment happen and I have no idea what to say now it has actually happened. But there is no silence. She immediately jumps into it with a big smile and a wide eyed exclamation. 'I can kiss Mark.' 'Yes you can,' I say, with what must be a pretty stupid looking smile as I try to act cool. So she does. And I do. Again and again. Then abruptly she stands up. Did I say stands up? She doesn't. From a sitting start she breaks into an impossibly immediate run, still holding my hand. 'What the h...' I say to the open air of the street. But I have no choice. All I can do is launch myself upwards, pulled by her own force, and run with her. Together, still holding hands, we sprint to the end of the close. Then we turn and sprint back to the house. With that completed she turns to me and takes both my hands in hers. Ever so slightly out of breath she says, 'OK. I'm ready. We can go in now.'

We walk into the house to just a little bit of a social anticlimax. Given Maja's hugely extended wait to get through security at arrivals, and the fact that we walked here from central London, we're arriving a lot later than I expected. Neither Sam or Cris are still up, and Jenn is only around to say hi, to give Maja the bedding things and other sundries we bought, and then she pretty much disappears. That leaves me and Maja to have a look at what she has to deal with in the room that is now hers. Despite all I did to prepare her, she's still stunned at how small the room is. Again, I did say but it really is super tiny; I will later learn that it's the same size, possibly even smaller, than her walk-in closet at the apartment she left this morning. Now I take in the state of the place. To give Elvin his due, by London house sharing standards he's actually left it in an acceptable enough state, but it's not quite up to Maja standards. So although she's had a long and emotional day, she insists we get busy with a full deep clean of the room before we can go to bed. Yes you read right. Before we can go to bed. OK. Let's get started.

Maja:

Yes. I do like things clean. Pass me some surface cleaner please, and oh my, have you seen the broken handcuffs behind the bed? Who lived here before?

THE DIARIES

Day one
Saturday February 20

Mark:

We barely move from the room today. Maja's at the very beginning of a journey which is all about recovery. I know that she's felt tense and almost emotionally hunted for a long time. She's now out of that situation but the effects and feelings run deep and do not disappear just like that. But she says that last night was the best night's sleep she's had since she can remember. Actually the first time since she can remember that she slept all the way through the night. A notable event in itself. She was just restful and relaxed, for the first time since she can remember. With that she has a wake up call of just how much she needed to get out of her situation in Sweden. So yes. Right now is about rest with absolutely no obligations to do anything. For a full 10 days. In fact, she's essentially legally obliged to do practically nothing for the next 10 days, or at least not to go anywhere. It's also about processing. Lots and lots of processing. I spend the whole day listening as Maja talks about what she's been through over the past year or so. As she talks, it's clear that she's talking to fathom things out for herself as much as engaging me in her thoughts. There are so many branches and avenues down which we can drive and I gently nudge her into a few of them, leading us to explore, in detail, quite a few smaller parts of the big picture. Through all this I basically just try to put pieces together and make sense of it all. It helps that we've spoken so much on the phone over the past week and I've at least got a handle on some of it, especially the more up to date stuff which I heard about more or less in real time.

We also touch on a few tiny details of our phone calls in the past week, including some of the little hints we dropped to each other which led to bigger hints, which have all led to where we are now. In between, Maja gets to meet Cris, the leader and vocalist in Wild Child, the Italian heavy metal band I play and travel with, and Sam. The guys are massively friendly and welcoming to her, and when they talk I do my best to stay firmly on the sidelines and let their own conversations develop. Basically, I want these interactions to be organic, with no input from me, and they are indeed organic as Maja charms them with her enthusiasm of being in a whole new environment with new people to hang out with.

These little interludes aside, the two of us talk so much that we totally forget about eating until it around 8pm and we realise we've made no plans. The last thing Maja ate was breakfast yesterday morning. I'm not that much different, although I did manage to grab a small thing at the airport once I realised the security holdup was happening. She asks if it's possible to get takeout sushi at this time in London. Yes it is, but I have to leave right now if I'm going to get to Camden before the place closes. One mad successful dash later and we have something resembling dinner and the first thing Maja has eaten in almost 36 hours.

Maja:

I wake up alone in the small bed, looking around myself in dislocated confusion. Where am I? It's hard to remember just what happened last night. I turn around and look at the room, it's tiny. The walls are white and have specks of dirt on them, the ceiling is white and somewhat patterned, like someone's been painting it with a drippy paint that wouldn't quite stick on. There's a closet that's small, but proved to fit all my clothes without any problems. By my feet I find a little shelf, over the bed next to the window. Under the bed there's three drawers. I rest my eyes a little more, squeezing my face down in the pillows, looking up again. Yeah. The room is the same. It's not my room in Stockholm. This is a minimal room, that would barely be enough for a child's room. But. It's mine. The bed feels wonderful, it's soft. And from it I can see out of the window. Outside there's a beautiful tree, and it's in full bloom right now. I feel exhausted, but also rested in a strange way. I've slept through the night for the first time in such a long time, which is a noticeable event in itself. The room is tiny but I don't care. I'm just so happy that I'm here.

I search for my toiletries and try out the shower. It's a nice shower, shared with all the other tenants, of course, but it even has a bathtub and I'm pleased to see that it is kept clean. Showered and dressed I go down to the kitchen, where I meet Mark.

Good morning, we say as we sheepishly look at each

other, and soon afterwards we go back to my room to get to know each other a little bit better.

In the evening I ask Mark if he could go out for sushi. Of course he does, and when he gets back I'm very careful to eat only a little bit of it.

London, day two
Sunday February 21

Maja:

I'm in London. It's a surreal fact to me and every time I try to reflect on it, it hits me forcefully by surprise. I am quite excited about being here. I'm not really sure what life has in store for me here, but that is of less concern. Right now, I'd just like to rest and talk. I spend most of the day with Mark, staring at the ceiling, telling him about who I am and listening to his stories as well. All while looking out the window at the beautiful tree. We joke a lot, and one of our favourite subjects here is that since I can't go out at all due to the enforced isolation, I could be anywhere. I could be in Brazil for all I know. And we continue to joke about how cold it is in Brazil this time of year.

We have a garden I can use even though I am in isolation, which is lovely. So we go out there, just for a little while. But apart from that, we're just in bed. Resting. Talking.

Mark:

Maja really opens up her heart to me and I start to gain a far greater understanding of where she is and how vulnerable she feels right now. All this makes me feel like I need to take care of her even more, and make sure she gets the rest she needs to recover.

In between all this talking there is a little flurry of activity sometime mid afternoon as we suddenly remember, just in time for today's post, that Maja has to do the first of the two Covid tests as part of the legal requirement of her quarantine. It's a good job there are two of us as it takes both of us to figure out how to do this thing, mostly how to put together the flat-pack cardboard box she's been sent to post it all back in. In between this and intense conversations, we eat nothing at all until evening, totally forgetting to do so as the idea of food just slips off both of our to do lists. Again.

When evening time does come and we realise we should probably eat something, Maja decides it's time she gets into the spirit of being in England a bit and wants to try something typically English. Hmm. What could that be? And given that it's quite late by the time I'm going out shopping, options are limited. What is typically English food anyway? I'm really not sure. I browse the shelves of the supermarket and there they are. Supermarket bought, so not fully authentic, but nevertheless, English. I bring back small individual pork pies, scotch eggs and a quiche. In case you don't know, here's a little introduction to all three. Pork pies are characterised, at least as far as I see it, by the type of pastry used to make them. So you have kind of minced pork meat in a dense crunchy pastry very rich in pork fat. Scotch eggs are a full egg wrapped in sausage meat which is then covered in breadcrumbs and deep fried. So yes, these two things really do have quite high calorie counts. Then there's quiche, described by Maja when I get back, as an egg pie, but sorry, no. But it is again a pastry based thing containing cooked egg and usually some kind of meat and cheese. And onions. So again, quite high on the calorie scale. I introduce all these to Maja along with that great cornerstone of all things British, brown sauce, a kind of rich, spicy vinegary sauce without which bacon, eggs and most types of British sausage are somehow incomplete. That might just be me, but you get the picture.

I suppose it could be said that I might have been a bit more judicious and delicate with my food choices and gone for things that were a little lighter maybe, but really, if you're looking for traditional English food, it does generally lean towards the, shall we say, higher caloried side. But maybe I could have at least added a salad.

Maja:

By evening, I ask Mark to go buy me some English food, I think it is time for me to try something English. I've been here for two days now, and haven't really tried anything yet, so it's time. Off he goes, I fall asleep and when I wake up he is back. He's bought a couple of things and is in the kitchen preparing them. When he's done, he calls me down and we eat. For the first time today. And we didn't eat anything at all yesterday. We just had a little bit of sushi yesterday. What I didn't expect is that English food is quite heavy. And I've been really bad at eating recently. So I sit in the kitchen and Mark serves me this decent sized meal, so the polite thing is to eat it, which is what I do. It's good, the pork pie, scotch egg and quiche are all quite nice. Although not really any extreme flavours or anything which is great, but just quite fatty. I eat maybe half of the meal, and then I sit back, waiting for Mark to finish. Doing so, I can feel how my stomach starts to act up. It starts to cramp. Slowly at first, but soon more and more violently. I'm getting cold sweats and am really wishing Mark could finish up his portion so I can excuse myself. As soon as he does, I tell him that I want to go rest, and I hurry up upstairs and lie down. It's painful. Really painful. I can't remember what happened any further than this, everything that remains is the memory of pain. My consciousness must have faded away.

Mark:

I get back and she's very interested to see what I've bought, and keen to try everything so we get to it. So far so fun, and I'm really quite tickled that she seems to really like it all, especially the brown sauce which many non-English people really don't understand or remotely like.

Then, as soon as we've finished eating, Maja says she needs to sleep. This, I will discover, will become a pattern as her body recovers from barely eating for the past however long it's been. But right now, I am in no way prepared for what is about to happen. Almost as soon as we're in the bedroom the convulsions start. I ask her what's wrong but she can barely speak, at least not enough to tell me anything useful. Her whole stomach seems to be contracting and as it does, her head flies back, her eyeballs also shooting up and back as it does so. In between is the most horrible, at times high pitched hyperventilating. I try to get her to concentrate on breathing normally, at least, but I get little reaction to that.

Otherwise, there's absolutely nothing I can do but watch, horrified, not even sure yet what could possibly have caused this. As I watch helplessly, my hand is on my phone and I wonder at what point I'm going to just call it and hit 999. This goes on for about five minutes but it feels like 55. Then slowly everything starts to slow down, back to normal-ish. Her breathing slows and she looks at me like, 'What the hell happened?' Like she's just arrived in the room to the aftermath of some dramatic scene she played no part in. With that she closes her eyes and falls into a sleep I'll best describe as restless. But asleep she is. I am not. I stay awake for an hour or so until she wakes again, all the time watching and making sure functions are all normal. Or at least normal enough that I don't have to return to my phone and thoughts of 999. Those thoughts are with me almost every second of that hour.

London, day three
Monday February 22

Mark:

Last night we didn't speak much about what happened, but today we get into it, especially now I've seen first hand how bad things have physically gotten for Maja. I'd been told of course, but I guess I have to admit that until last night when I saw it for myself, I really didn't understand how bad it all really was. I still don't fully, until she reluctantly admits why what happened last night happened. The way I understand it is that she was caught in a double fix of not wanting to hurt my feelings and of genuinely wanting to try everything. For the past few weeks, along with insomnia, she's barely been able to eat anything above survival rate, often going days or maybe even weeks of eating below the recommended calorie intake, and almost forcing herself at that. I also feel guilty at having introduced such fat-rich foods to her so soon, but I really had no concept at all of how much those kinds of foods could have affected her. That they could have caused such dramatic events was inconceivable to me. And I know what inconceivable means.

The one time we eat today, again quite late on, all we have is a super bland veggie soup. That's a generous description. I just boil some vegetables until they're supersoft and keep them in the water I did them in so that it can be called soup. Not even any salt. And some white fish fried in the absolute tiniest amount of oil. After all this, Maja has another very tired reaction. It is this that triggers her to finally admit to the problems she has with eating, and I realise that I have to tone it down even more when cooking for her. No seasoning of any kind, and absolutely no oil. I really do have to treat her as though she's properly sick with a body incapable of digesting anything beyond the simple. In that, this is like reintroducing someone to food who has been starved of it for so long for whatever reason. Within that, I've decided to eat only what Maja eats. It isn't a wonderful diet but it really helps with the solidarity of the situation.

Talking about all this, today we focus on what stress has done to Maja's body and general habits and the picture painted really isn't pretty. We also decide that what she has isn't an eating disorder. It's more like the inability to be able to eat, which is quite different. And as she's becoming more relaxed here, she is actually starting to want to eat and is even enjoying it a little, as much as one can enjoy bland boiled veggies and white fish. Although I have to say, I did do it quite well.

Maja:

I need to say, I love my family. I love my husband. With my whole heart. A lot of things have happened that have led me to where I am today. But this is one thing I am absolutely adamant on making clear. I can't be angry at you, or blame you. I would never wish anything bad of any of you. I miss you. I love you so much it hurts my whole being not being with you. Every day. Always. I love you.

I'm used to being seen as this strong woman that can do anything and never has any real issues, which makes talking about the issues I have really hard. I'm bad at talking about it. I am even bad at admitting any issues to myself. I'm fine. Nothing's on my mind. Everything is wonderful. I am not vulnerable. I am strong. I am smart. I can handle myself. I can do anything.

Yeah, you get it, I'm that kind of person.

This can sometimes lead to loneliness and isolation, even in normal times. Add to that, Covid, which has meant it even became frowned upon to meet friends and family. Meetings become sparse and, since I'm usually the one instigating meetings, they become practically non-existent. But I am not good alone, I need people around me to function. I get it if you don't understand how I can be both at once, but I can. I feel alone even when I'm with people but I am very sociable and need to have people around me.

I've often felt alone and I have had a hard time feeling properly understood. So I often only tell maybe one person how I feel, or I don't tell anyone. It's hard enough to admit to myself if I have any issues, and if I tell someone and they don't understand me or take it lightly, I find it so incredibly hurtful that I might not want to speak about it again.

I always try to be openhearted and explain to people close to me what is going on. I would never purposefully hide my intentions. I just don't have it in me to deceive anyone. Mark describes me as purehearted to such a level that I can't even understand how people can have bad intentions. How people can want to hurt people. I can't help but agree, I don't understand how people would like to do that. I know some people do. I just would never want to hurt anyone. Ever.

I'm very selective about who I trust enough to talk about any issues, and I rarely even mention anything to anyone. Much easier on everyone. So the problem becomes when I can't solve the issue by myself. That's why I've been very stressed for a long time now. I've been very alone in a situation that grew worse, and I've not felt understood in why I've taken the decisions I've had to take by those I've confided in. Which makes me feel like I'm taken lightly in a bad situation, leading to further stress and isolation from the world around me.

I hope that explanation of my personality makes it a little easier for you to understand why the story has come to where it is today.

I've been having a hard time recently, and I have had a hard time getting that understood. This has led to me feeling very stressed and I seem to be one of those people that have a problem eating if I get too stressed. It's like I just can't eat at all. Usually I am on the other side of the spectrum, alway having to control myself so I don't eat too much and make sure I eat healthily. So during this period I've lost weight a little bit quicker than might have been advisable. I've stayed mindful that this is a problem, trying to not completely skip eating and I've drunk a lot of water to help me stay alert. A little habit I used to have from years back, is to take a bath when I'm cold, to heat up. I used to do this often, especially when trying one diet after another. A lot of diets can leave you feeling really cold, so this time when I've had these problems eating I've taken a lot of baths to heat myself up.

Today I tell Mark about how I got to this place and that I want to return to ordinary eating habits as quickly as possible. He got really worried from what happened last night and I want to calm him down regarding that. I tell him about the stress and how that has made me unable to eat. And that this stress has been there for quite a long time by now, so my body needs to gently get back to normal eating habits.

Mark listens. Actively. It feels nice to feel heard. I'm not sure how much he understands, but he is starting to piece together an image of where I'm coming from. We talk for hours and hours. Of how I feel both mentally and physically. A lot of the subjects I bring up seem to be outside of his normal experiences but he is a great speaking companion. It's great that he actively listens and tries not to judge.

Like I said a few days ago, my room is absolutely tiny. And so my bed is also too small to sleep two people in, so Mark still gets to sleep downstairs. But since we can't hang out in Mark's room because Jenn lives there, we're spending all our time in my room.

Mark:

After dinner I cry in front of Maja for the first time. I have a chunk of my tongue missing. A piece of the tip at the front. It got ripped off in a hospital accident when I was five years old, maybe four. And yes. I was totally conscious. I've told the story many times, but have only cried once while telling it, which was during a counselling session when I was deep into my fibromyalgia years. Today I cry not for myself but for thoughts of my mother and the ordeal she suffered as a result of my own trauma of which I have very little memory. She was only in her early to mid twenties at the time and what she saw would have mentally scarred the most battle hardened of people.

I was in hospital for what was something of an experimental operation on a cleft palate which came as part of the deal of having a hare lip. This cleft is essentially a hole in the roof of the mouth, near the front. The aim of the operation was to close that hole. To do that, the idea was to cut open the skin up there, do the same to the end of my tongue, and then surgically attach the two together. The theory was that the two would then become anatomically fused. Then, in a second operation, the tongue could be cut away, leaving new skin behind, thus closing the hole. I was five, maybe four.

Naturally, talking was quite difficult after that first operation. There were some thoughts of me having a kind of signalling device for when I wanted attention. A whistle was the favoured option. I suggested a trumpet. In the end I got neither. Maybe what happened next happened too soon for that choice to be made. I'm also guessing the second operation would have happened relatively quickly afterwards and maybe in the same hospital visit because, well I've got my tongue attached to the roof of my mouth and you really don't want to stay like that for too long. We never got that far.

Although it was an NHS operation, I had a private room. I often did when I had operations at Booth Hall hospital where I was very well known by most of the staff, at least on this particular ward. My physical facial progress since birth had been so good that there were pictures of me on the wall in the main corridor to show it. This was among the pictures of many of the other young patients unfortunate enough to have to frequent a place such as this for the same reasons. My surgeon was the legendary John Lendrum, known to me then and deep into adult life, only as Mr Lendrum. His work in the treatment of hare lips and cleft palates was revolutionary and experimental and I believe he spent some time working in developing countries in this very field. I never saw him again once my time in his care was over, which was probably around the early teenage years. He died in 2015 leaving behind a considerable legacy.

I think this is an excellent opportunity to post up my own selected excerpts of this tribute to him which I found on the website livesonline.rcseng.uk

He was appointed as a consultant plastic surgeon to the North West Region at three widely separated hospitals.

These were Booth Hall Children's Hospital, Withington Hospital and Rochdale. It was a good thing that he enjoyed driving, usually fast, in coloured sports cars, with the top down. The stories of his car parking activities in the various hospitals were legendary. My mum said that this sounded exactly like the man she remembered.

J L was a skilled surgeon. He taught all the time and enjoyed watching young surgeons develop under his guidance and inspiration. He hated management interference with his ability to provide the best possible service for his patients. He was not a committee man and never sought high office in any association, but was elected to the council of BAPS in 1984 and did much useful work chairing the manpower planning and development committee, shaping the future of plastic surgery. John was elected an honorary member of BAPS in 1995. He was an honorary associate of the University of Manchester.

John enjoyed painting and retirement enabled him to paint more. He described himself as an artist with a 35-year interruption for a surgical career! He was a member of the Medical Artists' Association.

John was a colourful individual; he was loyal and generous, took great care of his patients and staff, but could be rebellious and outrageously incorrect!

I have no idea what that last statement means, but I'm sure you get the picture. What I take away from this is basically a man who knew what he was doing, cared deeply about it and what it meant to the people under his care - one of whom was of course me - and had absolutely no time for people who had no idea what they were talking about interfering in any of his business in any way.

So back to the story. I was sitting watching TV - Lassie since you're asking. I remember that detail like it was yesterday - when a nurse came in on her own. I was five years old, maybe four.

I didn't know exactly what she wanted, but she was holding a syringe. I'd had all kinds of injections since birth so the sight of needles was already routine. It held absolutely no fear for me. But this lady was alone and that did scare me. Worse, she didn't even say anything. Instead she just came towards me as though I was an object she could just stick things in. I wasn't having that and moved away from her. She wasn't having that and moved closer to me, at speed. I moved away from her again. She wasn't having that and came again until the two of us were walking, then running round in circles around the room. Yes, a grown adult, in some petty state of thwarted authoritarian petulance at having been disobeyed by a small child, was now chasing said small child in circles around a tiny hospital room brandishing a needle. I said no, no, no. Then more. I was five, maybe four.

I screamed.

Yep. Everything just came apart.

I have no memory of that. I remember watching the TV, I remember her coming in, I remember the running round in circles bit. Between that and my mum and her mum (my mum's mum, not the nurse's mum, incase you were wondering) entering the room - walking or running I have no idea - I have nothing. For what happened in between I have to rely on the memory of my mother, who wouldn't even talk of this to me until almost 30 years later, such was the trauma it inflicted upon her. I'm only realising while writing this that my grandmother never spoke to me of it at all, and I can't believe it's a topic I would never have raised with her. What they encountered was me screaming, a bemused nurse, and blood. Horror movie levels of blood. All in my mouth, all down my chin, all over my white hospital gown and all onto the floor. Enough to slip in. I know that I was quickly sedated, then anaesthetised, then immediately operated on again as an emergency case. The end result was that I lost the end of my tongue, and the roof of my mouth was significantly collapsed and similarly scarred. The hole that they were trying to patch up was also worse than it had been when it started, although over the years it has mostly closed, just by dint of my growing, so they could have just waited for that to happen and spared us all the - quite literal - pain, not to mention the, again quite literal, sweat blood and tears.

The nurse, I have no idea what happened to her and don't want to speculate. The operation as intended was abandoned as far as I know and, due to my own selective amnesia of the episode, I was spared the full trauma. So I've always been able to tell the story with a bit of a jokey demeanour. But today I tell Maja of it from the point of view of my mother. It's too much to think of and I'm barely through it when the tears come. Another little thing that brings us that much closer together.

Maja:

After getting back after dinner, Mark approaches me with what I think of his harelip. I tell him that I don't really think that much of it. He continues with asking me, you must think something of it. No, not really. I mean, I can see that your upper lip is mainly scar tissue, and it feels a bit strange kissing you. It's not like kissing anyone I've ever kissed before. But I'm OK with that. Mark is really happy that I seem to be so unbothered by it. I mean it was a big shock when I first kissed him, it just felt a bit off. It's stubblier than usual. Yes, that's a word now. Since there's not much of the pink lip tissue, and the stubble starts just where the lip ends, the stubble kind of cuts into my lips when he needs a shave. And also, his tongue is significantly shorter than normal, which kind of threw me off balance the first time, before I knew what had happened.

When I've thought about this, I've seen and noticed the scar tissue, but things like that are deeply personal, so I haven't been wanting to pry. I decided to wait until he wanted to tell me the story and that seems to be now. So he talks. And talks. And I get the opportunity to ask questions.

To me this story is worse than I could ever have

imagined. So I just listen, and I feel with him, and hug him tightly as he cries. He cries, violently. For the loss of part of his tongue. For the hospital abuse that left him forever mutilated. For the trauma inflicted upon his mother and family seeing everything happening to him as they arrived in the immediate aftermath. For the time and time again of broken promises of surgically fixing the face. For the hope those promises gave, that continued being crushed. Time and time again.

To describe how it looks, his upper lip is almost nonexistent. The lower lip goes outward as a usual lip does, but the upper lip doesn't have much of that soft pink lip tissue. There is a ton of scar tissue that seems to be connecting the lip tissue with the nose. And that tissue is so tight he has almost no movement there. And the nose is completely surgically made as well, but that story is for another day.

Mark:

Let's make this the other day. I was born without a nose. How did I smell? Terrible. Bum bum. But really yes. I actually was born without a nose. Somehow, I have no idea how, it was constructed in the first days and weeks of my life. I think. Apparently my nose is ridiculously hard. Or at least Maja says it is. She thinks this is really funny. This is not something I've ever been told before.

Maja:

My nose is soft and moves all over the place, I can make the tip touch my cheek, but Mark's. Come on. It doesn't move. At all. Hard as a stone. And quite big. Stone nose. Iron nose.

His tongue looks like someone has chopped off maybe an inch or so and tried to sew it back together, so the tip of the tongue is missing.

Mark:

Which isn't far off what actually happened.

Maja:

The whole thing is short and still has visible signs of where the stitches were. Honestly, if you just look at him, you won't notice much of what I've been talking about, but I am still impressed by how well he manages to do everything, especially with respect to the many missing teeth, most of them being the upper ones.

Mark:

About those missing teeth. It's not all gaps and stuff, like a boxer's missing teeth, or the teeth of someone who's really badly neglected them. They do all sit together and meet in the middle. It's just that there are certain teeth most people have that I just don't. Like the two little bunny teeth at the top in the middle. You see, I have no gum there. I just don't. I know. I'm getting more attractive by the second.

Maja:

Just saying, I find Mark quite handsome. We've been discussing some of the drawbacks for a while now, so I thought it ought to be said.

I guess he has thought of the horrific tongue incident many times, but today he, for the first time in a long while, re-lives it once more. I feel honoured and happy that he wants to share his stories with me. It's also nice to not be the only one that is talking.

London, day four
Tuesday February 23

Maja:

Another day, another good look at the ceiling. There's really not that much to do when the room is too small to even stand up and stretch in. Not that we don't try to do that at times. It's quite refreshing, now that the stresses around me have started to reduce themselves. I can just be here. I don't have to do anything else. And the view from the window is great.

For me, it's not like I have any big purpose for what I am going to do here in London. It's not like I came here to do anything touristy, or even to work. I'm just here, right now, right here. Without plans, without purpose. It was hard enough to get to where I am right now, and I don't really fancy going anywhere else.

Mark:

Maja's now started speculating that she could be anywhere in the world; all she's seen for days is the ceiling of this room and the inside of the house. She hasn't even ventured out to the garden yet, or at least not for anything more than a little look. As for me, well I've not seen much more since she's been here. The furthest I've ventured is out to the shops, so I've only been out of the house for around 20 minutes at a time, and often even less with the most basic shops being just right across the road.

Our thoughts are turning more and more towards music and the possibility of her playing with me and Kylie. I admit to Maja now that Kylie suggested last week that she might play with us but I nixed that idea saying she wasn't experienced enough. But now I'm starting to think it could be possible; with me and Kylie being a bass only affair, there are all kinds of simple bass lines Maja could play below what I'm doing to give more depth to things. Now we're talking about this, we quickly decide we should start rehearsing on our own in the house so that we can turn up with ideas and sections to present to Kylie.

Now Mark's opened up with the possibility of me working with him and Kylie, I'm shocked. You can't mean me, joining you guys? Doing what? What? I was kinda expecting to maybe be able to go along to watch a rehearsal, but really, I wasn't even expecting that. I'm a beginner, and I play bass, the same instrument as Mark. So what am I going to do? Mark has been thinking that we both could play bass. He has some kind of concept that he is starting to build up in his mind which, a concept which apparently won't be too advanced for me and would support what he's doing. Amazing.

This talking about playing together with Sarah then quickly and seamlessly morphs into, 'why don't we do our own thing as well?' Oh, we really are going and getting excited now, and we start to talk about songwriting and our own relevant experiences here. Maja became the main songwriter in Mad Box, her band in Sweden, and I have my own adventures which we will come to in here. They're deep in the past, but nevertheless, they are there. Could I be about to start revisiting my songwriting bits again? I used to be really serious about it but I haven't written a song for almost 10 years. Well, we're soon talking about this properly and wondering about what kinds of songs we would even write.

Straight away we remember a conversation we had this morning before we got up. We've been doing that quite a lot actually. Silly little conversations suddenly springing up supposing all kinds of nonsensical scenarios out of nothing. This morning Maja started musing about how you could get someone to love you and we started to think about how that could magically happen. Some kind of special object maybe? Before too long we come up with the idea of a magical beanie hat you could buy that would have the desired effect if you were somehow - and presumably appropriately - able to get it onto the head of the person you wanted to love you. Now we're talking about writing songs, we realise that has pretty good potential as a lyrical concept. We have our first idea.

Maja:

OK, Mark. Enough crazy talk here. This is crazy. Me, who is just starting out, starting an originals project with you. I'm just not good enough. But it's not really like there's anything else happening right now, and I might just be crazy enough to entertain this idea.

It's a fun idea, and there's nothing really that beats the thought of lying in bed, joking and writing down the silly thoughts that come out of our jokes. Like, what'll happen if you put a magical hat on someone to make them fall in love with you? But it'll have to be a beanie. In my head I hear the melody of Baby Love as I sing Beanie Love.

Today I also call a couple of my friends in Stockholm to tell them I'm not around anymore and why. They turn out to be very emotional and hard phone calls to make, but nonetheless necessary and good to do. I'm met with sympathy and, although I'm happy about that, I feel kind of strange. I'm not used to that kind of behaviour.

Mark:

Right. How do we go about all this? I have my bass and Maja will of course be buying a bass soon, but maybe we need an acoustic guitar. Then it suddenly comes to me. I have one. Or at least I think I do. A few years ago I bought a really cheap second hand guitar especially for a hint of a songwriting opportunity that never really happened. I don't have that guitar now and I start to wonder where it could be. It's possible that I somehow left it with Dan. Why I might have done that I have no idea. He has enough guitars and he wouldn't have asked to borrow it. Maybe I was going out to a jam with my bass after rehearsal with him one night and just left it at his place and never bothered to get it back. If that's the case, he probably isn't even aware he still has it. I should call him, see if I did leave it with him and if he even still has it.

Now we've decided we might actually do something musical together, I take a walk round to the shop to buy notebooks. I come back with three. As soon as I put them down we're like hungry people frantically tearing at food packages. The words can't come quick enough as we immediately start writing lines and ideas that have been occurring over the past few days. Before long whole chunks of potential lyrics and song concepts have been generated and the notebooks are already starting to acquire a used, lived-in feel.

I guess this is the point in the story where it could be written that the guy and the girl are in their room all the time just doing drugs. But we don't do anything like that and know by now that that's something neither of us is into at all. In these four days we haven't even had a drink. Neither have we watched TV. Not even so much as a Youtube video. No music either. Playing or listening. If we have anything you could call a drug it would be just ourselves and being with each other. And we might just both be starting to become addicted.

Maja:

I think there's a song in that. Addicted to love.

London, day five
Wednesday February 24

Maja:

I just know that I'm falling in love. I want to be with Mark, and I really enjoy talking to him, being with him. Right now, that's everything I want. I just want to be here. Right here, right now. Is that really that bad?

We're definitely more than friends now, right?

Mark:

We have no choice. We have to acknowledge that we're in some kind of relationship. Or that we have something. We have no idea what, but there is definitely a something here.

But yes, Maja is married and very much just on a break of which she's vaguely said would be in the region of two months. When I suggest that she can just go back when she's ready, if that's what she ultimately decides to do, she says that with all that's gone on between us just in these past five days, she can't go back now. So where does that leave anything?

It might seem like there's been a whole lot of serious analytical chat going on and that would be right. But in between, sometimes even right in between serious conversations, there's been a whole lot of laughter. I've laughed with Maja more and harder than I've ever laughed with anyone. And by now we're also starting to realise that we react the same way to a lot of situations. Maja already knew about some of this from reading certain Diary episodes. And of course we're learning a lot about each other within these four walls and under this ceiling. One of the biggest things we're learning about is the many parallels we have in career trajectories and the breakdowns we both had.

I used to be a journalist and rose very quickly - once I finally made it in. Journalism is ridiculously and notoriously hard to break into, to the point that it can actually start to seem impossible. It did to me anyway; I didn't get my first full time media job until I had just turned 23. That not going to university thing and trying to get into journalism before university leaving age didn't quite work. Instead I mostly did things like washing dishes and working on factory production lines. But within a year of finally managing to land my first media job I had doubled my starting salary, and before I was 25 I was a magazine editor in central London, and foreign correspondent for another magazine which sold a million copies a week. I carried on for quite a few more years, continuing to progress and loving it loving it loving it. Then, as I approached 30, I realised I was declining physically and mentally until I just simply couldn't properly function in the job anymore. A low point came when I was called into a management meeting. Myself, two editors and an executive - and told in a diplomatic roundabout way that I was slacking and letting myself and the team down. I kind of already knew this myself and I can't say the conversation was a surprise. I certainly don't remember feeling blindsided or ambushed in any way. If anything, I was probably thinking, 'Fair enough. I was wondering when you were going to notice.'

They did offer some kind of solution though, actually saying that if I had some idea of what would work best for me and if readers really liked it, then they would pay me more. The other side of that coin was the hint that what I was currently doing wasn't worth what they were paying me. I think this could be called a professional intervention. A few weeks later, barely even being able to type by that stage, I was done and out of the media game.

Maja:

It's interesting to get to know a little bit more about the Mark from before his diaries, and he shares many stories which I listen to intensely. I can't help but discover a lot of similarities between our professional lives. What's extremely telling is that we both entered very highly advanced fields, worked and thrived there for years until we ran face first into the wall. We both know what it feels like to have your head deep into that wall, not even knowing that it was there, and then the inevitable crash that comes afterwards. You don't realise when you're well past the point of no return. At least we never did. You go forward, doing everything you used to do, perhaps adding a lot of fitness training to take care of yourself because you think that might give you the something more you need to keep going. But apart from that, you're completely oblivious of the full damage your stressed out lifestyle is inflicting upon you.

Mark:

Oh yes. The training thing. When I first realised I was deep tired, I was already training twice a week with a semi-professional national league rugby team, plus playing in their third team with an eye on progressing, to maybe even the first team one day. But my response to being tired? Cut back on training? No. It was just obvious to me that I was tired because I wasn't fit enough. So the response - more training. Maja laughs quite bitterly when I mention this.

Maja:

I never knew until it was too late. Neither did he. I continued to work, train, do band rehearsals and meet friends, because that's what you're supposed to do. I planned every minute of my time, trained 11 hours a week, band rehearsal maybe 7 to 10 hours a week and didn't get home until after 10pm almost every day and was out again each morning by 7am. All the time. I was emotionally available to anyone needing to talk, and took good care of everything I had to take care of. On top of all this I always did my absolute best at work, and had a top salary for my age, with huge responsibilities and a good reputation.

It's special to talk about this with someone who has experienced the same things, albeit in a slightly different way. For him this was years ago, and he found his way forward through yoga and music, even managing to return to journalism in a limited capacity. For me, this is right here and right now.

I'm still stumbling.

Mark:

I hear today that the big story in the Diaries that really resonated with Maja, and which confirmed her thought once and for all that we shared very similar wavelengths, was the day me and Paul rescued the 14 year old girl who was lost, desperate and on the verge of being homeless at Euston Station, one of the very last places in London you would want to be a young girl who is lost, desperate and on the verge of being homeless. As Maja read that, she realised that she would have acted the same way as I did pretty much from the beginning to the end of the episode. That is, I was initially cynical yet open minded, which gave way to acceptance, openness and help. Then when Paul had to leave to catch his train, I stayed with her until she had got on a train to the house of a relative of hers who I'd been in communication with since the first few minutes of the encounter.

Maja:

For me this story proved an important judgement of character. I actually have a similar story, helping an eight month pregnant lady asking people for help in a supermarket. I still think of her at times, wondering how she's doing. I hope she's well. I can't remember the exact circumstances but she'd been at a house viewing, forgot her wallet somewhere so she couldn't take the train home to another town. Her phone had run out of battery and she was hungry. I was sceptical at first, but then realised her situation. We got into my car and I drove to my place where I gave her some leftovers from the night before. She was able to rest and charge her phone, and then I gave her money so she could take a train home. She was immensely grateful and I felt a little bit guilty for not having believed her right from the beginning. Everyone she had asked before had looked the other way and I almost did too. I'm really glad I didn't though. So reading this story about Mark really made me feel like he reacted in the same way as I would. It felt honest, but not risky. Wise in a way. This little story, which he posted ages ago, made me feel a little bit like this was a nice guy. Probably trustworthy.

Mark:

Since Maja arrived we haven't left the tiny room together for any sustained period of time. Most of it has been spent in there with just bathroom and shower breaks, punctuated only by trips to the kitchen for food. But even there, eating has been ridiculously sporadic and mostly still taken place in the bedroom. The weather hasn't been great to be fair, it is February afterall. But just as I type that I see it's now sunny and nice. With that, Maja really wants us both to go out and sit in the sun. So out we go and join Sam, who Maja joyously chats with. There have been one or two chats with Sam and Cris and when it's been one on one with Maja and one of those guys, I've pretty much stayed out of it, allowing them to get to know each other without my input. I've spoken enough to all of them. It's the same now as we lie back in the deckchairs and take in the February sun. This is something Maja is really having a wonderfully tough time to process. February sun. Back in

Sweden they're still up to their waists in snow and battling temperatures touching minus double figures. Really, just like she was less than a week ago. Yes. She's not even been here a week yet. Now, here she is wearing sunglasses and the bare minimum of clothes, reclining in what she was jokingly referring to last week as tropical London. I was like, tropical? Yeah, right. Well today it really is something of a dictionary definition of tropical as far as anyone in Sweden would be concerned.

Cris joins us now and it's clear that him and Sam have been starting to come to the same conclusions the two of us have been coming to, with Cris revelling in jokes about the lovebirds. At this, me and Maja just look at each other and laugh. The whole scene gives way to a really warm garden hang with us providing the tunes from Maja's phone for an early summer soundtrack.

Maja:

It's been nice hanging out with Sam and Cris a little bit as well. I like them both, they're great. I don't think Sam is out to be good friends. With him I feel more of a nice flatmate vibe. Which is cool as well. I'm a bit more curious about Cris, who is the singer of one of the bands Mark plays with at times -The Wild Child. He is teasing us a little bit, calling us birdy birds. But he is rarely at home, and I look forward to getting to know him better at a later stage.

Mark:

Inspired by the music, when we're left alone, Maja turns the conversation round to basses and suggests we start looking at what she could buy. For the first time, we're looking at the same screen as Maja starts thinking about what her next bass could look like. Then she surprises me by asking, 'What kind of bass would you like to play? I'm now thinking of buying two.' Her reasoning is that if this is the case, she might as well buy at least one I'd really like to play. I'm good with just my Washburn to be fair, but I'm happy to give my input here and start to think about something I would also like to work with.

It takes a while, but we finally settle on a Lakland and a Sadowsky and both pretty much mid to top of the range. Of course we're not able to try either out, but they look beautiful, very classy, and it goes without saying that the actual quality of them will be right up there with the best. Will they be nice to play? Impossible to say but I'm sure we'll get used to whatever little differences we find. Maja hits the buy button with complete confidence. With names like these, you really can't go wrong. Worst case, she reasons, if she doesn't like one, she'll at least like the other. Then I can make myself like the other one.

Maja:

Before I was going to England, I played a lot of bass and was just starting to get serious with it, so I decided that I would buy one to have while I was here. I had kind of decided on a decent budget for this already. Since last autumn I've been eyeing the Fender professional II J bass. I played it in the music store, and it was just something else. So I thought that I could use the money I'd put aside for that bass to buy something in London instead.

So we start to look at online music shops, and I realise that instead of buying one bass, I can afford two decent basses, so I could just buy one that Mark would like to play as well. Maybe. Looking around I find a Shadowsky and a Lakland that look really nice, so I decide to go for both. Since I can't test them in the store because of Covid, I could at least send one of them back if I'm unlucky. But they are great brands, so I'm sure it'll be fine.

London, day six
Thursday February 25

Maja:

Mark is supposed to have his rehearsal with Kylie today. Apart from that, we haven't been playing much music since I got to London, which means it's time to start now. Mark has a riff he's been playing with Kylie that he needs to remember for today. It's a simple enough riff; it's just that he's been finding internalising the phrasing kind of hard. So what better way to internalise new melodies than to teach them to someone? That's the thought when he starts teaching me the riff for the song White Rabbit. It's simple enough, but the repetitiveness of it makes it easy to get lost in it, and that is why he needed to rehearse it some more. And for me, it's quite amazing to be able to be of any kind of help. And I finally get to try the iconic Washburn that Mark has been using for all these years. It plays beautifully. It feels so special to have it in my hands. The bass that's been accompanying him for all these adventures during all these years. Playing it, I feel more connected to Mark.

Mark:

Yeah. That White Rabbit thing. No idea why. It has just refused to stick in my head. This is where listening, listening, listening comes in but it still refuses to stick. No panic. I'll get there.

In other, perhaps more significant news, Maja stops me cold and short today when, somewhere in the middle of chatting, she asks me if I'd be up for having kids. 'I'm not saying I want them now,' she says, 'but if I'm to start a relationship with anyone, I have to know this is something that could be a possibility in the future.' I get it. But the crazy thing is, not only do I not think there's anything strange about the question, but I say yes straight away. Again, not now. But sometime in the future. I'm saying I would not rule it out and that's the closest I've ever come to even entertaining the idea in my whole life. Since I was little more than a child I've said that I would never have kids and I've never come close to changing that viewpoint.

Until now. This actual moment. And it feels totally natural to say that. What the hell is happening here? Apart from anything else, yesterday we were talking about not knowing where we were, and now we're talking about kids. And a relationship? Well, this is certainly a something.

Maja:

I'm enjoying the time we spend together, talking, reflecting on life. And before any commitment, I'd like to know how Mark stands on some of the big things of life. Like kids. It's only natural I ask. I'm relieved when the answer of yes comes back, with full confidence. It's just such a shame that we don't have that much longer to talk about it, because it is time for Mark's rehearsal. Good luck.

Mark:

But, more than just a rehearsal with Kylie, today is the day we're going to do a full recording of our show to see what we have and maybe have a template to start to show people.

As usual I'm taking all my gear including amp, so Kylie is coming to the house to help me carry it to hers. Yes I can manage it all myself but this is a nice little regular gesture from her and it does make things a little easier. But she has a slight ulterior motive this time which she has not been at all shy in hiding. She wants to meet Maja. Maja very much wants to meet her as well. Afterall, this will be her first encounter with any of my London music friends, and so her first real encounter with the actual scene. Yeah. I think this really is quite significant.

Maja:

I'm a bit excited. I haven't really met any people since I arrived apart from Mark and our flatmates, and rightly so because of the quarantine. I'm still allowed to be on our premises, which includes our front small yard area, so I'll be OK to go out and say hello to Kylie. When I hear the knock on our door, I follow Mark upstairs, getting all nervous. He opens the door with a key. Wait what? He uses a KEY??? From the inside?! I don't have a key yet. Does that mean I haven't been able to get out all this time? What kind of house needs a key to get out? This is all very strange.

Mark:

Right. I have to address another strange thing about this house now. It's upside-down. Which is why you have to walk upstairs to the front door. I've come to see it as all normal, but it is really has freaked people out at times. When you come in the front door, the first thing you see is stairs going down to the first landing, turning left at a right angle halfway down. Apart from the top entrance, there are no windows as you walk down those stairs and if the doors are all closed meaning there's no natural light, it can be a bit unsettling. Once you enter one of the three bedroom doors in the hallway - Maja has the middle bedroom - although you've come downstairs, you'll see the back garden another floor below. Yes. The stairs continue from this landing to go down once more to the kitchen, and a large room downstairs which has been mine and Jenn's for the past few years; we've lived in this wonderful house for six years, the past four years in that fantastic big downstairs room with our own door to the garden. From that room, or the kitchen window, you enter the garden. So yes. If you've followed all that through, the house is built on a hill meaning the front is up at street level while everything else is down below, with the ground floor being at street level again, which is where the garden is. Then beyond the back fence you have the rest of the estate area with the whole central section being walkways between trees, bushes and flower gardens. It's a really cool, calm place hidden at the back of an almost central London area; even our street can't be seen from the main road as it sits back behind a small parade of shops. You could walk or drive up and down that main road for years and have no idea that behind that little strip of shops is a large car park area, and then a whole other world of houses and grounds. Really. Here we are in Kentish Town, just up the road from Camden and central London beyond that, and we live in an area where small children are able to play outside practically unseen by the wider world. And that upside-down house thing. Yes, people have come here for parties after a night out and found it just hilariously magical that after going immediately downstairs upon entering, they still find themselves upstairs when they reach that first lower floor.

Now back to that key thing. Oh yeah. I totally forgot to tell Maja about this, and it didn't even crossed my mind that I should have got one cut for her before she arrived. What if she really had needed to get out for any emergency reason? But even apart from that, without a key, she's not just willingly in quarantine, she really is actually locked in. Oops. I've accidentally kidnapped Maja.

Maja:

Outside, a very excited and giddy girl awaits us. She looks so excited to see us. Like a little child she is bubbling and bouncing with excitement. Hello hello hello. I get all shy and try to act normal, say hello and everything. It's obvious that she wants to say hello with a hug, and who am I to resist? We do some small talk, and then it's time for them to leave for rehearsal. Both say goodbye and they start to leave. Wait what? Just like that?

'Hey Mark, can you come here?' Mark comes back to the door, I grab him by the collar and kiss him. See you later. I can see how he turns all flustered and red as he says 'see you soon' and locks the door.

I'm quite tired now so I take a nap, but I can't stop thinking: What kind of house needs a key to get out of??? I know I'm gonna get one, it's just been forgotten about since I'm self isolating. But still, what if a fire started or something? I just don't get it. What about guests? You lock people inside the house?

Mark:

These are all very good points and I have never thought about any of them. The answer to all those concerns is yes. It would all be totally like that, although you could climb out of the kitchen window and into the back garden if you absolutely had to get out. And from there, over the fence if you absolutely had to leave/ escape. Remember those handcuffs? But it really is actually quite normal to have doors like this in the UK. Don't ask me why, it just is. Now Maja brings all this up, she's just right. It's not OK. As a result of this system I've found myself locked in the house plenty of times, like when I've been just about to leave and not been able to find my key. And yes, then managing to make myself late, or even very late for whatever it was I was about to leave for. Which, when it's time to go to the bar and I'm in charge of opening it that day, really isn't ideal.

I'm all packed and ready by around 5pm when there's a knock at the door. 'She's here,' says Maja. Indeed she is. We walk upstairs, I open the door, and Kylie's standing there, all totally expectantly. 'Are we hugging?' We are. With that, the two of them are out in the small front garden hugging and talking excitedly like sisters who are meeting again after a long time apart. I leave them to it and go and get the rest of my stuff from downstairs. When I come back up, they're still there and still both talking a hundred miles an hour. Finally, Kylie says, 'OK Mark, are we ready to go?' Yep. Once again, Maja tells her that but for the quarantine rules she'd love to be coming along. Next time, Kylie promises. Yes, of course. Next time. I'm kinda playing it cool with Maja, not wanting to be too 'public' in front of Kylie, so I just say goodbye and Maja goes into the house and we start to walk away. Then Maja calls me back to the front door. Oh, OK. I go back and she gives me a goodbye kiss right there in front of Kylie who, as I turn back, is looking on open mouthed, in stunned, delighted shock. 'No,' she says. 'No.' 'Yes.' With that she goes off on a celebratory skip down the road before returning, giggling like someone 20 years younger, to help me with the gear.

On the way I tell Kylie what me and Maja have been talking about and I think we could incorporate her into the act in a way I didn't think was possible a few days ago. Kylie is well up for the idea, saying it is much more about attitude than playing, and that if Maja has one thing based on what she's just seen for the first time, it's attitude. 'And you guys are just right together,' she says. 'I could see that straight away. Now, if you can take that chemistry and turn it into music, you have gold, no matter what levels of ability you're talking about.' That sets off a spark in me. Yes, this really could be something to think about. And with that, me and Maja have a project. And definitely something to talk about later.

But oh dear. With everything that's been going on over the past week, I am woefully underprepared for today's session in which we intend to do a full, recorded rehearsal of our short show, which is five songs all segued into each other. I've barely touched the bass all week. I had a tiny little play today just as I realised this, just to make sure I could remember the rhythmic parts of what we're doing and how each song goes into the next one. But as for the solo I have to do, I am way out of practice and am just going to have to make sure I'm warmed up, and fall back on what I've actually come up with rather than trying to improvise a bunch of cool stuff around it which is what I usually do. This is not a time for risk-taking in my playing. As it is, when we get to it I'm barely holding on to what I can play with her stuff. But that's alright. Kylie isn't in great shape preparationwise either which lets me off the hook actually. It looks like we've both let ourselves go a bit, but we do each have a lot of experience and technique to fall back on. All this means it takes six or seven takes to get a full one take recording of our show. In between we just go with it and have a laugh at our own little hiccups and mistakes which we pretty much equally share which means I can feel a little less guilty at not being as prepared as I would normally be. Of this, Kylie is totally understanding given what's been going on this week. More, she loves it and loves the story of where we are. Just as I'm about to leave, I realise Kylie has an acoustic guitar. Of course she does. We've been using it to get a few concepts together, and there it is in the corner of the room. Could I possibly borrow that please for me and Maja to work on? Of course you can, she says. Brilliant. With that, we're sorted.

Maja:

I fall asleep soon after Mark leaves for rehearsal, and I really need the rest. It's wonderful to spend time together, and I'd rather do that, but if I'm alone, I want to sleep. All of a sudden, I'm woken up by someone walking down the stairs and then opening my door. Yes! He's home! I sit up as quickly as possible and say hello.

In his hand he has a guitar, I wasn't expecting that. Cool. I guess he plays the guitar and has a plan, but I don't know that much about this yet. But it's always nice to have a guitar around, especially for songwriting.

Mark:

Oh yeah. Maja, I can play guitar.

Maja:

We soon make ourselves comfortable and continue talking. I'm not that good of a musician and I know that Mark pretty much only ever works with very skilled musicians. Now he says that he and Kylie spoke about the possibility of me playing with them today and concluded that yes, I'm going to join them. Now we're all about to start playing together. So apparently, I've moved to London, without any set plans, and within a week I've joined my first band. I could even say my first professional band, since we're planning shows and Mark and Kylie are, well, professionals. Just, wow. Or, wowsers, as Kylie would say.

Mark:

It's with some excitement that I return home and bring the guitar into the room to show Maja. And with it, the news that Kylie loves the idea of the two of us playing together with her. So it's game on. Me and Maja are starting to reach whole new levels now. We're talking about having kids, playing together in the same band, and also thinking about our own style and songs, which we can write on this new guitar we now have. Maja came to London to get away from something. Now she's starting to feel she also went towards something. 'What do you come to London for?' she asks. It sounds like she's musing rhetorically, but then she starts to answer her own question. 'For the music scene, which doesn't exist, but here we are talking about music. There are so many other reasons to come. But I just didn't expect to come to London and fall in love.'

What now?

She continues talking, musing quietly to herself really, with me as an incidental audience. But I've zoned out. I'm thinking about what she's just said and thinking how I should respond. Afterall, we've spoken about this being something of a relationship, and just a few hours ago we were talking about having kids together, or at least whether or not we were open to the possibility of it. And all the while we've been becoming closer and closer in every other way. As friends too. As close friends. As even best friends. Yeah. That's how it feels, with the depth with which we talk, and the highs as well. Filled with the kind of joyful spontaneous shared laughter I've experienced with very few people before, or maybe even no-one before. And she's said the word now. I think it's my turn. She's still talking but for once I'm not fully listening. She can see that because she comes to a faltering stop around the same time as I interject saying, 'Maja…' 'Yes?'

'I love you.' A breath, a pause. It's out there now.

'I love you too.'

Maja:

All of a sudden, when my thoughts and words finally slow down Mark says:

'I love you'.

I look him in the eyes, wondering where this came from all of a sudden. I stop to take a breath, to allow myself to think for a second.

'I love you too'.

Mark:

No more words are needed. No more words are spoken. This is almost too much to take. It kind of really is too much to take. I think it's really happened. The magical, elusive formula, the ideal of countless books, movies and songs. I'm in love with my best friend. And she's in love with me. To hopelessly paraphrase and misquote the movie Notting Hill, 'There are billions of people in the world and you're sent out to find just one of them that you love. Not only that, but they have to love you back. The odds of that are millions to one.' Yes. It really is something that seems impossible. Now, here we are. To steal again, this time from Jason Mraz: 'Lucky I'm in love with my best friend/lucky to have been where we have been/lucky to be coming home again.' As we settle blissfully into our new reality, I play this song for Maja. And for me. For us. And yes, as it plays, I cry in front of her for the second time. Just a tiny little tear trickle, but really Mark, pull yourself together.

Then reality comes back to us. 'Mark,' she says. 'Yes?' 'You do realise I'm still married?' 'Yes.' And I have Jenn, immediately below us downstairs. Different situation but even so. Maja stops and ponders all this, then explodes in a whisper. 'Boy, we're in trouble.'

London, day seven
Friday February 26

Maja:

Why can't things be simple? Just why can't I just simply be able to do what I want? What we want? There's too many whys here, and it just doesn't add up.

Mark:

Why isn't it spelt whies? Sorry. Not helpful. Carry on Maja.

Maja:

I just can't get what I want in a simple way. Why does it have to start off with an impossible list? Why do I have to navigate a way through the impossible, just to be where I want with who I want? Yes, I'm complaining a lot right now, but it really feels like this. I can't even stay here in this miniscule room for long, because of Brexit. Why does it have to be so complicated?

I'm feeling a tiny bit of whelm here.

So, what do I have to do?

Get a divorce, sell my apartment in Sweden, fix a new home for my dog Tommy, get a job in London, or some remote job at least, get an apartment in London. And get a visa to even be able to be here because of the stupid cursed Brexit. All of this, and I don't even know where to start with the first one. How should I even approach that? How should I even think about that? I mean, I love him so much still, but I can't be with him now. How do you even get a divorce? How am I going to be able to say that to him? How am I going to be OK? I don't know how I should handle this.

I just don't know.

This is impossible. An impossible list.

Mark:

Very quickly we're realising that we're going to need a bigger boat. We really have to take a pragmatic approach to what's going on here.

To start with that, we make a list of what we need to overcome. We quickly call this the Impossible List. It looks like this.

Divorce, which means she's going to have to make the actual call to say she wants one, and then have it granted and administered.

Organising/selling the apartment in Sweden.

Getting a job in London, or some remote working job.

Getting an apartment in London, and lockdown London at that.

Visa to be able to stay in post Brexit Britain, which will probably be dependent on whatever job she's able to get, and even then, it will be a huge ask.

Tommy - her dog. What will happen with him?

For my part, I have to deal with Jenn and how to break that, while still living here for the time being. Oh, mini reveal of what you probably already knew if you'd thought about it. Me and Jenn are still sharing a room. Yes I'm with Maja a lot, and in her room a lot, but the big downstairs room is still mine and Jenn's. In any case, the three of us are all still living in the same house. Awkward? You said that. I couldn't possibly comment.

Maja:

Yeah, come on. The whole Jenn situation is really not helpful right now either. How are you going to square this circle Mark? I mean, just how?

Mark:

If that's going to change, I have to figure out how the hell I'm going to make enough to pay my share of an apartment in London, with deposit. And if and when the move does happen, I also have to do the right thing which means, on top of that, keeping up my share of rent payments on the room here for at least a reasonable amount of time whatever that means.

In this area, and anywhere else this central really, property is truly expensive; in many parts of the country you could get a two bedroom apartment for the price of the double room in this house. A one bedroom apartment, which is what we'll be looking for, costs around twice the price of the room I'm currently paying for.

On top of all this, I'm currently on furlough. From a bar job. And get a new job? That could pay what all the above would require? Here? In lockdown, almost totally furloughed London? Don't think so. Which means we have to come up with an idea or ideas for how I could make more money to help fund the new reality and whatever comes next. Journalism is my field if I'm going to make any kind of even decent money, or media in general, so maybe also PR. But that would mean total re-entry with my last vaguely media job being advertising copywriting for a multinational communications company in Madrid back in 2009, over 10 years ago. So who knows what level I'd be starting at? And journalist? Is that even a thing anymore? I mean, it was almost an impossibility to get my first job when I started in the industry. I can only imagine it's multiple times harder now, and not nearly as well paid. But anyway, as I said, if I'm to look at getting a professional job outside of barworld on any kind of decent professional salary, I think that's my only option.

Combining our situations, pick any one of the above and you're looking at an insurmountable problem. As an entire list, it's impossible. Just impossible. There's no other word for it. We are totally deluding ourselves if we think we're ever going to get that lot ticked off and somehow sail into the sunset. But amazingly, we manage to solve all the problems almost instantly. We do this by refusing to think about them. Then we realise that, while this might feel nice, it really isn't a solution that's sustainable for any amount of time.

The first real biggie is the possibility of a divorce. It's huge that the situation has even come to this, but it is very much acknowledged that this would have been on the cards even without me, or anyone else; if, instead of coming here, she'd decided to go off to some island on her own to have her much needed break and to get her head around everything, she probably still would have come to the conclusion that the marriage was over and that she would need to deal with that. So no, I don't feel responsible for that and no, I don't believe that anything we have done or said has precipitated that. Nevertheless, it is something that will have to be addressed and something that will ultimately have to happen. Along with the divorce is the attached inevitability of her having to sell their apartment in Sweden and get all that stuff organised; of course, the mere fact an apartment exists means there are a lot of things in it and a lot of other administrative things to consider and get through. Where the hell do you start with all that? From here?

And if Maja is to divorce and stay here, we need to think about what that means. First, it means getting out of this room and into a place of our own. But she still has another three days of quarantine anyway, including today. So four days. Basically, she's only just over halfway through quarantine and is thinking of not just being able to go outside, but of moving from here totally. Which brings us onto the next problem of how the hell to get an apartment in London and how the hell to pay for it. To do that I really need to up my financial game, and how the hell does that happen? In Covid, lockdown London? As it is, right now I'm on furlough so I have some kind of decent income, but nowhere near what you would need to pay for half a whole apartment, plus deposit, plus keep up my moral obligations here for a little while. It's just possible, with me not having to work at my bar at the moment anyway, that we could look for a place a little further out, and so a little cheaper than the zone two we're currently in. But that still wouldn't change the fact that I would need to find a considerably better income than I'm pulling in now. How?

And even if we do somehow manage to get our own place, Maja still has to be able to stay in the UK to make any of it workable. Pre Brexit that would have been no big deal. She's European, UK was in the EU, not even a discussion. Live and work here, just like I went to Madrid to live and work all that time ago. Fully legally, with Spanish papers organised and everything. Almost did the same in Hamburg with Drunken Monkees; Hamburg, like other German cities, even had a welcome centre there - it was actually called The Welcome Centre - with all the bureaucratic offices under the same roof. Imagine. But all that's changed now for the UK. All Maja has, and all she can have, is a tourist visa which is valid for six months. Which means she can stay for at least that long. But she can't work. How the hell are we going to take that square and make it round? And all the other squares? Or circles? Or whatever the phrase is. All we have right now is a very bad game of Tetris where nothing fits but it's all coming down anyway.

But onto immediate issues. I have to tell Jenn where me and Maja are right now. She's out when the time comes for this, so I arrange to meet her nearby when she's on her way back. As soon as I make the phone call she knows something bad is coming and bitterly thanks me for ruining her day which she says was already a struggle because she's been worried about what's been going on here. Yes, we're just friends, but friends who have lived together and supported each other for a long time and she can see that we are now nudging at the end of an era. We meet in the empty beer garden in The Vine across the road from the house. I don't want to drag anything out so I just say it as soon as I can. 'Me and Maja said the three words last night.' I would like to say Jenn takes it well. She really doesn't. But she does say this has come as no surprise to her as she's been well aware of how we've been since Maja arrived. Bottom line, she asks to be given a few days to a week to process this new reality and then to maybe come round to accepting the situation. In that time, she says, I shouldn't be surprised if she doesn't speak to either of us. Fair enough.

Above I mentioned the fact that I have a bar job which I'm currently being paid for not doing. That reminded me that a certain amount of context had been missing from The Diaries, at least for people not familiar with Mark's Diaries, which is my thing before me and Maja ended our respective diaries and started this thing.

Practically my whole life in London, since I moved here from Madrid in October 2014, has revolved around bars, with my income pretty much evenly split between working in them and gigging in them; I played bass with various bands and also with my own cover acoustic duo The Insiders with my good friend Dan. I started that project with him when we were working together at The Oxford. When Covid hit, governmental stay at home advice saw bars, among other businesses, being forced to close. With that, wages, or at least a good part of them, continued through furlough payments. In my bar's case, these were based on average earnings over a given period before furlough began. With bars closing and work ending, my landlord also very generously cancelled everyone's rent in the house. At first he said he was suspending it and we could work it out when everyone was fully back at work. But then on that same day he came back to us and incredibly said, forget suspending it and paying it back. Until things are back up and running again, there is no more rent. Seriously, say what you want about landlords, but ours really did come through for us when the world went down. All of which has meant that I've been able to keep the wheels turning quite OK.

It also meant that I was totally available for all Skype calls with Maja when we first started communicating with the whole website/bass mentor trade off thing. And then it meant I was able to be available for phone calls anytime day or night when the wheels of her life started wobbling. And it means I'm 100 per cent around now too as she settles into the house and into London. So yes, Covid and its societal effects have been terrible. But for me and Maja, it really has worked for us. You could say we are children of Covid. Or at the very least, if it hadn't happened, we probably wouldn't have even made it to first base for want of a better expression. For a start, I wouldn't have been able to mentor her, or receive her website help, to the extent that I did, which, as you know, is how we really started communicating so much in the first place.

Maja:

Yes. If it hadn't been for Covid, a lot of things that happened to me just wouldn't have happened. It might even have been a trigger for why my marriage started to break down as well. And I certainly would never have picked up an instrument if it wasn't for Covid. So then I would never have started a band, never joined SBL, never found Mark's Diaries, never started my own diaries, never contacted Mark. And I probably would have lived my whole life never even wanting to go to London, nevermind live there. I mean, why would I ever have wanted to go there? I have my job, I work as a cloud engineer, my training is way too many hours a week - I do aikido training. If I was to do anything crazy and new it probably would have been going to an Aikido training camp in Japan for a year or so. But that never happened.

When the world came crashing down around me, so did everything that I knew.

London, day eight
Saturday February 27

Mark:

The basses arrive, along with a few accessories that were also ordered and it's like Christmas. They look as beautiful as imagined. But all of a sudden, the tiny room has got even tinier. That's OK. It's for the sake of new basses.

However, when we each have a little play of them, it's fair to say we're a little underwhelmed. This unpacking business has taken quite a while so we put our reservations down to high expectations and decide to leave them for now and come back to them when we have some time to really have a good look. Afterall, it could just be setup issues which could be easily fixed but which might need a little more consideration that we're really willing to give right now.

Instead, for the first time since we met, we do a new activity we haven't done yet. It's called TV watching. It's kinda fun and we don't do it for a great amount of time. There's some discussion about what exactly to watch and we settle on Maja showing me Melodifestivalen. This is Sweden's show to decide what their entry to Eurovision will be and it runs over several episodes and kinda looks like the final stages of The X Factor or American Idol. And it's all set in Stockholm with location links from the presenters, which gives her a little revisit to her city and an opportunity to give me a virtual introduction. As we see the presenters in various locations, she talks to me a little about the sights, most notably those of Gamla Stan, the historic old part of the city.

Maja:

It's fun to be able to introduce some things from my country to Mark. And if there's one thing we both enjoy, it's music. So why not take the opportunity to watch something live from Sweden, which encapsulates the best and worst of Sweden in the same short TV program without having to focus on really watching it? And we can have our own little guessing game. Perfect for tonight.

Mark:

But mostly we concentrate on the songs and, as with all other things Eurovision, have a great time making our own selections about who should be going through and who should be going home. And also with all things Eurovision, we have great fun seeing our favourite selections completely ignored while songs we thought were total duds get the go ahead. Oh well. Songs eh? Everyone's an expert and no-one knows anything. In fact, Ireland's top music TV and radio personality Dave Fanning once spoke to me about the minefield of trying to gauge if a song is any good or not. His conclusion was, 'No-one knows anything. There are no geniuses in this game.'

London, Day nine
Sunday February 28

Mark:

The day before the last day of Maja's quarantine and excitement is mounting at her finally being able to get out and about. Out to see London, maybe out to see a friend or two of mine, because outdoor meetings of small groups are allowed. And of course, the possibility of the two of us getting out to rehearsals at Kylie's.

Maja:

I'm way too excited about this. I've not seen anything of this new country that I am currently residing in. Not anything apart from the calm neighbourhoodly view from my window. My feet are itching to be used. The weather's been mockingly nice these last couple of days with the air bringing me a delightful spring taste. How will I manage to stay put during these last couple of days? Maja. Keep. Calm. You will get out. Soon.

Mark:

But also, with Maja still not being able to go out, the priority is to really have a look at these basses and to see if we hadn't been too harsh with first impressions. I'd had a look at the Lakland and Maja had mainly concentrated on the Sadowsky, but I think there's been just a little bit of

131

not really wanting to know because we didn't want to have to admit the reality. But we have a look now and quickly conclude the truth after the excitement of New Bass(es) Day. These are objectively terrible. Not that we don't like the setups or feels, but they are actually bad and should never have left the factory, let alone the shop. Both are full of fretbuzz for a start and no amount of tinkering with the action of either solves this problem. Then, the Sadowski's frets, all the way down, protrude sharply to the side, meaning any playing up and down the fretboard would start to cut your hands apart. So no. Unplayable. The Lakland has similar issues. If one single feature sums them up, it's that one of the screws in the Lackland body is rusty. Yes, actually rusty. If that's what it looks like on the outside, what the hell is going on on the inside? What kind of care can anyone who's had any part in selling this have taken with it? Really, how much confidence can you have in a new bass, a new anything, if something on it is rusty? Rusty. It's brand new - apparently - and something on it is rusty. No, we have no confidence in these basses at all. There are little physical alterations we could make to both, including truss rod adjustment, to realign the neck and maybe eliminate fretbuzz, But if any adjustment doesn't work, especially anything like attempting to file down frets, no refund would be issued as it would be argued that the basses had been physically meddled with. So they just have to go back. And not for resetups either. No. Nothing but a full refund will do. This particular shop will not be getting repeat custom from us. Sorry. I know it's Covid times and support local businesses and all that. But please. At least do something to deserve that support. But I'll be nice and I won't name the shop, but I should at least say that no, it isn't Camden Guitars.

Maja:

These new basses are just a disappointment. I can't believe how bad they are. I thought buying two would reduce the risk of this so we would at least end up with one that we liked, but this is just ridiculous. Beyond.

Day 10
Monday March 1

Mark:

On the phone to the shop and very little resistance is met. They will send a van to pick up the basses and, once they're happy we've not damaged them in any way, a full refund will be issued. OK. Fair enough.

We 'celebrate' Maja's last night of quarantine and anticipate tomorrow's London odyssey by ordering in pizza and going for what has become a real treat. Takeout cocktail bags from Ladies And Gents, the cocktail bar in Ktown built into a former underground toilet. Basically, they give you six cocktail measures in a large sealed plastic bag, and in another bag, you have the little bits of dried, seasoned fruit they would put in them. Then at home you put them together yourself. This is all a perfect accompaniment for our second attempt at watching any kind of TV - Maja's favourite - Doctor Who. We get 20 minutes in and give up. It seems TV really doesn't work for us.

Maja:

I've really, really looked forward to watching Doctor Who, because I haven't been able to watch the latest seasons in Sweden. No streaming service owns the rights to it in Sweden right now. So when it comes to things I want to watch here, Doctor Who is my highest priority. But we just can't seem to focus.

Come on Mark. You're just too much fun to be with. How are we ever going to get anything done?

Day 11
Tuesday March 2

Maja:

What a beautiful day. At least I think so. Being in self isolation since arriving, I haven't really been able to compare the days to anything. Today is the day we've been looking forward to. It's the day of the non-quarantine life starting! I'm quick about showering and getting dressed, since I really want to get out as soon as I possibly can. I am going to experience London today.

Shoes are located, and they almost look dusty from not having been used in ages. Or as dusty objects untouched for 10 days get.

'Mark, I'm ready to go now!'

'How do you feel, for your first London walk?'

'It's amazing. Come on, let's go now!!!'

I got my key a couple of days ago, and now for the first time I walk up the staircase and put the key in the keyhole and open up the door to lockdown London. My London. My mood rises even higher as I step out the door, and take a deep breath of the outside air. It tastes like freedom. I grab Mark by the hand and use my other arm to point in the vague direction of the city centre.

'Today, I want to go in that direction.'

'Sure. Today you lead the way.'

I've never been to London, and don't even have the slightest concept of where things are, but that doesn't matter. When I get to a new place, I like to just wander and see things as they come. I've done it so many times, in cities all over the world, at times alone, at times with someone else. One of my favourite things to do as a tourist is to go on the underground to a station somewhere and when I get up from the station I just go in whatever direction seems the most interesting. One thing I am careful with doing this, is not to read any direction signs, and certainly not any maps, since that is going to reduce the amount of surprises I get. If you are going to do the touristing in a Maja way, avoid maps and signs and just go. I recommend it. You might find something you otherwise would never have found if you had only gone for the big attractions. But if you do it like this, you might also miss all of the big attractions.

So off me and Mark go. In that direction. It is sunny but cold outside, a wonderful spring day. We find ourselves getting back to the Kentish Town area where a lot of people are walking around. Many of them are wearing face masks. I find Kentish Town a bit too busy and crowded.

We walk into Kentish town, which kind of starts at this huge bridge, which is so big you don't even realise it's a bridge. It includes a whole crossroads type feature. I take a sharp left turn, walking onto a smaller, calmer street. It's nice to walk in the calmer areas and I am fond of how the air feels a little bit easier to breathe and there aren't as many strange people to look at anymore. Being in crowds makes me feel a little bit suffocated, especially right now. So it is perfect that I am experiencing lockdown London, and not full on tourist London. I am needing a little time to adapt.

The town has turned into a little cute residential area, where just after walking a little while I can see Mark shine up like a little excited tomato.

We pass an old style apartment complex and he says, 'This is the first real apartment I lived in when I moved to London.' It's cool that the first place I manage to find is his first apartment. And it isn't really in a place you pass by that often. Mark stops by the local store across the road from the apartment to buy some fizzy water. I wait outside so as not to crowd the store, and as I peek in I can see him searching for something. It takes quite a while but soon enough he comes out with two bottles of fizzy water and some chocolate. Galaxy coins in a bag. I love that chocolate, Galaxy. It has rapidly become my new favourite chocolate. And he also brought us a Crunchie bar.

'I know this chocolate! My friend bought it for me once when I was young. It's really good and tastes like caramel, right? I saw you looking around in the store a lot, what were you searching for?'

'Oh, they didn't have it. I'm going to buy it for you later.'

I'm happy with what we got and enjoy my chocolate and fizzy water breakfast, continuing down the road to wherever.

We walk around a lot of smaller residential areas as I keep taking turns at unpredictable times, but I think we are getting closer to central London. Mark has promised me that he won't tell me any directions. Today it is I who takes him around London, not the other way around. We get to a little open cafe where they have moved the cashier to the entrance door, so you are able to buy a drink for take away. I buy myself a latte and Mark goes for tea, of course. Like the incurable Englishman he is.

Mark:

While we're choosing and paying for our drinks, I have a little casual chat with the staff. Just the kind of little pleasant exchanges that happen in places like this. And I tell them we're off out experiencing Maja's first day in London and that this is her first coffee shop. As we walk away, Maja again reacts to this. 'You really do talk to each other here,' she says. Yes we do. I guess it's in these little differences that you know you're in another country. That and the bridge right in front of us which has 'CAMDEN TOWN' painted all over it.

Maja:

We take our drinks and continue along, and I see Mark kind of squeaking when he realises where we are. I lead us on a little road that doesn't look that special, but on the left side of the road there is a little shop that Mark is taking significant interest in. I go closer and realise I've found my way to The Bass Gallery. The famous Bass Gallery is just here. Right in front of me. When I've just been casually walking around, expecting to find nothing. Wow. Just amazing. It is closed of course, we're in lockdown London, there are no stores open here. Expect pharmacies and food stores. We stand outside the store for a while, picking out some of the basses that we've seen online. No, we didn't buy the basses from here either, we just looked. I really wish the place was open. Oh well, there's no point in hanging around here for too long. We continue along, into Camden Town.

Camden Town. Oh my what a place, and I have BigNIC to show me around. BigNIC stands for, Big Name In Camden.

Mark:

I was given this very flattering name in my first year in London by the bar staff at The Oxford. It happened when they decided to come with me to The Blues Kitchen for the Sunday night blues jam. By that point I'd managed to get myself something of a reputation as a bass player in there and around many other blues bars in London. A couple of non-blues jam bars too. It also just happened that this particular night was very well attended by the regulars, and it also just happened that I got called up for some very prominent spots, including the climactic jam at the end of the night where I got called for a solo that I really went for. Up until now my bar colleagues had regarded me as a very junior staff member. Someone who had barely just started to know what he was doing after a very rough and uncertain start when it wasn't clear that I was even going to last at all. But when they saw me on stage that night, their whole perception and way of looking at me changed and they were like, 'Oh, we get it now.' Then it went a little bit further still and the BigNIC name was born.

Maja:

He is known in every bar, every club. The kind of guy that just can go anywhere and always have people to talk to. Mark really knows his way around here. The town of the crazies. With a seemingly non-stop nightlife. Everything is closed now, of course, and it is really eerie on the streets. When all the cool people have retired to their fancy houses in the countryside or other countries even, it is only the crazies left. The people I wouldn't really like to talk to, but they just keep on chatting to Mark. The place has a rundown feel to it, it isn't really that nice right now. So many bars. But if you look into the windows even the chairs are put away. There's nothing there. At times even the windows are barricaded shut with wooden boards. It's a sad sight. This once very lively city reduced to a shell.

We continue on our walk and arrive at an area with a completely different feel to it. Now the buildings aren't that rundown anymore, they feel more like the modern buildings in Tokyo, a place I know very well and compare things to a lot.

'Come on,' says Mark. 'I'd like to show you where we are right now.'

He leads me into a huge building with row after row of shops inside of it. All closed and dark and giving off an eerie feel. There is almost no one around. One or two people around the place, and everyone is wearing masks of course. It's a train station, and when I go up the stairs to the second floor I realise immediately where we are. This is Kings Cross. We stand looking at the international railway departure hall. And I've seen this place before, the first place I actually recognised. It's from the scene when Hagrid disappears after giving Harry his ticket to the Hogwarts Express at platform nine and three quarters. I know that they have a tourist attraction with the entrance to platform nine and three quarters, but it seems to be nowhere around here. Oh well, maybe we'll find it another day. I'm going to have Mark show me the way next time. I guess I am just that nerdy. I love the Harry Potter books. To me they are a big part of my childhood and I love them for all of the wonderful days I've spent sucked into the magical world of Harry Potter.

Kings Cross is a train station, and therefore one of the few places where they seem to be allowed to have toilets open. So we take the opportunity to use them. That's also something handy for you to put into your box of information you are probably never going to use again; in case you need a toilet in London in a pandemic, go to Kings Cross.

We soon find ourselves hungry and tired from walking. We're outside the closed British Museum and it's around lunchtime. It would be great to find a bite somewhere but everything is closed. We're now in the centre of London, which means the area that people don't really live in. We're close to the Marquis where you might be able to buy takeaway food as bars are at least able to do that now, so Mark tries to give his friend and Marquis boss Tommy a call to see if that is happening there, but there's no answer. Mark had an idea it would be cool to meet him up too, but anyways it might be best not to. So we need to find something to eat now. We go sit down on a doorstep in a back alley in front of the British museum and rest for a little while. Tommy didn't answer, so we need to find somewhere else. It's cold and we're tired and hungry. Let's go search for a supermarket or something that's open. After a while we find a decent sized supermarket. They have a sushi section which feels like hitting the jackpot. We buy sushi and some mango pieces, and then look for a place outside to sit down to eat. We settle on a beautiful wall right outside a building, finally resting a little bit.

'Mark, say aaaah.'

'Aaaah.'

And I put a big chunk of mango in his mouth.

'You know mango. It's bass player food. If you're a bass player, you can't get nutrition from anything else.'

'I didn't know that. That must have been why I've been losing weight recently. I haven't had any mangoes!'

After our wonderful meal of enough mango to keep us bass players healthy and some sushi for good sake, back up on our feet it is. We're somewhere central right now, and I have no idea where. There aren't many people out and about, but we manage to find a couple of cafes that are open. There is one selling bubble tea which seems popular, but I want to go to the ordinary coffee shop next to it, which is a wonderful fairly big shop where the barista Dario is working. Mark strikes up a conversation, we talk about the different coffee types and I go for a nice Brazilian blend. It turns out there really aren't many customers coming around here, and I suspect we might be his first customers today. And it is afternoon. Not long until close for a coffee shop. We talk about everything from me being new in London to his country in South America. After talking for a while, he says:

'Would you guys like some pastries?'

'Oh, yes please.'

'There really hasn't been anyone buying pastries today.'

He talks while he starts loading croissants and pain au chocolat into a paper bag, one, two, three. Oh wait what, how many is he going to fill them up with? He fills the bag to the brim, I think it is with about maybe 10 enormous pieces. Thankyou very much Dario. It's well appreciated.

We can't be standing there holding the shop busy for too long, so off we go, continuing left. I'm feeling the left direction today. That's the way to go. We walk for a while and then Mark informs me that the big building we see in front of us is St Paul's Cathedral. Oh, cool. I found a famous place! We take some photographs and move in closer, then turn into an almost completely empty wide open space called Paternoster Square. Or, given how it looks now, we call it Apocalypto Square. It is perfect for photographing while doing weird poses.

The cold is biting us now, so it is best to keep moving, but stopping for some nice photographs is a must. But I actually don't feel like I need to photograph everything all the time anymore. I mean, I'm not here as a tourist really. I live here now. At least for now. So I can go to central London whenever I want. Which feels so cool.

We find ourselves walking into Shoreditch, where we come across a sign on a path saying the place inside sells wine. This sounds very much like a bar, so we simply must go inside and see what they sell. It's a very nice little wine bar where you can actually buy bottles of wine to bring home. It's so nice to see a place like this, it must be so cosy here when it's open. The owner is really nice and sociable and seems so happy to see customers in the store. We ask if we could try any of the wines, and we're lucky, because we can.

So we get a couple of options of the already opened bottles presented to us, the bottles have been open a couple of weeks, but they're still fine. It's really fun to be able to try wine like this. This just isn't a thing for me, I've never really done it like this, which makes it all the more special. We end up buying a nice bottle of wine from the owner's home country, Hungary. They are currently renovating in preparation for the opening up. In the meantime they're continuing to operate as a wine store.

It's starting to be time to return home. I'm just too tired. We hop on a bus, and I finally get to try the double decker London buses for the first time. It's strange to get on a bus and see a staircase leading up to the second floor. We go up there, and we're alone so of course we sit at the front. Watching people all around town, going around in a bus that seems impossibly big for London's narrow streets. It's like an illusion, a magic trick perhaps. The buses are simply so big I can't understand how they can drive them on these narrow streets. It must be magic. Like that bus in Harry Potter that magically changes size fitting all kinds of openings. Yes. I've decided. That's how the London buses work. That must be it. We sit and rest and watch the people on the street from the front window on the top floor of the bus, and I see this guy dressed kinda bad with an acoustic guitar without a case in his hand. He jumps on our bus and sits down on the lower level and I can hear him start playing. After a while he jumps off and we're alone again. I guess things like that just happen around here. How cool is that?

Mark:

It's been a wonderful first day out in London for Maja and I'm not entirely sure who's shown who around. But really, with the newbie leading the way, we've seen a whole different London than we would have done if I'd been in front and brought us to all the usual sights, which I'm sure we'll see in due time anyway.

What we can't do so much anymore is talk about it. We've been talking so much in the past week or so that late in the day our voices just start giving out. It happens to me first, and then when I mention it to Maja, she says that yes, her throat isn't feeling quite right either. I know what to do about this and when we pop into a shop for water, I leave Maja to get that while I go hunting for honey and a small bottle of lemon juice. Out on the street we both have a little of each and instantly feel the relief of the rough throat disappearing and something like voice normality resuming. But really, I can barely talk anymore. I don't think Maja is that far behind me.

Off the bus and we're into Kentish Town, getting off a few stops early to walk the rest of the way home through a street that Maja has only seen once before and at night, on the walk here on that first day from the airport. We use the walk through town as an opportunity to have a look in the windows of estate agents to see what kind of apartments are available around here and what we would be looking at for rents. I have an idea of course, but Maja doesn't. More significant than the ridiculously high London prices, I have another ridiculous thought. We met less than two weeks ago and here we are looking at apartments together. Well, that seems to be where we are now. Yep, we haven't even spoken about it, but here we are looking for our own apartment, like something we're just taking for granted.

Maja:

It's interesting to have a look at the real estate postings, to see what the reality of living London life would be like. We need at least a two room apartment, so I will be able to work in the mornings in my home office. An extra room could also mean Mark wouldn't have to disturb my sleep after coming home at three or four in the morning after playing the bars of London. It won't be cheap, but it would be totally doable if I got myself a computer engineering job here. It's something to keep in mind for the future, but as of now I have a couple of other things that are more important. Like the impossible list. And also I want to feel a little less sad before looking for a job. Let's just live life in the moment for a while, I think I deserve that. I want to spend some time looking at options, and see where life leads me. I'm sure it'll be fine.

Day 12
Wednesday March 3

Mark:

Rehearsal at Kylie's today, and with quarantine over, it means Maja can finally go too, which essentially means that, on only her second proper day in London, she's about to have her first session with what will be her first London band. But physics intervenes and we don't make it.

Pretty much our whole house has been furnished with things found on the street. In London, if people buy new things and don't need their old things, which are often not even that old, they just put them outside somewhere so that someone can take them. If it's an electrical item, there will often be a note saying, 'this works.' Our whole garden was kitted out that way, with a little help from the Palmerston regarding the parasols and deckchairs which Maja has come to love so much. This is why one of our kitchen chairs is an office chair. She's sitting on it now and I'm kind of milling about doing stuff. Until I decide to sit down and have a little close time. So there we are, Maja sitting back in the chair, me straddling her lap facing the wrong way. All's going well and fun until we slightly adjust our balance and the adjustable chair does what it does in these kinds of situations and adjusts. That's not normally an issue at all. But then, it doesn't normally have someone sitting backwards on it. And that's the way I go now. Full on backwards, launched out of the chair. And Maja can't do anything about it because she's been thrown totally forwards. So now we're both going. This might not be quite so bad, except Maja was facing the radiator, which means I'm now unknowingly heading towards it at quite frightening speed. Or to be more accurate, the back of my head is about to hit it at quite frightening speed. And, according to my sources, with a particularly frightening sound.

Maja:

As the chair disappears from beneath me and we're thrown at a terrifying speed, I hear one of the worst sounds I've ever heard. Not quite a thud, more of a bash which is then followed by silence. Almost like a kickdrum. And just after that my forehead hits the radiator as well. It hurts, shoots right through me, but soon afterwards I feel OK. It's just a small bruise. But Mark, on the other hand, just drops down. Not quite immediately, but I see him losing a bit of power as he half sits, half leans on the radiator. It doesn't look good. A second or so later it's like he has regained some kind of control and tries to sit up and weakly repeats "I'm alright, I'm alright." Oh no mister. You're certainly not alright. Lie down now. I will accept no resistance. I gently but strongly push him down, holding my hand under his head to soften any possible further impact. I let him lie there for a while, almost under the radiator on the kitchen floor, while making sure he is OK. I think he's got a concussion. Almost definitely.

Mark:

That all happens and I crumple to the floor, my crumpling considerably hastened by Maja projectiling on top of me as she suffers her own fall. In this fashion we very messily complete our undignified drop to the floor and that's where the similarity of our journeys end. She's immediately up and I'm not. I'm kind of half sitting, half lying there on my back, head very clumsily and uncomfortably propped up by a hard, white slab of metal. My eyes are closed in pain and a little bit of shock, causing considerable alarm in Maja who's now looking down on me asking with some deep concern if I'm alright. With that I think I really should open my eyes and let her know I'm at least not dead. This proves a little harder than I was expecting and it's not too long before my eyes are more or less half closed again. 'Stay there. Do not move,' says Maja, her medical experience and knowledge kicking in. I do, and she makes sure no serious damage has been done before she gives me the all clear to stand up, where we do another cursory check to make sure all things are working as they should. They are. More or less, and I'm insisting that I'm alright. 'No you're not,' she says. 'That was a heavy fall. You have a concussion.' Concussion schmushon. I'm fine.

But no. She insists that we go upstairs and I lie down on the bed, at least until we can confirm that I am absolutely alright.

Very quickly after lying down, I start to suspect she might actually have a point. My head is hurting. A lot. It feels thick and heavy and I'm dizzy. So much so that the room isn't quite spinning, but it is at least moving backwards and forwards a little which it certainly wasn't doing before so it must be me. Maybe it really was a little bit more than an innocent knock to the head. I do hope the radiator's OK. Maja says nothing for 10 minutes or so and just lets me recover my senses (a questionable exercise at the best of times to be fair). Once I've come round a little more, enough to admit that yes, she's right, I say we should probably get in touch with Sarah and cancel today. Well, duh. So, instead of going off and having a musical session round there, we stay here and Maja sits by the bed, passing the time in my de facto absence by singing along to a whole bunch of her favourite songs. Which is how I discover that she can actually sing pretty well. For now I'll file that away for future use as I lie back and continue to be useless for most of the rest of the day.

Maja:

I'm glad I'm stubborn, because he is definitely not OK, I very much realise this when I have to help him up the stairs. Then, once upstairs I have him lie down while I check online for what to do if you suspect a concussion. I decide that he is not in any danger and will be fine if he just spends the day in bed until he feels better, so I keep him there. But in any case, he will certainly not be able to move around much today. Oh, what a bummer. We had all of those grand plans of going to Kylie's for rehearsal, and enjoying the second day out of self isolation and here I am having to stay in this room all over again. I feel a bit bored after a while, not really having anything to do. So I default to doing something I like to do while bored. Singing along to songs I like. Right now I'm into Red Hot Chili Peppers and Gorillaz, so I mainly play tunes from those bands.

Day 13
Thursday March 4

Mark:

I'm on a little trip out to the shop for milk and other basic things when I see a nearby house has left a whole bunch of garden stuff outside their front garden. I don't register any immediate interest and walk past it without too much of a second look. But on the way back, just as I'm reaching home, I glance back and see that there might just be something of interest. Not anything actually in the display, more what a portion of it is actually on. I walk up to it all and see that this section is arrayed on a small two level service-type trolley. A very dirty trolley, but quite interesting nonetheless. I wonder what this would look like cleaned up, I think. Only one way to find out. I have no idea what this kind of thing could be used for, but I think it's something worth having a look at at least. My idea is to take it into our back garden, give it a good clean, then chuck it back out into the front garden and then show it to Maja who can decide if it's worth keeping or not. I really expect her to say no but that's OK. Apart from anything else, it would probably just be more clutter in a tiny room. It might not even comfortably fit.

Oh well. Let's see. First, it really cleans up quite well and I can now see it in all its silver and gold shiny newness. Now it also finally looks like what it is. A cake trolley. I take it upstairs and place it in the front garden. Now to go and get Maja and see what she thinks of it. She comes up the stairs mildly curious. Before I open the front door I say, 'Feel free to say no. I'm really not sure myself.' I open it up and there it is. She's not hugely impressed but she's not dismissing it either, saying, 'Let's bring it in. You never know.' I didn't see that coming to be fair. But OK. In it comes. We now have a cake trolley.

Maja:

After receiving the perfect little gift of a cake trolley, which sits perfectly as a little wheeled table in my room, it's time to go out. Out to explore the world. Or more like: out to see Camden market. Yes, I know, everything is closed. But that is not stopping me. Let's go and see what we find. The streets are, well, not quite empty but almost. There's not that much movement around. It's a nice walk, the weather is fresh and the cold is slightly biting but not too much. Actually very comfortable. After a while we reach Camden again. It's a town filled with empty bars, and there's almost no one walking around. Mark keeps pointing out all bars, with trivia in the style of, in this bar this and that famous band started out. This or that band was signed in that bar. And, I played there with the Insiders, and other stories. I listen and can't help but feel a little overwhelmed. It's a lot. Just... A lot.

After a little while we reach Camden Market. It's a famous place that tourists usually go to. A sightseeing spot. It has restaurants, bars, food stands, boats and shops. Everything you can possibly imagine a sightseeing spot having. Except people. And everything is closed. Except for the food stands. London is currently open for take away catering, which means that food stands are allowed. But there is a catch here. You're not allowed to sit down, or even stay in one place and eat. So you need to eat while walking. We see this getting enforced by security officers walking around the area, and if they see someone sitting down for a little while on some steps or something they walk up to the person and ask them to walk along. I never see them enforcing it any stronger than that, but this really makes it impossible to rest, even for a little while.

Mark:

I'm sorry, but that whole you can't stay in one place and eat and have to keep walking is ridiculous. Just a ridiculous, petty, almost performatively vindictive rule. Just so pointless and all I can see it achieving is upsetting people and setting people against each other, like the possibility that people could just get angry at the security guards, then the security guards get angry back, but with authority, and the whole thing could escalate. Just because someone committed sitting down to eat. I actually feel sorry for the guards for having to enforce this rule and it wouldn't surprise me if a lot of them disagreed with it, but they have their job to do and I think the best way to help them is to respect it and just keep moving along. I should also disclose some professional solidarity with them here. We had a similarly absurd situation in barworld when the bars reopened for a laughably short time in December before being forced to close again to kick off the period of furlough we're in right now. When they did reopen, one of the new rules that came in was that people had to order food if they wanted a drink. And the minimum thing they could buy from us cost four quid - a scotch egg in case you're wondering, which had become quite the national debate if you can believe that. I told you it was absurd. So they had to pay a whole bunch more just to get a casual pint. Theoretically, this meant that we had to enforce the law and make sure they actually ate the food. At the risk of getting into trouble, I never did enforce the law to make sure they ate the food and so was quite happy to turn a blind eye to people committing drinking. But I did have to turn away people who said they just wanted to order drinks and really didn't want to have to pay the extra for food they didn't want. And I know that as I stood there and refused them entry they were seeing me as a petty jobsworth. So yeah. I do totally have sympathy with the security guards round here today.

Maja:

Since the food stands are open we walk around to see what they have open. There are a lot of different food options. Chinese, Mexican, all kinds of food from countries I can't remember and of course, fish and chips. I want fish and chips. I don't think I've ever actually had it before. It's just not something we eat in Sweden. We don't have a culture of deep frying things, so everything fried is quite new to me. I want to try it. We order one serving each, and we get this wonderful fish and chips with a nice pink sauce to it. It's really nice, and feels very very British. Mark starts a little chat with the chef in the food stand. It's obvious that these places have had a rough time. And of course, Mark and the chef soon start bonding over something specific to northern English people. I think it's about curry sauce with pineapple in it. Whatever they mean by that. I'm not quite sure. There's so many kinds of curry in this world that I can't even begin to guess.

We want to stand there and eat our fish, but the chef asks us to go stand by the railing of the river since they can't have people staying by his stand once they've been served. We do, but soon a security officer comes and tells us to continue along. So we do. This is where we learn about that rule being in place now. So we walk and try to eat the fish while also trying to not let it cool down too quickly in the slightly icy wind.

It's still a very good fish.

Time flies when you're having fun, and we realise it's starting to be time for us to return home to get our gear and walk over to Kylie's for our first rehearsal. Halfway home Mark gets a phone call. It's Kylie, cancelling the rehearsal once again. Well, it's fine, we'll just do it another day.

I'm not really complaining, it's nice spending time with Mark. We have a couple of stories to tell each other today as well. And the ceiling is starting to get a little bit lonely since we've not been there to look at it.

Day 14
Friday March 5

Maja:

I don't want to leave. That's the feeling I've been tackling these last couple of days. I really have started to like it here, and I don't want to leave. But really, what is it I don't want to leave? I don't want to leave Mark. I don't want to go back to Sweden just yet. Not now. Not when I don't even know what I really want just yet. Please, don't make me leave. Please.

I've decided I want to stay. Really stay. Beyond the six months I currently have on my visa. But how in the world will I accomplish anything like that? How will I stay in London now after Brexit has happened? I've been looking at different ways of how to stay here, but I've not really reached any good alternatives just yet. I'm used to working in English, so getting a job in London would be a piece of cake as far as language is concerned at least. But even if I wanted to do that, I would need a work visa. For that, I would need to go back to Sweden, somehow get a job in the UK, and then apply for the visa from there. First, by definition, that would mean leaving which we've established I don't want to do. Second, I came here in the first place to get away from my situation in Sweden, not to go straight back into it. And third, finding a job in the UK and then applying for a visa sounds like something that would take a long time. And after all that, there's a fourth. The application could simply be refused. What then? So no. Leaving is not an option.

But there is this one thing I've heard of called the Global Talent Visa. On the face of it, it looks like the perfect fit for someone like me. I'm a cloud engineer, which is one of the most sought after professions in the world, and the number one sought after profession in tech. Honestly, I'm confident I could get a job with a good salary anywhere. I also understand that a Global Talent Visa would allow me to stay without the obligation of going and getting a job immediately. It also seems to be a fairly quick processing period - three weeks give or take. So me and Mark start to delve into the details of how to apply for that visa.

Balls.

It doesn't take long for us to realise that the whole thing is just impossibly complicated and seems set up to fail. Also, there are too many bureaucratic requirement boxes I don't tick. Actually, it seems impossible that anyone as young as me could tick them all. And there seems to be a lot of coordination to be done from the employer's side as well. An employer I don't even have yet. And they make constant references to 'Your sponsor' without giving any information on what qualifies someone to be named as your sponsor. We spend a lot of time just trying to find some clarification on that one single point and end up being taken round in circles. It's here that we give up. No. This is just impossible. Even if it wasn't, I have experience in applying for working visas and it's just hell. There are also so many things that can go wrong and I really don't feel that confident about applying for anything in Brexit UK.

But I want to stay here. Or more than that, I'd like to stay with Mark. I don't want to leave him. I think I love him.

OK. I can stay here for now and worry about the six month thing later on. Until then, I really just could be here, living off my savings which I happen to have because I never really spent that much, preferring to be able to travel. Like many young people do when they save up and go travel the world. I want to do that, or at least my version of it. But for now I would really just be happy renting a room and being with Mark. I've had a high salary for quite a while now so I have a good enough amount built up. And if I was to go for a slightly more modest lifestyle to make my savings last longer, that would be no big deal. I saved most of what I earned when I was doing well, and it's not that long ago that I was a student and getting by on barely anything at all. Also, while I was far from deprived growing up, it's not like my family had any kind of great fortune lying around either. This is all to say that tightening up would not be a major challenge for me.

Of course, savings are always finite, and I don't know how long they're going to last. But for now, I'd rather live a little time stress free until I feel ready to go back to an office job, or maybe I'm just going to feel like doing something else. I don't know. I just know that right now, I don't feel ready to go back. Not just yet. I want to stay with Mark. Besides, if it comes to it, there are always opportunities to freelance in my line of work.

Can't I just stay here?

Does it really have to be this complicated?

Then it comes to me. 'Mark, can't we just get married?'

Mark:

By now we've decided that we're opposite sex versions of each other, with each one also covering the gaps the other has. An example. Maja really wants to do music but doesn't quite have the skillset or experience. Hello. To really do anything in music, you need to be quite good at technology and computers for recording, and internet stuff in general for all the other stuff. Did you read anything above just now that fits into that? Come on. Even my Mark's Diaries Wordpress site wasn't up to speed until she came along. We've also discovered we have very similar work ethics and approaches. With this, she's been starting to call me Boy Maja, an almost overwhelming feeling of approval given the total awe in which I hold her achievements, determination and aptitude. I guess that makes her girl Mark.

The idea of Maja staying in London beyond her six months has really taken hold and we're researching how she could get a visa. Her preferred route is through the Global Talent programme which basically means companies can sponsor people they believe have abilities beyond what are available in this country. But we're in the middle of a roadblock with that and Maja's trying to make a bit more sense of it. She's deep in thought and reading so I decide to go downstairs and make tea. It will be the most momentous trip to make tea I've ever made.

I come back to see how she's getting on, and kneel down on the bed in front of her to listen to the expected update. She looks up and all I see in her expression is exasperation. In a tired voice, she says, 'This looks really complicated and undoable. We should probably just get married.'

Oh. OK. Yes. That's it. That's my response. I nod and say, 'OK.' Then I realise two things. First, the actual gravity of the situation and second, that I'm already on my knees. Alright, not one knee but I think you can see we're already going about all this a little bit differently to expected convention. My expression morphs to serious as I look deeply at her and she lets out a little giggle as she realises what I'm about to say. And I do. 'Maja, will you marry me?' Another giggle. 'Yes.' There's no ring or anything. Oh, and there's the small detail that she is actually still married. But just like that, two weeks after we first met, we're engaged.

There's only one song to play to mark the ocassion, so I dig it out. The Counting Crows' Accidentally In Love. Seriously. When I went to the airport, I was going to meet a friend who was in a difficult time and needed to get away. I just happened to be able to provide a place to stay. Romance was nowhere in my mind, let alone the possibility that I was heading off to the airport to meet my future wife. But here we are.

This definitely has to be marked. This really is celebration time. So I go out and buy champagne, a purchase I augment with whiskey and ginger for cocktails. While I'm doing that, Maja orders in Thai food. A party for two, all set up on our wonderful cake trolley.

Maja:

I'm surprised when Mark, already on his knees, says, 'Wait, wait, wait. That's my line.'

He then grabs my hand and looks me deep into my eyes.

'Maja, will you marry me?'

'Yes.'

The rest of the day disappears quickly into happy hormones, champagne and Thai food.

I'm in love.

Mark:

So am I. Accidentally.

London, Day 15
Saturday March 6

Mark:

A gentle day after last night with a notable afterparty guest as our cat Toffee comes and joins us in the room for a while and hangs out on the bed. It's her first visit so maybe she felt a change in the force.

Maja:

Toffee is a little cat, with a peculiarly small head. I mean, her head is really small. Like too small to be true. But she is very cute, and I get to cuddle her a bit. But she is a scaredy cat. Any sudden movement and she'll jump to the other side of the room in a second. It's clear to see that she is very attached to Mark, who is an animal lover. Mark can be a little awkward around animals, but it's clear that he enjoys them very much. I think he really wants to have his own pets. Toffee barely counts since she was practically adopted from the street, and mainly lives outside. But Mark is really happy to have her around.

London, Day 16
Sunday March 7

Mark:

Before I go onto today's account, let's meet Toffee a bit more. It's all in Mark's Diaries but worth recounting at least a little here. First, she's a very striking tortoiseshell, hence the name. And yes she was adopted from the street. But more accurately, she adopted us. She turned up one day in the back garden in March 2018. This was after weeks of dramatic and freezing snowstorms which I can only imagine she had somehow survived through having been, again speculative, abandoned or whatever it was that saw her out in that lot. My favourite theory is that a family moved house and left her behind. Another is that she belonged to some old person nearby who died, maybe while Toffee was out, and that was that. Who knows? Anyway, the weather this particular late winter/ early spring was so notable it gained a media nickname - Beast From The East - and lasted from around mid to late February to mid to late March. The subsidence of the bad weather coincided exactly with Toffee turning up one day starving, dehydrated and with no voice with which to meow; only a pathetic half whisper emerged whenever she tried to. I thought she would have some food and water and leave. But she just stayed. On that first day she intensely guarded the back of the garden from the top of the fence because, I guess, she'd found this place and wasn't about to share it. Cats. Then she made furtive forays into the house, after a while feeling comfortable and safe enough to hang out in here. Over the next days and weeks we did all the appeals. Signs on lamp-posts and all that. Tried to get her adopted. Formally and informally. No dice. Then, once we'd accepted she was here to stay, we did all the responsible cat owner stuff. Which included having to have the whole neutering operation done because vets can't know this stuff without going in, which meant essentially having the same operation and recovery time as actual neutering. She had been neutered. Which meant she had come from somewhat of a responsible home, as we had suspected, deepening the mystery of how she'd ended up where she had. In all that vet stuff we discovered she was around 10 to 18 months old. As she grew considerably in the subsequent year, we settled on her age having been somewhere near the lower of those numbers. We also had her microchipped and began the general regimen of deworming and all the basic health and hygiene stuff. So yes. A preference for the outside, including at night where she found a place to stay very happily in our shed which was eventually kitted out for her, but you would equally find her hanging around inside, not least in the very convenient large cupboard space under the stairs. Somewhere in all this, after one or two farcical episodes, we had to own up to the private landlord that we had a cat contrary to the renting contract. He had no problem with it at all. With that, I considered Toffee officially living here.

On Tuesday February 23 we decided we were going to start to try writing songs together. Since then we've written something everyday in one of the notebooks - that's the three I bought at the beginning, and an extra A4 book. That something could be a few verses, or both of us writing whole sets of lyrics each, sometimes spanning up to four or five pages at a time. Translating the written word into a song is a whole other thing, but getting something out of a blank page is also progress, so ideas are there. And what we're telling is the story of us. Nonsensical conversations turned into fantasy lyrics, or just simply tell-it- as-it-happened lyrics, or say how you feel lines. All put together for a whole concept of what we see as just feelgood writing which we hope to turn into feelgood songs complete with singalong choruses. In short, we're attempting to musically bottle up what we are and somehow, we have no idea how just yet, take it out to people.

Maja:

I love writing these little lyrics. Just me and Mark, with a notebook and dreams and laughter. Cute little happy rhymes, mixed with dark stories about what we've been through. There's a lot of artistic freedom of course, I'm not saying that everything is based on reality, but it feels really good to put pen to paper and try to express feelings in rhymes. Wonderful. I've never really done this, and thoughts just keep on flowing out of my head down onto the paper in little bucket loads at a time.

Mark:

With that, we get started for the first time today as Maja sets up a studio in this little room. To set up a studio in this context means to turn on the computer, open up the recording software and hook up the external interface. The interface is a small rectangular box. On the front of it are some fundamental volume and balance controls and inputs for microphones and instruments. On the back are outputs which you use to attach it to the computer, and also speakers if you want. But the interface also includes a headphone jack, so you can hear all the sounds through there, both during recording and playback. And you can use that playback to play along with or sing along to, to put a new track onto a song. On the screen, among many other things, is something that looks like one of those mixing desks that the big recording studios use. So in this case, instead of touching all those faders which go up and down on the top of the desk, you move them up and down within the programme by using the mouse. And of course in the same way, you click various buttons, like mute or whatever, on and off.

Now that's all set up, it's time to tackle the first issue of how we're going to do percussion. One idea I've had is to try to get different percussion or drum-like sounds out of the acoustic guitar we borrowed from Kylie. I manage to come up with something that sounds like a kick drum - or bass drum if you prefer - and a snare. The 'kick' I make by hitting the back of the main body with the palm of my hand. I then produce the 'snare' with a quick, hard plectrum hit across all the strings while having them all muted with the palm of my left hand.

Now we get started with recording the 'kick.' To begin the process we set up what's called a click track, which is a computer generated metronome you set to the speed you want the track to be. Although it's called a click track, it can just as often be a kind of beep. As you set that speed, the virtual studio also sets and resets itself. So, assuming for our purposes here that each click is a single beat in a bar, each bar is made up of four clicks with the first of each set of four being slightly louder than the other three. Within the programme, if you decide you want your track to be faster or slower, those bars will readjust themselves to always be four clicks. Yes, there are different time signatures which would alter this equation, and you can also double the clicks which I sometimes find can help with accurate playing, especially with slower songs, but not everyone agrees with that. But for now we'll just focus on the general rock and pop rhythm of four beats to a bar and the same for the click.

We're now going to use the microphone to record my guitar 'drum' sounds. This means I have to wear headphones so that I can hear the click but it doesn't get picked up by the microphone. In this way we first record the kick drum track. Then we go back to the beginning and I record the snare track over what I've just played. This time, as well as hearing the click track, I can also hear the kick track I've just recorded. And now we have sounds in the programme, and they're all single isolated sounds as they're drum beats, we can slightly move any beats that I didn't quite play in perfect time to give us a solid rhythm track. With that, we now have a drum track to play along to and hopefully begin to create with. After this it's down to experimentation as we try different chord progressions and break out some of our lyrics to see what kinds of vocals we can come up with. It's all part of the process and I'm not expecting whole chunks of already written lyrics to end up fully formed in a song. It's just great to have got this started. As I thought might possibly happen, once a vocal line begins to emerge with one of the lyrics, we really get hold of it and develop it to come up with something different. We both have a go at singing lines as they come, to see where they can be taken, but we don't get a massive way into this; not long after we've got this far, we have to leave to go to Sarah's. But that's fine. We've finally started actually trying to do something with the lyrics we've been writing, and that is a really big deal.

Maja:

Being as my room is so small, there's no way that you could possibly even fit a desk in here. But we have the cake trolley that Mark found, so I could use that to set up a makeshift desk. Maybe. I search around in the room for anything usable, and behind the bed I find a couple of broken wooden bed slats. Perfect. I take the slats, tape them with some gaffer tape and put them between the handles of the trolley. Voila, a table! The computer goes on the slats, the interface beneath, and then we can connect the microphone to that. Perfect. Mark starts to do a lot of different things and all I can think is wooah. I have no idea what to do here, how to help. It's amazing and a bit daunting at the same time. Especially when he starts to play the guitar and totally goes all out in his singing. How does he even do that? I just don't know. How am I going to do that? It's a bit scary. And I get all nervous and flustered. So, not wanting to make a fool out of myself, I perversely manage to make an even bigger fool out of myself.

Mark:

No you don't. This creative thing is hard and you really have to put yourself out there. Pulling songs and ideas out of thin air, the key is to not be afraid to be terrible. Everyone does stuff that's terrible. You just do your best to not let anyone outside the room see your terrible stuff.

But of course, sometimes things do slip through the quality test and make it onto the stage. But even then, when you think you've done good stuff, you've just kinda got to hope other people agree. Or even then you could be deluding yourself and making a mess strutting terrible stuff all over the stage. On the other side, which is why you take the chance to put this stuff out there, a song you thought was terrible, or at least not up to your best, could be the one that everyone goes for. You just really don't know.

Maja:

Looks like you have a lot of experience of making a fool out of yourself. That's great.

Mark:

The very definition of an experienced person is someone who's made a lot of mistakes. So yeah. Maybe someone who's made a fool out of themselves a lot.

We get to Kylie's and she's all over Maja. Kylie has a new pet project called Geisha Rising, which she says will aim to promote all kinds of different artists. She's now blown away that into her life has walked a girl who embodies quite a few qualities of the Geisha; not only is Maja adept with a sword, being a proficient practitioner of Aikido, she also speaks fluent Japanese. And we're all stunned when Kylie shows us the logo she's chosen for her project and Maja really looks like the character contained within it. Kylie, a deep spiritual believer, feels a significant alignment of the stars. Not least where it comes to myself and Maja. 'You two are the real deal,' she says with absolute conviction. Me and Maja coyly look at each other and laugh.

'Well,' says Maja, 'We have some news.' Kylie takes a seat and looks at us. We look at each other again, each daring the other to say it. But before either of us has a chance to say anything, Kylie bursts out with what sounds like a one word sentence, 'You'regettingmarried.' We don't even answer. We just laugh hysterically and Kylie launches herself from the chair to envelope us in a huge group hug. 'I knew it, I knew it, I just knew it,' she says in between what are almost sobs.

Then all of a sudden she gets serious. 'How's it going over at the house?' she asks. My silence says it all, while Maja replies, after some hesitation, 'Not good. Really not good at all.' This part hasn't been written about so much in here, more kinda being a between the lines thing. But I should break cover now and say that Maja and Jenn don't talk. Not, aren't talking. They don't talk to each other. At all. They're never even in the same room. As far as I'm aware they've not said a single word to each other since saying hi on the first night. As for me, well, Jenn hasn't said a whole lot to me lately either and I'm now even knocking on the bedroom door before I go in. A room I called my own for over four years. Which I'm still paying half the rent for. But strangely, it does feel right to knock.

To just walk in would feel like an intrusion now. But it really is different for Maja. I've been in this house for six years and have known Jenn for 12. Maja is brand new in the house and didn't arrive in the best emotional shape as it was, so the potential for her feeling awkward and generally unwelcome is off the chart. As well as not having written too much of that in here, it really isn't something we've spoken about a great deal either. Oh, and the upstairs room is of course Maja's and not mine. So really, in this house I've lived in for six years and still live in, I currently don't actually have a room.

'OK,' says Kylie, nodding sagely, wheels clearly turning. She stares at us for a second, as if taking us in, then says, 'How would you guys feel about coming and living here? Rent free.' What now? Me and Maja don't even bother to consult. An instant, breathless yes is all that comes out of both of us. We rush to her and there are more exuberant group hugs. But Kylie isn't finished. 'That's really great,' she says once we've all broken away. There's more. 'I've been wanting to be away quite a lot for a while now but I've not had anyone to watch the cats. For a while I've wanted someone to just be living here and there's not really been anyone I know I would be completely comfortable with asking. But I look at you two, so much in love, and having a bit of a hard time of it with a difficult living situation and, well, Mark I know, but Maja, I feel such a great energy off you and the two of you together, well…

'The thing is, it's not just helping look after the cats

while I'm away now and then. I've been thinking for a while of just getting away from London altogether. I mean, to live. I've always seen this as just a temporary base for myself and I'm getting restless to go back out into the world again. Where, I have no idea, but within a month or two, and it will be for a long time. It would mean so much to me to know that my home and my cats were safe and that there was someone living here that I could really trust. And I just know that's you guys. All I'd ask is that you looked after the bills. Everything else is taken care of. And you could move in Thursday if you want. Would you be up for all that?'

We are now nodding frantically and totally disbelievingly, unable to take in what was being said as it was being said. It's just unreal. This does not happen. Yes yes, yes and yes is all we can say. And we can move in this week? On Thursday? That's mad. It's Sunday right now, to save you having to go back to check. 'My babies, that's just wonderful,' she says, grabbing us both in yet another huge hug. 'I just know this is going to be amazing. You guys are perfect for me and for this place. Before I go off on my travels, we can also work together, play music together, anything. Whatever you want. And this place will be yours, so treat it as your home. Whatever improvements or anything you want to do, just go for it.' She then says that she has to go out and meet someone now, so will we be OK if she leaves us on our own for a little while? And we can also take some time to think about it. Yes we will definitely be fine here, and no need to think about anything at all. With that, another hug and Kylie is out the door. As soon as it closes, me and Maja look at each other in complete, total incredulity. What was that? Did you hear what I heard? We have a place to move into now? And in a short while it's going to be just us? This is going to be our place? A large, beautiful three bedroom apartment in practically central London. For free? This is just too much. This just doesn't happen. Really? Has this just happened? It has, but we truly are having a hard time taking it in. So much so that we're convinced we must have misheard or misunderstood something. But we can't figure out what any of that could possibly be, so we conclude that we did indeed hear and understand the same things. Wow. OK. Time to check out the place. Our new place. That we'll be moving into in a couple of days. Only a few days ago Maja said out loud, 'I wonder what our place will look like.' I pretty much shut the conversation down as it didn't seem to be something possible so I didn't see it as being really worth thinking about. 'I was only thinking about it, it's fun,' she said. So I played along and we thought and talked about this impossible, mythical London apartment we were going to move into. All the time I was thinking, 'I'm on furlough, and will have to keep up rent here as well for at least some kind of respectable period. No. Impossible. Not going to happen, but hey, let's play pretend.' Well...

Kylie said the place is a bit of a mess and there's a lot of work to be done, but that's fine. We're up for it. And I know what our room will be. It has to be.

OK. Let's take you through it all. Kylie of course has

the main big double room with its view overlooking central London. Not the classic skyline and bright lights, but over and through the houses of north London you can see through Kings Cross to one of the prominent buildings of the city. The apartment also has what we've come to know as the main room, which is where all general hanging out and rehearsing takes place. This is in the middle of the apartment, with the small kitchen off of that to the left, and the bathroom off and to the right. From the main room there's a corridor with the toilet immediately on the right. A little way past that, also on the right, is the door to Kylie's room. More or less opposite this, so on the left of the corridor, is the front door. If you were to walk in the front door and turn left you would come to a small room which I happen to know is basically used as a storage for things belonging to Kylie's friends. Then, next to that is what I suppose would otherwise be the front room. This overlooks the street from which you enter the building. It's a beautiful room and really quite big. This has to be what will become our bedroom. We go and stand in there for a few moments trying to take all this in, spinning round, arms outstretched, in what will become ours. No more tiny room for Maja. This, then later on, the whole thing. And between now and then, we will be living with the wonderful, hugely talented singing Kylie in what will be just the most amazing three person house share ever. Me and Kylie already have our connection, personally and musically. And the way she's been drawn to Maja is just huge and instant.

For so long in my head I've been solving our ever growing impossible list by not thinking about it, just living minute to minute, day by day, in the delusion that solutions will just pop up out of the road as we come to them. Now, here we are with a few huge delusions realised in one hit. We've found an apartment in lockdown London which, despite all our optimistic noises to each other, seemed a totally insurmountable goal to achieve.

But now with this, we've also solved the financial/work situation of how the hell I would pay my part of it, and sorted out how I can keep paying my share of the room with Jenn. Just like that, the impossible is all taken care of; I can continue to pay my share of the rent I've been paying all along with the furlough I'm still getting and, er, that's it. Job done, impossible ticked off the list. All it took was for someone to offer us our own central London apartment for free. Pretty obvious when you think about it.

Maja:

Eeeeeeh. Wait what just happened? I don't think I quite follow.

London, Day 17
Monday March 8

Maja:

Today we have nothing planned, which is perfect and it means that we can just walk around and talk about everything that just happened. Which I still just can't believe. Nothing really makes sense to me anymore. We need time to realise what just happened, and how better to do that then to take a wonderful walk around the neighbourhood. To Camden Market maybe? We find ourselves a wonderful little coffee shop in a charming little record store where I'm finally able to satisfy my coffee cravings with a wonderfully made flat white topped with amazing coffee art in a takeaway cup. After wandering around and taking in Camden Market, we start to make our way home again. 'Hey, Mark. I don't want to go back just yet. Can't we continue?' And so we do, ending up in Waterlow Park where we see the ducks swimming harmoniously in the pond. Then we go and find a bench where we sit and enjoy the view of our London. We've been out for way over three hours. We return home excited about whatever is going to happen next.

THE LONDON DIARY
THE FIRST MOVE

Day 18
Tuesday March 9

Mark:

We're chilling at home when Kylie calls me. 'I'm going out for a bit so if you want I can give you the keys to the apartment. But I'm leaving pretty much now. So, if you're up for it, say 20 minutes at Tufnell Park station?' I don't even bother to check with Maja. I just say yes we'll be there. I go to the kitchen to find Maja having a good chat with Cris. Apologising for interrupting, I say, 'Maja, we have to leave right now.' I explain what's happening but my words clearly come out too fast because once we're out of the house she says, 'Where are we going?' Oh dear. Sorry. OK. I tell her properly this time and get a much more excited response to the fact that we're now getting keys to the apartment. Moving day will still be maybe Thursday, to be confirmed, but to be about to get the keys makes it so real because, frankly, the thought of getting this place for free has seemed a bit too good to be true. But now with keys about to change hands, we know it's actually happening. We get to Tufnell Park tube just two minutes before Kylie, who gives us a huge greeting before handing over the keys. Then she's gone into the night and we head off to the apartment.

We're hanging out just chilling there a few hours later when Kylie calls. 'Guys,' she says, 'I've decided I'm staying out tonight. Do you mind staying there and I'll see you in the morning?' Maja hears this, we nod to each other, then I confirm that yes, that will be alright. I hang up and then me and Maja have a moment. Oh, we think simultaneously. This is it. We've moved in now. Just like that, it has happened.

Thoughts now turn to how we're going to have dinner here, and the fact that we have to get a little something extra to mark the ocassion. We decide to order in from a local Greek restaurant which I'll pick up while taking a detour to one of the finest wine shops in London which is right around the corner. When I leave, I can't help but to take a celebratory sprint to the end of the street. Me and Maja are in sight of having our actual own place in almost central London. A three bedroom apartment in view of the city. And there's no rent or deposit to pay. All we're being asked to do is cover the bills. We're literally on the verge of being given a free apartment. Even before it becomes our own whole apartment, we have a proper big room. Again, for free. This is also us moving in together, and into what will be a totally musical place, just two and a half weeks after we first met at Heathrow airport.

Maja:

I can't believe we've just managed to do another impossible thing. It is impossible to live rent free in London. It's just impossible. And it seems beyond wonderful to live in this musical collective. Cheers Mark. To us and to our bright future.

Mark:

Impossible to live rent free in London? Try impossible to do that anywhere. And just to get an apartment in London. Or lockdown London as it is right now. You might as well put that on the impossible list too.

Day 19
Wednesday March 10

Mark:

When Kylie arrives at the house this morning she's absolutely delighted to see us there. We all live together now and we get to talking about musical plans. Kylie really wants the two of us to join her as essentially her backing band and she has big plans for us to really go to town on rehearsals now we're all in the same space 24/7. There's talk of reshaping the main living room area into a studio/workspace, but that will come later once we've got the apartment into a bit more order. To this she says,

'Guys, this is your place. I'm not going to be staying here much longer so whatever you want to do, just do it. Treat it as your own home because it is.' While we will be working together, hopefully a lot, Sarah's fast moving on with her plans to be moving on and out of London. And with that, she gives us an even bigger surprise than she gave us last night when we discovered we'd accidentally moved in. She wants us to have her room. The main double room overlooking central London. 'It makes sense,' she says. 'I won't be living here much and you guys will, and eventually the whole place will fully become yours anyway, so we might as well get that started now.' Besides that, she reasons, we're two people and she's just one so it makes sense that we have the big double room and she moves herself into the single room. No, we were not expecting this at all. I've long known the single room was for storage of things for her friends and was not to be touched. There is another large room in the house at the front looking out over the street and we assumed that was where we would be calling our own. But no. The whole place is to get an overhaul and we're to play a big part in that. And all while staying in the big double bedroom. With our very own central London view.

To make this all happen, there is a hell of a lot to do so we do the only thing there is to be done. We get started. This new place is a 15 to 20 minute walk from the house we're leaving. So, while Maja cleans and organises, I get busy with making shuttle walks between the two places carrying all our stuff. This is, indeed, moving day.

Maja:

Under the bed are a couple of drawers in which some men's clothes are stashed. I carefully place them in a box for the cupboard as I ask Sarah, 'Who do these belong to?' She explains that they belong to a TV celebrity. I, a Swede, have never heard of him, but this is where he stays whenever he has to work on a TV show or something. I'm not sure if it's a good or bad thing not knowing who he is, but the bed I sleep in now is the very same bed a famous person has regularly slept in.

Mark:

Once we've got to what we can call a conclusion for the day, we settle in at the window and pour ourselves a massively earned Orange GnT. We have to do that in our room because Sarah has very recently decided she doesn't drink anymore so would like to not have the temptation. However, she's been emphatic that we shouldn't let that stop us, as long as we keep it to our room please. No problem at all. And well, with a view like that as well to share between just the two of us, that's actually just fine. More and more this is all getting too good to be true.

Maja gives actual action to that thought as she tells me she's going to continue paying rent on the room in the house we've just left. 'Incase things burn here,' she explains. I respect the decision and don't say anything, but really, why should things burn? This is a beautiful situation with the beautiful soul of Kylie and us two. What could possibly go wrong? But yeah sure. Nothing wrong with having a little back-up plan.

Maja:

As we finally lie down, we're in a celebratory mood. We live here now. Kylie has settled down in her room and now this is the first night for all three of us to be here. Mark quickly falls asleep next to me and I remain awake for a while, reflecting upon the weirdness of all the things that have been happening lately. My former life and my future life. I'm getting sleepier and sleepier. I'm close to really dropping off when I notice a strange sound. It's coming from down the hall. From Kylie's room. I quietly sneak out of bed and peek into her room. Next to her is an enormous speaker, but it is way too far away for me to dare to go in and turn it off or down. So I sneak back into bed and try to accustom myself to the new sounds I'm going to have to listen to tonight. 'Aaauuuumm, aaauuuummm, ching, aauuuum'. Some kind of meditative chanting. I hate these kinds of sounds. I find them terribly unnerving. As the tracks continue on I realise that I'm stuck in an infinite playlist of Youtube hell.

Mark:

We won't find out what this all is until morning, but what's happened is that Kylie's fallen asleep to something soothing on Youtube. Whatever that was has finished and now the continuation playlist has been activated. Either the video she was listening to was very quiet, or the next one was very loud. In any case, what's happening now is that the whole apartment is filled with eerie, extremely unnerving Gregorian chanting. It feels like we are inside and living the soundtrack to a horror movie. I have a few unnerving moments when my imagination tells me we are actually in a horror movie. We're totally encased in it and sleep is impossible. It goes on and on and we have no idea what to do. We don't want to intrude on Kylie's room and turn it off or down. Instead, we comfort each other and endure in varying levels of desperation and exasperation. This goes on until about 8am when it suddenly gets turned off with Kylie waking to do so. We still don't intrude. Instead, relief and benign gratitude washing over us, we go to sleep. But it's somewhat of a qualified relief because we're left wondering if this kind of thing is normal around here and something we're going to have to live with. Oh dear. Day one and I feel our first little chat approaching. We have to know what the hell all that was about.

When we're all up and about I bring it up with Kylie, who casually says, 'Oh, if that ever happens just go in and turn it off. I just fall asleep and never know what's going to come up next.' Oh. That was easy. A horrible, horrible and very unsettling night, especially given it was the first one, but really, we can leave it there.

Day 20
Thursday March 11

Mark:

New Bass Day for Maja and she's totally thrilled with it. A Washburn, the exact same model as mine, but a different colour and just a few ever so slightly different specs, but essentially the same bass. And it plays wonderfully. It's ridiculous to think two new, high end basses were sent back to the shop in disgrace, while this second hand number has turned up, costing about a quarter of the price of either of them, and is just out-of-the-box brilliant.

As Maja's joyfully contemplating and trying out her new acquisition, for some reason I decide to look at the serial number on my bass, something I've never done before. I am stunned beyond to discover that the first five numbers of it are 92102. Maja's birthday: 1992, October 2nd. Even Kylie, with all her tuned in spirituality and encouraging words that the two of us are meant to be, is struck into total silence by this revelation.

After all this, me and Maja have a few drinks then, at 1am, we decide to go out to the local town of Archway and continue out there. We fill a backpack with selected bottles and cups and take off. It's in some state of enthusiastic exuberance that we bounce along the road, coming across a shop protected with a purple shutter and adorned with stylish graffiti. Maja is wearing a purple raincoat. It is far too good an opportunity to pass up. The resulting photographs are every bit as spectacular as we hoped they would be.

We continue right to the end of the high street. There, opposite the tube, we find a late night kebab takeaway place. Across the road from that is a very attractive and socially laid out group of benches. Just perfect for a party of two.

Day 21
Friday March 12

Mark:

Another trip to Camden Market. This really is becoming a thing and that's the main item on the agenda today, alongside the continuing huge job of cleanup and organisation of the room and apartment with Sarah enthusiastically joining in. She really is going for it now, saying that she expects us to be there for anything up to five years as she keeps going off on her travels. She says once again that she's only ever considered it as a temporary base anyway and had long been looking for someone who could come and take the place over, but didn't know anyone who quite fit what she was looking for. Then Maja came along, the two of us needed a place, and Sarah saw a perfect fit in all directions. And now here we are. I told Maja things happened in London, but within less than three weeks of arriving here, she's landed a relationship, what looks like being the beginnings of a full time band with one of the most connected people in town - I'm talking about Sarah here - and a free apartment. By any standards, this is just ridiculous.

As for all the other stuff, this time I really have solved it by not thinking about it. I've returned to walking around in a state of denial and delusion that somehow, magically, the other obstacles in front of us will just fall away. After all, we've just landed a free apartment. Surely the rest of the stuff will take care of itself as well. Yep. OK Mark. You just keep telling yourself that. But really, I think I've boiled it down to, you're OK today and that's about it. It comes down to that. One day at a time, so today is just today.

On a little wander out to the shop today I bump into Rafael, who lives above my bar. He says he saw us making all our trips the other day and says I should have asked him to help, as he has a big work van. I knew this, I just didn't want to ask. 'You idiot,' he says. 'Ask next time, please.' I don't know whether to thank him or apologise. He seems almost hurt. I promise I'll ask if there ever is a next time. Of course there won't be, but why hurt his feelings further?

Day 22
Saturday March 13

Mark:

Our first 13th of the month. Do bad things happen on days of 13? I don't even believe that Friday stuff, but I can't help but have a little muse first thing this morning.

If anything, today is a bit of a lucky day. It's the first day we feel really in any way settled in our new place. All the moving has been done, as well as a large part of the organisation and cleaning. Today, for the first time, we feel like we have something of our own space. Our idea is to just take that absolute relief at having landed somewhere and do very little. Maybe a little bass and music practice, but very much as and when the time and mood takes us. If we're to be totally honest with ourselves and you, we fully intend to spend today doing absolutely nothing but chilling and thinking nice things.

With those thoughts and our very newly discovered domestic wonderfulness, we settle down for a simple lunch of soup and bread using the desk just outside the kitchen and next to the bathroom as we haven't quite got round to fixing proper dining arrangements in here yet. But it all still feels fantastic. It's a beautiful, practically central London day and the vibe is untouchable. What could possibly go wrong?

There's a little sudden furry flurry of excitement as Kylie comes running through to retrieve Ron, her younger cat who has just run into the bathroom. When that happens, it can only mean one thing. Ron has gone under the bathtub. It's a frustrating process for Kylie to have to get him out and once she does, she says that the cat is possibly just feeling a little unsettled at having new people in the place. She often seeks refuge under the bathtub, Kylie explains, but she's apparently been doing it a little more than usual lately.

So Kylie says that it would be good if we could be extra vigilant for now and leave the bathroom door closed at all times. At least just until Ron settles down and hopefully starts to feel a little more comfortable with us. No problem. With that, Kylie lgoes back into the bathroom, emerges a few minutes later and walks away, without closing the door. Well, why should she automatically think of doing that? It's a brand new thing, right? I kinda notice the door's been left open but I don't really think too much of it. I'll close it. Yes I will. In a minute. In a minute, I'll get up and close it. No, really, I will. About two minutes later, Ron comes running back towards us and goes, yep, you've guessed it, into the bathroom.

Balls. I knew I should have shut that door straight away. I really don't want Kylie to know the door's already been left open long enough for the cat to get back in there. And kinda on our (my) watch. Alright, it wasn't me who left it open, but I've been here with an open door all this time. All two minutes of it, at least a minute of which the door should have been shut. I was sitting right next to it.

Why didn't I just do it as soon as I saw? I know Kylie won't be too mad at this having happened so soon after it became a brand new thing, but she might be like, 'Come on guys, what did we all just agree?' and fair enough. I'd rather avoid even that. Let's just deal with this quietly and quickly, and then make sure we don't forget again.

So I go into the bathroom, and there Ron is, faithfully under the bathtub, just two red eyes hovering and staring at me with benign malevolence in the darkness. Yes, she has red eyes. The eyes of the other cat are yellow. Which is how you tell these two almost identical white cats apart. I reach in with my hand trying not to scare her, but still trying to make her uncomfortable enough to run out. With my own cat Toffee, who I've now sadly left behind with Jenn at the old house, the faintest of movement inside a hiding place is enough to have her scurrying out in fright. Ron is clearly made of sterner stuff and knows she's perfectly safe in there thankyou very much. I reach further and further in, but she just isn't having it. She's now gone deep and I'm almost lying on my belly trying to reach in. There's a bunch of semi damp rags under here and, as I reach for Ron with my left and arm, reaching round a bathtub support to do so, I inadvertently move the rags away with my elbow. I'll worry about that later. I should be worried about that now. Very worried.

Seeing something I haven't, and very much realising something quite significant has just happened that I have no clue of, Ron suddenly makes a dart for it. Great. She's decided to come out. She disappears behind the support I was just reaching around and that's it. She doesn't emerge from behind the support. She just disappears. Down, it seemed like. Did I see that? Did she just suddenly lurch downwards? Surely not. It happened so quickly it doesn't seem possible. Still not massively overly concerned, I crawl a bit more under the bathtub and peer in, up to and around the support pole. There's no cat. She's simply ceased to be. Just like that. Oh no no no no no. In a split second I realise what's just happened and how and why. Those rags. They were stuffed into a hole in the floor. That cat, well, she's gone through it. And is now, very most likely, on her way into the depths of this building. It's around two hundred years old and has been knocked all different kinds of ways into different apartments over a substantial amount of years. The walls and floors in between are nothing but impenetrable labyrinths, unseen by human eyes in generations. And I've just seen Sarah's cat, no, I've just helped send Sarah's cat, jump into that black void from which escape or retrieval may well be impossible. Did I mention today was the 13th? Oh balls.

There's nothing for it now but to tell Kylie as soon as possible what's happened. When I tell her, the look of shock and panic on her face is total. I don't know it yet, but this has long been one of her worst fears and now it's happened. Not yet having really taken it in and not yet fully ready to be rational either, she refuses to believe I didn't do anything intentionally. I of course had no idea the rags hid a hole but, at this immediately early stage, she's understandably somewhat hysterical and convinced I pulled them out myself, exposing the hole and allowing the cat to go through it. She does the talk to the hand motion and says she can't talk to me now but I'm not leaving it like this and insist that she believes my truth. Once she's had a frantic look under the bath for herself, she sees how this actually happened. At the same time I'm also telling her I'm sorry but I didn't want her to know the door had been left open just two minutes after a very specific conversation about keeping it closed at all times. This is all happening so quickly and is so bewildering and I know that none of my words are registering. Less than five minutes ago all was bliss and fluff. And now we're in this total chaos and rage panic. With that in mind I don't add that it was Kylie herself who really left the door open almost the instant she'd insisted on keeping it closed. Somehow I really don't think that would help matters right now. Having composed herself a little, but still very clearly shaken, Kylie tells us that this happened to another cat in here five or six years ago. She says that he was gone for two weeks and came back black. 'That's hundreds of years of tunnels and who knows what down there,' she says. Yeah. The reality of that is starting to hit both myself and Maja. 'Guys,' she says sadly, pleadingly. 'Please, you can't be here right now. I think it's more likely Ron will come back if it's just me here. Can you just go to your room?' Still totally stunned by this wrecking ball that's crashed into our world, we comply without thought or hesitation. But as soon as we're there, we look at each other with a realisation which I give voice to. 'We've just been sent to our room.' Maja nods sadly. 'This is really not good,' I continue. 'That cat could actually die. It might already be dead.' I'm thinking of so many scenarios right now, some of which I mention, others I don't. She might never be able to find her way out and could starve to death in there. Essentially an indoor cat, she could possibly find her way outside. If she does that, she'll have little to no idea of how to behave in this car-filled area. Then, if she were to somehow survive that gauntlet, I don't see how she finds her way back to the apartment. Even if she does somehow find her way back, it's not like she's going to buzz the downstairs intercom and gain access to the building. She has no idea what number apartment she lives in. No. Sarah's baby, the so-called light of her life, is gone. Disappeared, dead, or at serious risk of death, or with little chance of finding her way back if she somehow doesn't get/ hasn't already been killed. I might as well say it now. It will be me that will have killed/ lost her. Happy Saturday 13th.

Where the hell do we go from this? My first thought is that we're going to be needing Maja's insurance policy already. The fact that she's not given up the small room we left. After just four days. How can we carry on living here if the cat doesn't come back? I don't see how it could be possible. But even if she does come back, that might not be until tomorrow. Or two days, three days, a week, more. How tense will the atmosphere be like in here all that time? No. I just don't see it.

It's with all those thoughts swirling round my head

that Kylie comes knocking, enters the room and says, 'Guys, I don't want you drinking in here anymore. I just don't.' Then she leaves. That does it for me. It might seem trivial, but if she'd said at the outset no drinking in the place at all, fine. We could have taken or left it, and we would have taken it. But to let us in and impose a rule like that now, after one incident, I'm really not happy about that. Apart from anything else, what house rule is she going to spring on us next? And after that? My immediate thought is that I suddenly don't want to live here anymore and I say so. Let's just move back to the house, however horrible that might be. At least it would be our horrible. Maja says we shouldn't make any decisions like that in the heat of this moment and she's totally right. Above everything, we just have to get out to clear our minds for a bit and make sense of all this. Kylie couldn't agree more that we shouldn't be here right now. But before we leave, she makes a point of telling us that she's spoken to a good friend and neighbour about this and has come to realise that it wasn't my fault at all, that she should have told us about the hole being there, and she totally accepts I exposed it completely accidentally. She also apologises for coming slamming down on the non drinking rule, saying, 'I'm sorry, I was just lashing out and looking for things to blame, but this is your place and of course you can do what you want.' Lovely to hear and an equilibrium of sorts has returned. But none of that changes the fact that Ron is still gone and probably won't be coming back. We thank her for her thoughts, wish her luck and leave.

Maja:

Everything was all fine until a minute ago, I think to myself as I quickly get dressed to leave. The soup we were having for lunch has been quickly moved to the bedroom and is now going cold, forgotten. Because once again I know that our little world is going to crash. Again. We need to get out of here now. Before it gets even worse. I put our essentials in a backpack and off we go. Half kicked out with neither of us having any idea of when it might be appropriate to return. Even then, how are we going to be able to continue living happily here if it turns out we have killed the cat?

And the new rules suddenly imposed. It's not like we're rowdy teenagers. We're all adults here. We should be able to respectfully have a quiet nightcap at home if that's what we want. This is just getting weird now. The lovely musical collective that we were supposedly living in is now a, yeah what to call it, a really uncertain and fragile way of living. It might blow up at any moment, and that weighs heavily on both of us as we try to find somewhere to be during the day. Avoiding home. Knowing that a crisis will be looming as soon as we get back home.

Mark:

Out on the street, Maja says, 'Wow. Our first crisis.' Yes, no other way to put it. It very much is. We walk slowly to Hampstead Heath, all the while trying to take it in but we just can't. I just say over and over again, 'I've killed her cat.' I don't see any way back from this. We talk about the prospect of moving back to the house, which would mean moving back in to live with Jenn which Maja is not keen on at all. The two of them did not speak a word to each other all the time Maja was there and she does not want to return to that atmosphere. Option two is staying where we are and dealing with whatever fall-out that entails. Not a good secondary option at all. We really, truly, do not know what to do about this. The one thing we're lucky about is that the weather is nice. This is Corona, lockdown London. Once you leave the house, you're outside and that's it. If it was raining or cold, there would be nowhere to go and have a sit-down in. No cafe, bar or library. Nothing. We probably would have ended up riding the bus or tube just to get out of the weather, but thankfully we don't have to think about that. Instead, we have the wonderful Hampstead Heath to roam about on. I've never enjoyed being here less. But there's no escape. No matter where we go, nothing can change the situation or the crisis clouds that have now gathered all around us.

We walk around like this for four hours, never quite leaving our dazed, bewildered, slightly scared state. It's around the four hour mark that Maja says, 'I think it's time to go home.' Home? I suppose it is, but for how long? With foreboding, we make our way back, each step taking us closer to whatever the hell we're going to find upon opening the door. We arrive at the street and I pull Maja back for a few pep talk words. 'We're about to walk into the fire,' I say. 'We go in there together, and face whatever we come up against together.' She nods with defiance. We're going to front up to this and we're going to do it now. We pause for a few seconds to individually steel ourselves and then turn and deliberately walk towards a world of doubt, confusion and possible retribution. Chaos, grief, anger? We have no idea what we'll be met with. But we're about to put ourselves right in the middle of it all and accept whatever comes our way and whatever that could mean. Our minds are blank. We have no idea of any of this so can't even see a way to the immediate future, that future being just seconds away. We enter the apartment block and walk up the stairs, heads held high but stomachs brought to a ridiculous low. This is climbing over the top of the trenches territory. We're in no-man's land now and any moment the machine guns are going to open up. Will we make it through? At the front door I turn the key and look at Maja. 'This is it. Let's go.'

We enter the apartment and it explodes.

'Guys, guys, did you get my message?' We didn't but this is not at all what we expected. Kylie's happy that we're back. Jubilant even. She runs out of the main room and calls to us from the end of the corridor. 'She came back. She came back.' She's almost crying with relief as she says the words. 'Half an hour ago. I sent you a message to tell you. Oh I love you guys. You must have really been through it.' Oh, we have. Her relief shoots through us like a wave of lasers and we run to her to be enveloped in the hugest of group hugs. Oh wow, oh wow, oh wow. It's over, it's over. From what we can gather, and no-one can really be certain anyway, Ron never went very far into the hole and so the nightmare scenario of her becoming irretrievably lost in the labyrinth of Victorian architecture never happened. And when she was ready, she just jumped back out again and into the arms of a disbelieving, hysterically jubilant Kylie who is now full of joy and how wonderful she thinks the two of us are all over again. In short, it's like the whole episode of horribleness never happened. But me and Maja look at each other and we know. We've been seriously tested today. We've stared at the fire, held hands and walked, together, right into it. And here we are on the other side. All happy again, harmony in the apartment once more restored. Oh, and while we were out, Kylie and a friend did the underside of the bath and plugged the hole up properly with tiles. So, no more hole, and no more damp rags under the bath hiding a mystery in the hope no-one would one day push them aside while a cat was under there.

Maja:

The emotional whiplash is hurting me. All of a sudden it's all happy go lucky, everyone is best friends forever again, and nothing is ever gonna go wrong. We'll be the group of three living together until we grow old and die and everything is awesome and will always be awesome.
Wait what? Really? That's what's happening now?

Day 24
Monday March 15

Mark:

Oh wow. How relaxing was yesterday? Do you know how you can tell? Go see. The last entry was two days ago. I think there was some drama about a cat or something. Yep. No entry yesterday. That's the first day since I don't know when. Certainly the first time in this Diary. There was nothing to write about yesterday and it's noteworthy that that's noteworthy enough in itself. And yes I'm aware I just wrote about yesterday in the same sentence I said there was nothing to write about about yesterday. Now onto today. Today.

Kylie doesn't have a fridge. She's vegan and doesn't use conventional milk so doesn't really have things around that can go off. Cooking, for her, is mostly a big pan of vegetables and beans and things that just sits there on the stove for whenever she wants it. She's shared it with us, and told us to help ourselves to it whenever we want, and it really is very good. In fact, this is kind of how the whole experience here is developing. Food, and just about anything else, is just there for anyone to help themselves to whenever they want. It really is developing into a kind of communal living thing, right down to the three of us all hanging out around the place naked at times, although we do have to be just a little careful in the main room because we have a mildly strange situation there where the window

199

looks out onto another window just a few metres away. This is very much not the conventional house sharing situation. We even just pop into each others' bedrooms for casual chats. Yes, naked.

Maja:

Mark is more comfortable being naked around here than I am though. I'm not quite yet, but sure. I guess this is where I'm going in life now. Maybe at some point I'll start to get comfortable with living in a situation where nakedness in a community is just expected. But for now, not yet. I guess I just have to fake it.

But what I am really bothered about right now is the lack of a fridge. I like being able to have milk in my drinks, and to be able to store food for longer than a couple of hours. If I'm gonna stay here for any longer, that's gonna be one of the things I'll need. And off I go on my phone to try to find one. I mean, there's no harm in getting a fridge for the place, right?

Mark:

Fridge. Oh yes. I was talking about the fridge, or non existence of one. Well, me and Maja have decided we would very much like the existence of one. In London, many people, if they can help it, don't throw anything away. Instead, as we saw with the cake trolley, all kinds of items get put out on the street for people to come and help themselves. When we were arranging our room here, it contained a big black, kinda broken couch that didn't quite fit the room the way we wanted it. It didn't fit anywhere else in the apartment either so we put it out on the street. The next day it was gone. A ridiculous amount of furniture and kitchenware in our old house came from the street. There are also websites where people will post stuff for sale, or also often for free if you can go and pick it up. When we first came here I registered with one of these sites to see what we could get, and yes, I did do it with the hope of seeing a free fridge. That crazy idea stops being crazy today when Maja does indeed see a free fridge on offer. We make the call and it's still available. We can pick it up tomorrow.

Day 25
Tuesday March 16

Mark:

The lady who has the fridge is called Marcella and she lives in Holloway, two to three kilometres away from us. We've talked about hiring a car for the job, but I have another ridiculous idea which is that we can take the trolley I've used to carry amps all over London in what now feels like another life. We'll just wheel it all the way back home. Will this work? I have no idea. We're just going to go there, see if the trolley thing works, and if it doesn't, decide what we need to hire to do the job. We've figured that even if we pay up to 50 quid or more for a hire car, or man with a van or whatever, it will still be a lot cheaper than buying a new fridge, which is what we're getting here for free.

We get to Marcella's house and she's delighted to see us, and to see that the fridge is going to some people who need and will really appreciate it. We're also helping her out because she had no idea how to dispose of a fridge. Why it's being disposed of we don't quite get to the bottom of, but that's none of our business. It's not a little thing though. It's a full on fridge freezer, one of those things that's taller than the average person. And it looks brand new. Incredibly, we discover the trolley can take it. Which means that now we're about to set off and wheel a person sized fridge through a few London neighbourhoods, down busy Holloway High Street and all the way back home. This means going very slowly with me pushing the thing, totally blind to where I'm going while Maja walks in front, gently guiding me left and right as obstacles appear. The most notable of these is a full sheltered bus stop full of people right in the middle of a London high street that we slowly, and quite literally, have to negotiate our way through. Then, when we do finally make it all the way home, we have to carry it up two flights of stairs. Oh, that is fun. Then, once in the apartment - what a lovely triumphant moment that is - it's back on the trolley for the final leg of wheeling it into the main room to place it lovingly in the corner where it quietly and joyously hums away. Kylie can't believe it when she comes home. She marvels at our resourcefulness, effort and determination at even being able to find such a thing in the first place, never mind the sheer force and energy required to get it all the way here. The next day, in something of a celebration, I write a set of lyrics commemorating the event, called Marcella's Fridge. I really hope we can do something with it one day.

And this really is what we do now. Live life and write about it. In this diary and in our songs. Or, at least in our lyrics, which we fully intend to turn into songs when we finally get the time and space to sit down and really look at songwriting. We keep thinking we're going to get to that, but then something else happens that demands our attention. Songwriting. It really is the thing that happens when you have nothing else to do. For whatever reason that is. Yes, I know, there is the avoidance issue that even some of the most successful have. Sting says he avoids it like the plague and even Paul Simon says it's never fun. For us, at least as far as lyrics are concerned, we write write write all the time. We've taken the David Bowie approach of just writing everything down. All of us, we're surrounded and blessed by genius. People saying great and funny things. All the time. We just don't write it down enough. Think about it. You don't sit down at your kitchen table and think, 'I'm going to think of something devastatingly funny now.' No. It just happens when you're with your friends. Someone says something, you react and everyone just falls about the place. The same goes for genius observations, and just comments in general. And of course it's not just what you say, but what your friends say and also what you overhear in the world around you. All. The. Time. But mostly it all gets lost to the ether. Well, we're trying to gather some of that ether up. Or at least catch it before it becomes ether. For this, we have pens scattered all around the apartment and we take notebooks everywhere we go. A conversation on a bus, a daytrip, a chance encounter, an image of London. It all goes in. And what doesn't I know will stay with us to emerge at some later time. This has led to some bizarre situations. Meeting friends in the street while one of us was walking along oblivious to the world and writing away in a notebook. And in supermarkets while one of us has continued shopping while the other stands deep in thought in the middle of an aisle. Clean up in aisle five? For us it's write up in aisle six. Just a few sheets of paper and our writing sticks. It's all we need. Never in my life have I seen notebooks fill up with lyrics as fast as ours have in the past three weeks or so.

But here's the other thing. As a former songwriter, I have written plenty of lyrics as pieces on their own, with a thought to using them later but very very few of those pieces ever see the light of day as actual songs. By this I don't mean that I don't try. I do, it's just that while I usually think it will be an easy, almost lazy thing to do to just put some chords together and sing what I've written over them, I almost always end up writing whole new lyrics to what I'm coming up with melodically and rhythmically as I'm coming up with the melodies and rhythms. But it's still great of course to have all these lyrics lying around as a resource, and just great that we're writing full stop. Even the concepts of them, and individual lines. Which is another thing. Apart from whole sets of lyrics in those books, we also have individual lines from things we've said or heard, and sometimes simply just concepts. As for what we'll end up doing with them, who knows what Maja's approach to actual songwriting will be when we get there? Or mine for that matter. I really haven't done this for almost ten years.

Maja:

We're finally off for a little outing to meet and hang out with someone. Since it's still deep into Covid times and the bars are closed, we decide to meet Mark's friend Matt in Camden and have a couple of beers by the riverside. It's fun to get to meet Matt, he is a very lively person with a ton of positive energy bottled up in his chest. As we stand in the winter cold, cheeks bitten by the wind, I get to hear a ton of lovely stories. About a city that was once alive. A town that was bursting with musicians, tourists, and the people that used to make this place, until recently, the music capital of the world. The city I missed. And my heart hurts knowing it will never be the same again, so I will never get to experience it. The before Brexit and before Covid London.

But I am happy to hear the stories from the people who were there. By the musicians that made up the tourist attractions that people would travel to see. To hear about playing at the Blues Kitchen, Ain't Nothin' But… and of course the 100 hour jam. Who gets to hear about stuff like that?

That's what I think while I let these talkative guys go on and on. Sipping my drink. Enjoying the atmosphere. At the side of the empty canal next to Camden Market.

Day 26
Wednesday March 17

Maja:

I'm woken up by Kylie entering our room in some state of lovely excitement, bringing me a present. When she woke up that morning, she was a bit chilly, so she put a jumper on. That jumper was an official Gorillaz jumper from their tour a couple of years ago, which lead singer Damon Albarn personally gave out to only musicians and crew. One of the touring musicians was a friend of Kylie's. The character on the jumper is Murdoc, the Gorillaz bassist. I'm beyond happy about it. What a way to wake up.

Gorillaz is the band I've been listening to the most this last year, so it's very fitting. And Murdoc. The bassist. Perfect. I play the bass, as does Mark, who is my bass mentor and now Kylie's bassist, so what could be more fitting?

Mark:

After a wonderful morning, we're hit again by reality in the evening as we sit down to really go through visa possibilities for Maja so that she can stay in London. All it pulls up is despair, despair, and despair. The two options we seem to have are by marriage, or something called the global talent plan. We spend three hours forensically going through both, and whenever we feel we can overcome one obstacle in the scores of requirements, we come to another which cannot possibly be met. The whole thing is just looking totally impossible. In fact, we conclude that both routes are deliberately written to set people up to fail. One piece of information in particular that keeps coming up is the need for a sponsor, with no indication at all as to what would constitute a sponsor, no matter how much we research it.

The marriage road looks like this.

Maja has a six month visa as it stands right now. She has been here just about a month. You can't apply until you're actually married. We discover you have to formally announce an intention to marry, and then you can't get married for at least 70 days after that. If we were somehow able to make the formal announcement tomorrow, that would take us more than three months into the six. But you also have to have a venue booked at the time of making your announcement, so even in this hypothetical scenario, that will probably not happen tomorrow. Especially not when you throw Covid regulations into the mix.

The application process takes up to two months to receive a reply. That's five months right there. Oh, and before any of this can even begin, Maja first needs to get a divorce which also has to go through the courts which will take at least another month. If it begins today, which it won't. So there's your six months. Minimum. And it's not even a given that a visa would be granted on those grounds even if we managed to jump through all the hoops and tick all the boxes within the available time.

In a moment of clarity, we decide to solve the Visa problem by deciding we're not going to depend on it. We're going to do this by simply not living in the UK. With that we start to look at countries where it's easier for Europeans to go and live. This leads us to seriously consider a few countries in Asia, South America. We've been on this visa thing for hours now so we'll look at these new options more closely another day, but it's great to have had this thought.

As we're discussing this and I'm considering an option or two, Maja suddenly stops me cold. 'Oh, I have an idea,' she says breathlessly, wild excitement in her eyes. Oh wow. This sounds like it could be something. I exit my train of thought instantly. We're in a desperate state here and her entire expectant face tells me she's just about to unleash the magic thunderball that will blast the whole thing wide open. I take a mental step back to allow full space for whatever she is about to say to wash and crash right into. She hits me with it. 'Will you go travelling in a camper van with me.' Wow. I didn't see that coming. But I don't hesitate. 'Yes.' 'Wow,' she giggles. 'That's a bigger commitment than agreeing to get married.' Yeah. I guess it really is.

Maja:

Having to deal with visas is the worst. Just saying.

I've been thinking about camper vans for a long time. As a way to travel around and still keep my life with me. So why not now? Mark can be in Europe for 180 days a year and I can be in the UK for 180 days as well. So we can travel and live that way together. We just can't work that way, but that is a different problem. Maybe we can solve that in some other way. Only this way, we can stay together. I hope so. That's really everything that matters to me right now.

Mark:

Instantly this has become our fallback option and we've now decided not to let the visa thing stress us out at all. If it happens it happens. And even if some circumstances arise which miraculously facilitate a visa solution, we might just follow through with all this anyway. Because, as we talk more and more about it, the whole thing starts to make more and more sense. Almost seamlessly the conversation coalesces into an actual plan for what we really want to do now and what we are now going to do.

Which is to write songs, tour internationally with them, and write about it.

So far since we met we've spoken about kids and marriage. We've moved house together. And now we're committing ourselves to working together as internationally touring, diary writing musicians and songwriters. Can I please remind you, we first physically met less than four weeks ago.

Day 27
Thursday March 18

Mark:

We tend not to talk about Kylie related stuff in the apartment, good or bad. Today while we're out and about, we agree that while we love the touring idea, we're not just going to look at upping and leaving as soon as we can. We've been given this opportunity of our own apartment based on Kylie needing someone in it, and to take off anytime in the next few weeks would be a bit of a betrayal of that. And besides, should the visa situation be sorted, it would be no hardship to stay here in London for a while. I kinda had similar thoughts when I first came to London with that office job Paul had got for me while I was still living in Madrid. The boss there really came through, giving me the job on Paul's say so, and on the strength of a one minute phone conversation with me. Although I was itching to dive into London's music scene and really start my journey there, I decided to commit to that job for at least six months, maybe even a year, maybe gently working myself into music at the same time. As it happened of course, it all fell apart after just two weeks which blew all my good will apart. As a friend said at the time, when the hurricane was still at its fiercest, that was the best thing that could have happened to me as it left me free to follow my London path. I had already begun to harbour such thoughts myself and did my best to agree, but damn it was hard to do so.

Maja:

So if I'm going to stay in London, as we know, I need a visa. Our lovely friend Kylie is very well connected and one of her friends is a lawyer. So she says she'll do what she can to help, which is to see if he will do what he can to help. First things first, she asks me to write up a CV so she can send that to her friend and he can have a look at how to make this happen. I do, she has a look, and she's mighty impressed. She discovers now that I'm a well qualified and experienced cloud engineer. As we talk about this, we come upon one possibility we haven't fully looked at but that I have been aware of. A working visa.

So why don't I just apply for a working visa? Honestly, I'm not quite ready for that yet. I'm going through a divorce and am generally overwhelmed with life right now.

I might apply for a working visa later though, but for now, I'm prioritising having freedom in my life. I have a bit of savings, and would like to just live life and feel free for a while. However, I'm also acutely aware that working visas keep you tethered to the same job and on strict terms. I just want to be with Mark. I want life to be easy for a moment. Is that too much to ask for?

Mark:

Kylie's met a guy around the local area called Lee. She had him round the apartment a few days ago for a bit of a social and really liked his vibe and where he seemed to be going musically. He's into production and rap and she thinks he could be a good fit for us, whatever 'us' means. So we settle on a rough rehearsal time - all times are rough around here - and by around 6pm, all four of us are in the main room and ready to see what kinds of sounds we can make. Me and Maja have been rehearsing a little by this point and have worked out something of a system for jamming and this is our first chance to try it out. It works quite well and there really is something of a special vibe with the two of us playing together. Bass is all about feel, and that's exactly what we're talking about here. We settle on something simple with Maja playing single, steady root notes and me playing grooves and solos over them. Well, I've never had such a feeling playing over such a simple beat. There's real emotion in those single notes and I'm able to feed off of that and produce some really great feeling grooves. All this sets Lee moving all over the place and singing and rapping like it's the most effortless thing in the world. His vibe bounces back into what we're doing and we hit a new level, which then sends Lee flying even more, and so the cycle goes. As it builds and builds, Kylie starts to sing as well, so we have the two of them really going for it as me and Maja keep things burning here, with Maja holding the full bottom rhythm as I play off the two singers while keeping the groove going for them at the same time. As this continues, as the dual basses pump and rumble, the dancing starts and we feel the start of something really special coming together. We jam through a few more bits and pieces for twenty minutes or so and then stop to collect our thoughts. Kylie has seen enough. 'This is serious,' she declares. 'The power and vibe of the four personalities in this room is just huge. This is on. We all look at each other and agree. Myself, Maja and Kylie already feel like we have a massive collective personality, like we could take on anything, and Lee has just come and fitted right into that, while adding a whole new dimension of positivity. Apart from anything else, he loves the energy given off by me and Maja, loves the whole feel of the two of us playing bass, and, as a particular fan of bass, really likes the way I play individually. There's so much more that can be tried as well. This really looks set. 'Guys, we're doing this,' says Kylie. 'Twice a week, maybe three times a week, in here for two hours at a time, no messing about. Yeah?' We all look at each other and smile. Yes, it's on. This is happening. On top of everything else, Maja is now in a band. But there's more. A member of an international chart topping band has expressed an interest in joining us. But not just that. This is someone from one of Maja's favourite bands. Kylie tells us about this, but warns us that if it happens, this person might well try to take it over as their project because apparently, that is what he does. We look at each other again. No. This is ours. Don't care who it is, no thanks. Maja leads the charge on this. So now, not only is she in her first London band, she's now also turned down the opportunity of working with someone from one of her favourite bands. This is all getting a bit surreal.

Day 28
Friday March 19

Late morning and we hear strange voices in the apartment. We don't bother to go and see who it is, or what's going on, but we don't need to. After about ten minutes, we hear whoever it is leave, and then Kylie comes into our room, barely able to hold onto herself through the tears of laughter. 'Guys, you're not going to believe this,' she says. 'The neighbours downstairs have just had their ceiling fall in. It has to be because of the bass frequencies and the dancing from last night. We might just have to tone it down a little.

Day 30
Sunday, March 21

Maja:
I am new in England. I've never been to England before and they have their dishes they are very proud of. Such as the English roast dinner. So as a welcome, Kylie decides

to cook one for us. Kylie loves to cook, but recently she hasn't had that many reasons to cook, with living alone and being a vegetarian. So she offers to cook us dinner, a wonderful pork roast with crackling and roast goose fat potatoes. Brilliant, thankyou very much.

Me and Mark go about our day, having a lovely walk, writing some lyrics, and time flies. When we return home Sarah greets us with the most lovely roast dinner, and it is amazing. Absolutely brilliant. Roast pork with a thick layer of crackling. Yorkshire puddings. The most amazing roast goose fat potatoes cooked from scratch, golden and crispy on the outside with the softest inside you can imagine of a potato. Of course served with roasted veggies and gravy.

I would have loved to have shared this meal with all three of us, but Kylie says she would never eat something like this. She says she just made it for us to enjoy and that's all she wants from it. With that, she leaves the apartment to hang with one of her guys and we are left alone. This feast is one of the best meals I've ever had. Me and Mark enjoy it fully and after we put things away, we go to sleep.

When Kylie comes home, she can't resist having some of those incredible duck fat roast potatoes that she had made. Soon after she decides it just doesn't sit right with her. They just don't fit with her new strict healthy living vegan regime so she decides to fast for three days straight to set things right for herself. Not long before we came here, she'd also decided to stop smoking. Other things have gone too, and all good, but now on top of that she's having a three day fast. It's just too much. She is trying too hard. This just does something to her personality, making her fragile and unpredictable and ready to pick any argument even if you're agreeing with her. There will still be moments of fun and togetherness, but all punctuated by too many down moments. This quickly marks the beginning of the end for us here, and no matter how much we try, things will never really be quite the same again.

Day 31
Monday March 22

Mark:

We always knew this day was coming. The Lord Palmerston sends out a group message, through my friend and assistant manager Duran, to ask when we'll be available to be back. I answer I'll be ready as soon as needed. This is the first sign that the furlough, which I've been on since mid December, and which even made this thing with Maja possible in the first place, could soon be coming to an end but there's no indication of when that could actually happen which would be nice to know. Alright, it's supremely frustrating not knowing but I suspect even the company doesn't know exact details yet so I'll just have to leave it for now.

There's more frustration as Kylie tells us we can't shower anymore as water is now dripping into the apartment downstairs following the ceiling collapse. We have no idea what is going on structurally, but there are some large holes in our bathroom walls, and it seems drops of water are going through them, collecting then dripping downstairs. We are told we have to have just baths from now on. Bugger. Far from ideal, but we'll have a go.

Maja:

We try to have a bath while Kylie is out. Sorry for not being more grateful with the whole free rent thing, but it's the most disgusting bath ever. There's mould everywhere, and you have to sit in the tub trying to get clean. After getting up from the bath the water is black with mould and dirt. It's making me sick. And apparently I'm not allowed to do anything about this situation.

Mark:

It could just be that the bath was filled so much that with the water going up and down, it reached the overflow as it seems that's where everything comes from. Maybe we just shouldn't fill it up so much. Afterall, I'm sure Kylie doesn't have baths in this black stuff so maybe we've done something wrong. But no. Not ideal.

Day 32
Tuesday March 23

Mark:

Wow. There have been a few brief re-openings of the bars but today incredibly marks the one year anniversary of the announcement of the first lockdown in the UK and here we still are. But it's also fun(?) to note that yesterday was the day we got the message that we would be opening up again, again.

Meanwhile, our daily experience really is going up and down. It goes up this morning as Kylie stakes another claim for best housemate in the world by bringing us breakfast in bed. And I mean the full real deal. Bacon, duck eggs, toast, tomatoes, and beans. And of course, obligatory by law when providing an English breakfast, steaming cups of tea which keep coming as required.

We get all that down us, chill a little while longer then, with the apartment's milk supplied depleted courtesy of Kylie's breakfast teas, pop across the road to pick up some more milk. Almond milk, mind. It's really lovely and sunny and we are very well fortified so we feel like staying out and getting a bus into town. So, back at the apartment building, Maja waits outside while I run the milk upstairs. We're just going to get the first bus that comes along and see where it takes us.

Here it is and we see it goes to Victoria, which means I get to surprise Maja with a walk down what looks like a nondescript street along a mysterious barbed wire topped wall. What's behind that wall? She discovers when we round a corner and there it is. Buckingham Palace. A walk from there, then up the mall to Trafalgar Square and once there, we simply have to go round that corner to give Maja her first look at The Marquis, sadly closed, but there it is. Also round this area, Leicester Square and Piccadilly Circus, up a little to Carnaby street, and then a general walk around. A few hours of this and we're almost done. But then just as we're thinking about taking a bus back home, we come across Fortnum and Mason. Means nothing to Maja, but I've never been in here and I really think we should, so we do. What we find is the most spectacular food and drink shop, complete with its spiral staircase going down to the most colourful fruit and veg display I've ever seen. Through all this we find the whiskey and brandy section and we simply have to have a look through all that. This is kind of like a mini Harrods. Like a Harrods but just a big food and drinks shop which happens to have a bottle of brandy that goes for 23 thousand quid. Shop assistant Andrew takes us through their ranges with Maja really keen on finding a good peaty whiskey. She settles on a high range bottle of Ardbeg which you would definitely not find in your average supermarket. After this, it's onto the cheese section where she finds a perfect Gruyere to accompany a bottle of red wine sometime.

Then it's onto a sunny bus home. This really feels like the first day in a long time where there have been no events to bring us down at all. Everything is just fine and stress free and here we are having a lovely walk round Londontown.

Maja:

Today's date day in London town is amazing. It's a sunny dry day, warm for March, and it is absolutely lovely to be walking around town. I also suspect Mark finds it amusing to introduce all these places to me, someone who doesn't have the cultural references that he is used to.

As we walk through Mayfair, or honestly I'm not entirely sure where we are, I'm looking up at the buildings towering over me. The huge old buildings that look like nothing I've ever seen before. 'Hey Mark. I'm feeling a little bit of whelm.' He smiles at me. That's a funny way to express yourself. 'Just a tinsiest little bit of whelm.' And we keep on laughing about my lack of knowledge and fun way of expressing myself for the rest of the day.

Day 33
Wednesday March 24

Mark:

Kylie continues the breakfast theme and wakes us this morning with toast and tea. We will really have to be careful to not get too used to this.

She tells us she's decided that if we can patch the shower up so that it definitely, definitely does not drip anywhere, we can use it. This is something of a relief so we get to work. We go out to the local hardware store and buy what we think we need to do a patch up job. With different types of cut out parts of bin bags and shopping bags, along with new shower curtains and a lot of tape, we fix the holes around the bath where water has been leaking through. It isn't pretty but it sure looks effective. It looks like we're back on.

Maja:

Well. As long as I don't do anything permanent I should be able to find a way of making the shower usable again. So I drag Mark to the hardware store. I'm going to fix this. I'm not allowed to actually fix the cracks with grout - that has to be done by the council that refuses to come - so I'll have to find a solution that works without doing anything permanent.

I return home with three of the cheapest available shower curtains, some tape and a load of bags. With which I fully waterproof the bathtub area so you can shower. As I finish, it is once more usable, and no water will fall on the floor, or drip down onto the neighbours. This is a big accomplishment for me. Only one thing. The bathroom is left looking like one of those rooms that people use for murders in horror movies.

Mark:

Through this job we've discovered a couple more things that we could get on with. One of them is to maybe replace the lino in the bathroom. This seems like quite a big change so I think it's prudent to ask Kylie if it would be OK. She's almost offended by the question. In a weary tone, bizarrely managing to snap at the same time, she says, 'Mark, I've told you. This is your place. Do what you want. I couldn't care less what you do. Stop asking.' Despite the tone, I guess there's a kind of love in that response.

We haven't heard at all from Kylie's lawyer friend, but she says he can be a bit like that and not to worry about it. Then, standing in the centre of the main room, she says, 'Hang on a minute.' She closes her eyes, goes into deep concentration mode and faces her head towards the ceiling. When she opens them again, she looks at us with total confidence and says, 'I just asked my guys and got the answer back. You two will be fine. Maja isn't going anywhere.' Two words. O and K. When I speak to Maja about this later, she rationalises it, saying that what Kylie is actually doing is concentrating and going on gut feeling and claiming, or actually believing, that that is coming from some other place to give her a message.

Since it was declared that we would rehearse two or three times a week, no messing, we haven't yet managed one follow up rehearsal. There's an attempt at it tonight with a rehearsal declared, but with no explanation, we later learn it's been cancelled. Oh well. We take the opportunity to instead take a bottle of red wine up to Hampstead Heath to sit on our favourite bench on the top of Parliament Hill and look out over the beautiful and spectacular city centre view with some Gruyere as a perfect accompaniment. A wonderful escape from what is increasingly feeling like a chaotic, ever changing and unpredictable lifestyle. Oh yeah. Lee apparently lives with us now. We've not been working with him so much but he has been spending more and more time here. That was cool, but then today Kylie announced that he's moved in. Fine. We guess. Whatever she keeps telling us, it is of course her place and she can do what she wants with it, but what's happened to the thing where she was never going to be here and it was to be our place to do what we wanted and then she was going long term travelling and leaving it all to us? This is increasingly looking like not being a thing. She hasn't even been away once yet. Instead, what we've experienced is being told a whole bunch of times that she had plans to go away, then those dates have come and gone, completely unobserved, with no mention of any kinds of plans or cancellations. Again, totally her prerogative of course, but it is all a little strange, slightly unnerving, and starting to veer ever so slightly off course from the brochure message we received at the start of all this.

Day 34
Thursday March 25

Mark:

Oh dear. Kylie's on the unpredictable path again. She comes into our room today, pretty much unannounced - fair enough; that's how it goes in this communal, walking round the apartment, into each others' rooms naked, food sharing thing we have going now. But it's far from a friendly visit. Out of nowhere she says she doesn't want to work with us anymore. The reason? We read her some of our lyrics yesterday and she's latched onto one line, totally misunderstood it, and put her own interpretation on it. She's saying that it was our subconscious way of telling her we didn't want to work with her anymore so she's deciding now that we won't. Er, what?

Maja:

Not again. What now? I don't even know how to act anymore. This is definitely a place where your subconscious decisions can matter almost as much as your conscious ones.

Mark:

The offending line is. 'With others it's not the same.' This is a line comparing our relationship with the way we, or most people, are with other people; external stimuli are usually required to hang out - TV, drinking, music, video/board games, sport, whatever. We're saying in that song, and it's quite clear, that for me and Maja to hang out with each other, we often require absolutely no external stimuli or diversions. Remember those first five days? The two of us and the ceiling. No TV, music, reading or alcohol. Nothing. There's no-one either of us has ever spent time with that way. With others it's not the same. Most people need activities to do when they hang out. Even the best of friends. We often don't. With others it's not the same. Without even talking to us about this, Kylie has decided it means that we work well when it's just the two of us, but when others become involved it's not the same. Meaning, according to her, we think that when she's involved it's not the same. Who would deliver a message like that in such a subliminal way in the first place, and then expect it to be understood? This is totally twisting words we've actually written down and read to her. This is not the last time she will get angry with us for something we may or may not have been thinking. The difference is that this time we're able to persuade her that she's got it all wrong. She eventually leaves the room having been convinced of that, saying she loves working with us and hopes it continues and continues. Well, that's what she's saying now. But working with us? We've done one 20 minute rehearsal and had every other rehearsal since then cancelled. But at least we've averted a bad atmosphere. For now.

Maja:

An artist comes over to leave some art supplies and Mark says hello. I spend the time singing. Afterwards, we talk a bit more to Kylie, who has been talking to a female friend of hers who is currently living in Scotland. This friend wants to live in London and Kylie says she's offered her a room here so she will probably move in with us. So now, from being offered our own apartment, it's gone to Lee has moved in - although we've yet to see evidence of that - to someone else might be moving in. At this rate, even if Sarah ever does go away saying it's 'our' place, at any given time we feel there could be a knock on the door and it could be someone we don't know saying they live here with us now.

We feel a little unsettled about all this, but are still resolved to make the most of the opportunity. We go back to our room and decide to practise some easy singing. This is where Mark puts on some music, plays along to it on the bass and I sing along to what's playing. First we go for a couple of Jack Johnson songs, then we try Laleh which Mark totally doesn't get, then we go for Red Hot Chilli Peppers. I'm used to singing RHCP, so when I do that now, I can finally get some power in my voice and it feels more like it used to. We're trying to make out some parts of Californication and are feeling pretty good about it when Kylie comes into our room, all fun, positive and excitement, saying she wants to film this great vibe we have going. But all we're doing is singing along to famous songs. This really isn't something we want recorded and put out there. This is also totally destroying the flow we'd got into. But OK. Mark decides to go for what she wants, but with our own thing rather than singing and playing along to recordings. He says A1 - we've developed a few shorthand codes for playing together. A1 is a particular type of simple groove that I play and then he solos over it. So I have to grab my bass, tune up and find a groove. It takes me a while to get in tune, and all the while we can feel Kylie standing there waiting for us to do something, and our flow is slipping further and further away. I end up just playing A. Mark tries to solo over it, but his concentration after having his own momentum broken as well isn't quite having it. We both feel pressured and frustrated over the situation and we have to tell Kylie it just isn't happening and to please not use whatever she's just recorded. She says, 'No problem. Deleted.' Great. Sometimes you try to record things and it just doesn't work. We try to get back to what we were doing before she barged in, but with frustration now in the air, it just isn't happening. We look at each other with a sigh and just know. So we stop, take a shower, and go on a walk just to refresh our minds. It's lovely outside, but with the frustration in the air, it just doesn't feel nice. All we can think is that we had finally started doing something and it felt good, and then that feeling just got stolen from us. And put onto virtual videotape. That, along with everything having changed from what we were originally told when we first moved in, has really taken the shine off the whole thing. Exactly where is this all going?

Day 35
Friday March 26

Maja:

Good morning London. Today it's time for another panic walk. An early one.

I just need to get out of the apartment. Just be somewhere else where I can talk to Mark without being afraid that any and every word I say has the potential to be another crisis. And also the place we live in is really starting to wind me up. How can anyone think that that flat is livable? Every shower we take leaks into our neighbours' bathroom no matter how much care we take with the shower curtain. Just imagine how much black mould there must be in the walls and between the floors if that is the norm. There are holes in every wall. The taps look dangerous to use. And I have zero trust in any electricity in the flat. It feels nothing short of dangerous. There are no handles on any of the doors, which means if you close one accidentally you're effectively trapped until you manage to push in a broken spoon handle or something to force your way out. Yeah. All the doors have spoon handles in the holes where the actual handles should be and that's how we open them. I need to vent. I need to just aggressively state my opinions, and I can't do that inside. Ergo, panic walk. Now.

The walk never seems to end. Hours pass and I get an idea. Tape and more plastic curtains. I think I could make a complete watertight shower area by covering every little area with curtains and tape. That might just work. For a little while.

Let's see where life takes us, and if we get to a good place here, this might all just become a little fun story to talk about.

Mark:

Early today we go out on another of what Maja calls our panic walks, or at least crisis walks, as we continue to take in the thought of yet another person being offered a room here in what we were promised was going to be our own place. What is going on? We were told that this would be ours. Fine, again as we've said, Sarah can do what she wants with her own home, we totally get that. But please don't promise something that isn't going to be delivered. Rent and deposit free? Damn yes. That was unbelievable enough. With that, we would have completely accepted that other people would be around as well. But that's not how it was sold. We were told she would be travelling and we would have it all to ourselves. For years, she's even said on a few occasions.

This is all starting to feel like it's kind of falling apart around us. No, we definitely did not sign up for this.

Downstairs is leaking again. What we did should have been good enough, and Kylie thought it was, and even agrees that it looked like we'd blocked all the possible leaks. But there's so much going on with these walls it was clearly impossible to catch them all. She requests we stop using the shower again. With that bath we had the other day, just not happening. We will sort this. There has to be a way. Maja comes up with it as she has the idea to first buy more shower curtains. We do that, and then return to put them up around the whole inner bath area. So now we really have created a fully sealed, totally unleakable shower. A sceptical Kylie comes to have a look and loves it, which is a big relief because it's one thing not being able to shower, a whole other thing to think of the prospect of that bath we had the other day.

The fact that we have a shower again feels like something of a new start. Our space isn't quite as much our own as we thought it would be but it could yet get there.

Maja:

This space isn't under our control yet. But you know what? We can take control over something. We can own time. We could completely make it our own. What do you think about that Mark? Right now, we don't have any real reason to be aware of time. We can remove it from our lives, and wouldn't that be wonderful? Come on, let's cancel time. We don't need it anymore.

Mark:

Yep. With that we decide to cancel time. No more clocks. We've realised we truly don't need them.

Day 36
Saturday March 27

Maja:

Yesterday we did everything we could to cancel time. We decided we would avoid looking at clocks in public spaces and on our phones. There, we even set different time zones on each others' phones so that we wouldn't even know which time zone had been selected and so wouldn't be able to work out what time it was. I took Mark's phone and set it on +9 hours, and he took mine and set it on something else. That way, we could start to confuse ourselves with time but still be able to use our phones. It works. And no time means no alarms. Oh my gosh. It's an amazing feeling to just be able to sleep until we wake, eat when we're hungry, go wherever we want and spend all our time together, refusing to count the seconds ticking by and without even being aware of them at all.

I love you Mark. I love all the little things about you. How your brain works, the way you smile and how you make me feel. I'm getting small rabbit punches in my belly just looking at you. Removing all pressure from the outside, cancelling time and everything else, makes me see what matters most. You. And how you make me feel.

Mark:

This cancelling time thing is seriously cool. We really are going about our day with absolutely no idea what time it is, which is incredibly liberating, if a little frustrating when you inadvertently catch sight of a clock - which makes the big one in the main room a tad inconvenient. I've been on furlough for a while now - on and off but even so - and have generally got up when awake, slept when ready to sleep, and ate when hungry so time hasn't been a massive factor in my life for quite a while. But now, we really are working to the rhythm of our own clocks with no idea even of how long we're doing a particular activity. It should be acknowledged right now that this whole thing is made easier, or even possible, by the fact that we're very central within London. We really don't have to pay attention to any public transport timetables. Here, apart from in the latest or earliest of hours, any bus or train comes within ten minutes, usually within five. Even night buses can be as little as 15 to 20 minutes apart, especially when you're looking to get back to Camden from Trafalgar Square from where you can catch four or five different buses. Easy.

Well, it is all easy until Kylie knocks on our door at 1am and says, 'It's really cute and fun and all that that you guys have cancelled time, but the people downstairs haven't. Did you know it's one O'Clock? And you really are being a bit too loud.' Oh sorry, we really didn't have any idea. OK. Fair enough.

We might have to think a bit more about how to do this. We conclude that if it's light we can assume we can be as loud as we want, but if it's dark maybe be a bit more mindful.

Day 37
Sunday March 28

Mark:

I made a full English breakfast for me and Maja yesterday while Kylie danced and sang in the main room. This will be the backdrop to the greatest disaster in the apartment yet.

First, Kylie's been doing a lot of dancing and singing in the apartment lately. Brilliant. It's added a greatly energetic vibe and we're very happy to be living within it, even on a day like yesterday when she dominated the main room with it. Great. Go for it. We'll stay out of your way and do our thing, inspired by your thing. And it really has worked so much the other way with Kylie saying we have inspired and lifted her mood so much just by being here and just by being us.

So yeah. Yesterday. Full English breakfast. Me and Maja eating that in our room at our window overlooking our part of central London. Just brilliant. The kitchen, as you know by now, is tiny. So Maja walked back to our room and past Kylie while I carried on in there while Kylie danced away to her music while checking out her form in the full width mirror. On the way, Kylie caught Maja's eye through that mirror. The wrong kind of eye apparently. I'm about to find out just how wrong.

It begins to unfold first thing in the morning with a disaster we already had in waiting that we had no idea of.

I'm up and going to the toilet and Kylie, all warmness and blessings, calls me in. I ask her to hang on, pay my visit, then come back and pay my visit. Kylie's temperature has dropped about 10 degrees. She is no longer all warmness and blessings. She's all fine with me though, she assures me. Oh yes. All fine with me. It's Maja that's the problem, she says. What the hell is this? 'I received some feedback from some friends this morning about your video,' she says. What video? What friends? 'The one I recorded in your room a few days ago.' Oh. OK. Not a great start. Didn't we agree that was to be immediately deleted? Didn't Kylie herself look at us actually say it was deleted there and then? While she was standing there holding the phone in her hand? Well apparently, not only had she not deleted it, but she sent it to people. By all accounts, very influential people. Her people. People, she says, she's been hoping to persuade to work with us, the three of us. Maybe even get funding from. Yeah, this is a thing that's been mentioned a lot and I have absolutely no idea what it means. 'They've come right back and asked what the hell I'm doing letting that negative energy in my house. They've told me I should not have that energy in my house.' You're talking about what exactly? I don't say anything. Kylie calls up what she now knows as the clearly offensive video on her phone and shows it to me.

'Look at that,' she says, zooming in on Maja's face - Maja, who at the time was being suddenly filmed deep in concentration and in some mild distress while she was struggling to come up with something on the spot to jam. And yes, feeling intruded on while we were very much in the middle of something else. 'Look at that scowl. That negativity. In my house. People have seen this and have said this is a bad vibe that I should not be having or allowing in my home. And do you know about yesterday morning?' I do not know about yesterday morning. When we were loving your vibe and making and having a great breakfast while you were loving our energy? That yesterday morning? Please tell me what disaster befell us all while that was going on. 'It was the same again. Maja walked past me as she came through the room and looked at me in the mirror like I was some piece of dirt or something. Just a look of aggression.' I have no idea what Kylie's talking about and I just know that if I mention this to Maja, she will have no idea either. I'm in a state of disbelief. To deny anything would just be to admit there's a problem. To apologise would be to admit there's a problem. To say I'll talk to Maja about it would be to admit there's a problem that needs talking about. To tell Sarah she's imagining it all would cause a problem. If I say nothing, I'm kind of admitting it's a problem. I say nothing. So Kylie continues to talk, confirming that yes, there might just be a problem here. 'Maybe living here isn't the best thing for you guys,' she says matter of factly and suddenly with a hint of sympathy in her voice. Maybe you'd like to think about looking for somewhere else.' She speaks that last sentence with something approaching compassion, like she's doing us a favour. It's not kicking us out. It isn't even remotely asking us to leave, but it's the first time anything like this has been suggested. And once a conversation like that has popped up, it really doesn't go back in the box very easily. Leave to where exactly? Wasn't getting this place the impossible?

For the first time I have the realisation that Maja was totally right to keep the rent up on her room in the house to keep it open. But surely no. We won't be needing that. This, whatever the hell this is, can be worked out. I gently tell Kylie I don't really understand and that I'm sure things are all good. She smiles sweetly and says, 'I'm sure they are darling. I'm sure they are. Yeah. You go and talk to Maja.' I'm grateful for that hint that the conversation is over and I leave Kylie's room and head back to ours. Which, until very recently was Kylie's. Until she gave it to us and she came into this tiny room to sleep on a mattress on the floor.

Back in bed and Maja of course wants to know what I was speaking to Kylie about. Is there a problem? Hmm. I really don't want to cause a panic here so I say that things are fine, but there may just be something of a misconception that could be cleared up. Maja's listening now. I tell her about the mirror incident. Get me. Incident. Damn. She's stunned. It wasn't something she'd even thought about. I've already decided I'm not going to mention the video. I think that on top of everything else, that could really cause a blow up so I'm keeping that to myself and Sarah. For now. Maja says she'll go and talk to Kylie now about whatever this misunderstanding is. Before long, I hear them both giggling away and talking affectionately. By the time Maja returns, it's clear that all is sweetness and light again. But for how long?

We get ready without any real hurry, then decide to go out for the day. We have no particular destination in mind, just catch the first bus that comes along. We take that bus to Kings Cross and then just get the first bus we see from there. Which goes to Elephant And Castle, quite a long way south of the river. Us north Londoners don't cross the river too often - the South Bank doesn't count - so this is a rare excursion into unknown territory. It's just cool to be out and to take in some different streets and scenery. That area also boasts the Imperial War Museum. It's closed, of course, but the out front display is still there - an enormous double field gun, which we take time to marvel at and get some photographs with.

After a few aimless wandering hours, we see a bus heading to central London so hop on that. From Trafalgar Square we walk all the way back home, but when we arrive at our street we just don't feel like going in. So we carry on walking and end up going all the way to Holloway, where we continue walking aimlessly until eventually we see a bus coming towards us and heading to our area. Yeah. It's time to go back. We've walked over 11 miles today.

Maja:

I absolutely can't believe that happened with the whole mirror thing. Really? How in the world can a confused look cause such an amount of feelings and such a multitude of problems. It shouldn't be possible. This demonstrates to us just what a fragile state we are currently living in. And someone completely based on imagination and feelings in the ether maybe isn't the best person to be dependant on.

I am aware of how quickly I need to turn Kylie's frown upside down, and I do the only thing I can think of. I write a poem to apologise. I read it to her, sincerely apologising for making her uncomfortable.

I'm glad we have the little room as a backup, because we might just need it.

Day 40
Wednesday March 31

Mark:

A reminder in case it's needed, that with all bars in the UK being shut due to Covid, I've been on furlough from the bar since late December. Today I discover I'll be starting back at the bar on April 11. This happens in the form of a text message for us to check the rota. I go and see mine and it covers two weeks of around 30 hours a week. When I tell Maja this she just goes quiet. I go and make a cup of tea, and when I come back I encounter a very pensive looking Maja. Something is clearly up. I don't even ask, I know she'll start talking when she's ready. When she does, I'm totally stunned.

Maja:

I really don't like the prospect of Mark going back to the bar. It would change our life right now, and I really wouldn't like to be by myself again. What would I even do while he was there? I wouldn't really feel good just doing nothing here by myself at Kylie's. We wouldn't be able to make anything progress either if he was just gone all the time. And right now, more than anything, I just want him to be with me. I don't want to be alone. And, I mean, I have a little bit of savings. I could just pay the way for both of us while we figure this out.

'Mark, I have an idea.'

Mark:

'I don't want you to go back to the bar,' she says. What? How the hell is that supposed to happen? She reads my unspoken question and continues. 'I have enough money for both of us to get by for a considerable amount of time.' How long, she doesn't exactly know but says that can be worked out. But she's done the emotional maths, saying that whatever the hourly rate of the bar is, she'd feel much more value in that time if it was dedicated to her, to us and to what we're working towards. As long as I'm not here, whatever I might be contributing financially, I won't be contributing in time. And time I can spend here, she's decided, is worth so much more than whatever bar company economics has decided my time is worth there.

She's done the equations and feels they really don't add up. I start to speak, but she asks me to please not allow pride to come into it. 'I know you feel it's important for you to pay your way,' she says, 'But you will be. In the way I've just described. And I know you want this too. Please don't fight it and just say yes.' What can I do? I'll see what I can do. But really, this is huge. Enormous. Game changing. And an unbelievable show of faith in my abilities and very much also a show of faith in us. Apart from anything else, I've just been asked to quit the day job to concentrate full time on music, and been told the resources are there for me to do that. And also to spend this time with, and working with, the girl I love. But more. It's all but been demanded - in the very best usage of the word - that I do exactly that. Isn't this what I've always wanted? And so so much more that I could never have thought of. I mean, there's a beautiful, practically identically minded bass playing singing songwriting girl in the equation as well.

Day 41
Thursday April 1

Maja:

As yesterday's chat settles, a budget gets done today and we estimate we can last for a little while with nothing else coming in. However, if and when the live music scene picks up again with the reopening of the bars, Mark can be available for any gigs there. We have something of a plan, and it involves making what we do, whatever that really is, our full time job. Our life. Our everything. From now.

Day 42
Friday April 2

Mark:

Me and Maja are aware that, as bad as the past year or so has been for society, we have all that and the subsequent lockdowns to thank for everything. I totally get that's a controversial view given the pain, suffering and just pure inconvenience that has been caused everywhere, but really, it breathed us into being and has continued to breathe us to be. It was Covid and the resulting furlough from barworld which gave me pretty much 24/7 availability. And it's this availability that allowed me to be there on the phone whenever Maja needed me while she was still in

Sweden. And then I was able to continue to be around all the time when she got here. If I hadn't been so available, our initial phone chats would never have the happened in the way they did, and I probably would never have even got to the part where I said 'You could come here,' let alone be in a position to deliver on the kind of support she needed in making such a move, both in the week before, or in the weeks after.

But as the resurgence of Covid has given, so its apparent regression always threatened to take at least a little away; our time together, doing what we want at any time of any day, has often felt like a bit of an illusion. We always knew the call for me to go back to work was inevitable. Now that call has come, Maja has instead decided to turn the illusion into our reality.

When I tell Kylie of what we've spoken about and that I'm going in today to quit the bar job, she's ecstatic and full of admiration for us taking this momentous step.

After being frustratingly unable to yesterday, I get hold of Moni, the bar manager, today, and arrange a meeting of just the two of us for this afternoon in which I will announce I'm leaving. Moni's massively intrigued as to what I could have to say. I have a thought, which I have of course shared with Maja, that I will be asked and expected to honour the posted two week rota, although I also expect I will be given the opportunity to cover myself for as much of it as possible. Which I suspect will mean that any arranged cover will have to be organised by myself. So, my rota, my business. I think. Some managers don't like staff swapping their hours around between themselves and will often actively refuse rota swap propositions. I don't see what difference it makes but there you go. However, I'm not a manager and if I was, maybe I'd discover the reasoning and I wouldn't like it either. Other managers have the attitude that as long as someone suitable is there when needed, they really don't care who it is no matter what person the rota said was supposed to be in during that time. I think Moni falls somewhere between those positions, but leaning more towards the latter. So, do the hours or get them covered. However, as I'm a supervisor rather than just general bar staff, I wouldn't be able to just blanket offer my hours out to anyone. It would have to be a bit more considered than that, so not quite as straightforward as it might seem. I sit down with Moni in the bar and drop her my bombshell news, telling her about myself and Maja in the process. What comes back is exactly as I described above. What else comes back is a lot of happy thoughts from Moni about what's happened and how things have panned out. And now Moni even goes a little further, as she offers to cover some of my more managerial type duties if I can get suitable people to fill the rest of those days. This gives me much more leeway, so as I said the other day, I'll see what I can do. I think this arrangement will see me doing about half of what I currently had. But who knows? I might yet manage to get the whole thing covered. And it's not like I have the deadline of April 11 to do this; any day after that could be covered a day or two before, so even if April 11 turns up and I still have my full complement of rota, so much could yet change.

I also say that, although I'll be leaving, Moni can leave me on the rota if she wants, to call on me should I be needed in a real pinch. She really appreciates that but fast forward a few days later she tells me she's checked this out with the higher-ups and I actually have to formally resign. This is because if I'm kept on the rota but not working, I'll continue to receive furlough payments and the company has decided that is just not on. I hadn't thought of that. Fair enough.

Once all the practical details have been covered, me and Moni continue to have a lovely personal chat as I fill her in with more details of what's brought all this about, and I leave with her very best thoughts. Time to go home and tell Maja about all this. The process of me leaving barworld to work full time on our project has begun.

Maja is delighted to hear me declare: 'I just quit the bar job.' Then of course I have to fill her in on how it's actually going to happen. But no matter. It's done. I'll take the days off I manage to fill, and happily do the days I don't.

Maja:

I am so happy to hear that Mark managed to quit the bar. Right now I just want him close to me as we figure this out. Just please Mark. Stay with me. Let us make this work. I want to just...be here, with you, all the time. Please.

Mark:

But when it comes down to it, I do genuinely enjoy bar work and have always loved The Lord Palmerston and felt a great deal of pride in the place. So I really do want to do a few more days in there. It would actually be a little bit sad if it just ended without ending. I wrote many times in Mark's Diaries about the benefits of bar work to a musician trying to get on the ladder while still needing a regular settled income, and the Palmerston, and Moni, and previous managers there, really have fit into that model of giving me enough hours to get by while totally respecting my need for flexibility regarding gigs. And I have to say that across the board the staff have been equally supportive and willing to swap shifts when I've need. All of the above, including my love and respect of the place, was also true of The Oxford in Kentish Town when I worked there during my first year in London. For locals, not The Oxford Tavern which it became later, but The Oxford, as it was known from 1861, although it did change names back and forth a few times in that hundred or so years.

With today's chat done, what we're doing has now become truly real; there's always been that reality check that all our time to ourselves has been a Covid/ furlough granted illusion. But once this up coming period in the bar is done it will no longer be an illusion. Our time really will be our own. But with that, we'll have the responsibility of making it work. Which means financially. What we're doing, at some point, has to become viable and self sustaining.

So, with me fresh from the bar talk, me and Maja have our first business meeting. Which is planning for how to really decide exactly what our thing is and how to monetise it.

What we do very much conclude is that, while we have to fully acknowledge that Brexit is not very helpful for us and accept the reality, we will not be restricted by it. If we have to get round the new visa situation, we will. We're just not sure what that means yet.

Apart from that, it's acknowledging that, with our songwriting and diary writing in tandem, we have a music and writing career now. Which means we have to work out a way to really practically go forwards with it. Basically, how do we generate income and make all this actually real? First, we know that this will be no quick fix. But what we can do right now is come up with an actual plan of where we want to get to as a first base and set ourselves in motion to achieving that.

The plan looks like this.

Maja to complete Maja's Diaries which could possibly be published as their own book at some point. When they're completed I'll need to edit them, mostly from an English grammar standpoint.

Me to finish Mark's Diaries which may, in parts at least, also be physically published in time.

But yes, they still do need to be finished as we begin

the process of merging our writings going forward as one joint diary.

Related to the above, we have to decide on what actual day The Diaries will begin. Will our own respective stories end on the same day? How will they physically merge? We're really almost there with how this will happen but not yet fully decided. There's time for that. As long as we know it's on the think about list.

As for the music side of things. we'll need to get at least three full original songs ready for what we're now referring to as the package.

Then there's the thought of the presentation of our own, as yet untitled diaries within the package. Whether this will be with a synopsis with teasers, extracts, or what, we have no idea. But something to give it a good presentation.

This presentation part of it will be incorporated in our website, which we will clearly need. Again, we're not too heavy on the details of any of this just yet. But really, the overall idea is to present the three or four songs we will have, then both diaries, especially the parts where they start to merge towards the ends, then our joint diary. And the website.

By the end of the discussion we still don't know how any of this gets monetised.

We both bring different things to the table in how to hopefully develop everything. I have my media background and network of London music contacts, while Maja has her vast knowledge of the internet and how to really utilise that.

We may choose to look at agents or other kinds of companies for gigs, beyond what we could generate ourselves, and then there's how to get this thing into an actual book form. No idea how we want to do that, but it's now on the table as a tangible goal to aim towards. Spoiler alert. We did that.

Our professional flow of obligations now looks like this:

Play music and write songs...

Which creates opportunities to...

Have interesting experiences and live life...

Which creates material to...

Write diary

Monetise this. Somehow.

Gigging and publishing are the main ballparks we're aiming towards. But really, the bottom line is generating the raw material, the bedrock of which will be our songwriting and performing. Without our own music and the attendant stage show to back up what we're doing, there is no story and therefore no project. And even once we have own music and stage show, that still has to then go out and make contact with reality; it has to have real audience appeal. We absolutely must write good songs and perform them well. We don't yet have one single song.

Maja:

We have a plan! I have no experience in the creative arts whatsoever. But we have a plan now, and that is absolutely momentous. It's amazing. We're going to actually give this a shot. And we're starting now. With a plan.

I feel the stress drip away from me and my shoulders relax. I can't believe I'm looking at the possibility of a life where I don't have to be an engineer.

Mark:

Within all this, we have to develop our feel for playing together and really, to reconnect with our own instruments and musicality which have both been greatly neglected for the better part of two months. We decide to ease into this by identifying songs that are in our ballpark in terms of playing and singing. Oasis is high on the list for that, along with Kate Bush and Red Hot Chilli Peppers.

That's it. That's our plan. Where to go, what we need, how to do it, and what to do about it all right now. This new reality is coming at a very opportune moment; for the first time, we're about to have the apartment to ourselves for a whole weekend. Kylie is off on a walk of spiritual discovery, from Salisbury to Stonehenge. She leaves today and plans to be back on Monday. As me and Maja conclude our first business meeting, Kylie returns to the apartment from her latest errand just in time to pack and go. While she's doing this, she breaks away for a few moments, curious to see how my thing went earlier on. She's beyond thrilled when I tell her. This is it. I've given my notice. 'Oh, I'm so proud of you guys,' she says. 'You're taking your destiny and making it your own. You can't ever do more than that.' Then I add, 'And if I ever need to go back to the bar, the manager said I can call and...' Kylie cuts me off. 'Don't even think about that. You've made your decision now and done something about it. Only be thinking about moving forwards now, not backwards.' So that's her position pretty clear. And yes, she's right. If you've got a safety net you'll be tempted to use it. She finishes saying, 'Guys, as I go off on my spiritual journey, I love what you're doing. And taking this huge step and commitment towards it is just so inspiring.'

After this brief chat, there's just time for time for a group hug while she congratulates us again, and we wish her all the best for her odyssey. I think the feeling between the three of us right now is the best it's ever been and we wish her nothing but wonderful vibes for her trip. Then she's gone and the apartment suddenly falls silent as this scene of hopeful jubilation hangs in the air. It's now Friday afternoon. Until sometime Monday, this place is ours.

Maja marks the occasion by claiming full rights to the kitchen and making lasagne. Cue Liam. I'll pick you up at half past three/ We'll have lasagne - Digsy's Dinner by Oasis in case the reference is totally lost on you.

I must have the official record record that the lasagne is great.

Maja:

It's a relief to just have the space and time to do some cooking tonight. It feels great to have the beginning of a plan ahead of us. And, I'm finally getting to know some of these music references. Thank you Mark, let's turn Oasis up on the speakers. We'll have lasagna!

Day 43
Saturday April 3

Mark:

We wake to an apartment in which we are alone and really take it in. Kylie has stressed over and over again that this is our home and that we should do with it as we please. Things have even calmed down about all that talk of different people moving in. Lee certainly hasn't for some reason. We were told he had, then it just wasn't mentioned again and nothing at all happened. Also, the general feeling has veered towards Kylie deciding she wants to come good with her promise after all. Now, it feels like this weekend is a bit of a dress rehearsal for when the place actually becomes ours. After a wonderfully relaxing morning, me and Maja settle into our room and into our large corner window overlooking the city. Sunlight is streaming in, creating the most spectacular workspace. It is here now that we will create, write and rehearse. We also plan to supplement that by taking ourselves to various parts of

London, and indeed to other parts of the country, to do the same. We get to it now. A lovely joint diary writing session as we remind each other of the details and minutiae of various events, and then a really chilled little rehearsal as we continue to shake off the cobwebs of singing and playing. Yes. This is how it was supposed to be. Panic walks are a thing of the past. We're on our way now. This feeling of liberation greatly inspires our thoughts as we exchange messages with Kylie throughout the weekend, both voice and text messages. We have our thing going on, and she's on her wonderful, liberating spiritual walk. The connections and good wishes between us are at an all time high. We love encouraging her to keep going and she loves every idea and any random thought that emanates from either of us.

Maja:

There's a hallway you need to go through every time you have to go to the toilet or to the kitchen. And on one side of it is a huge rack messily filled with clothing items. We have to battle past all those clothes whenever we walk down the hall - which is a lot. Carrying two bags of shopping down that hallway to the kitchen? Forget about it. I've been thinking to myself for a while now that it would be lovely to first move that rack into the mostly unused front room, and then I could arrange the whole thing a lot better. So I go ahead and do exactly that. I carefully take out every piece of clothing and gently hang each one up on the clothes hangers. Shirts to the left, dresses in the middle and jackets to the right. I tenderly organise them, to reduce creases and to prevent clothes hanger marks getting on the garments. After I'm done the rack looks stunning, easy to use and nothing has been discarded. It means I've transformed what was a messy rack in the hallway into a stylish clothes rack in the front room. And the whole passage is now totally clear and easy to walk through, just like it should be. Kylie will be delighted. I have no doubt about that.

Day 44
Sunday April 4

Mark:

We have to re-engage with time today because we have plans with Cris, and Maja's going to have her first London car outing. This is a trip to Crystal Palace with two friends of Cris who I also have a great relationship with - Rob and Jade. Crystal Palace is an area in south east London named after an actual crystal palace that was almost unimaginably large when it was constructed in 1851. However, all we have of it now is ruins as it was destroyed by fire in 1936. Instead, we have the site markings along with a few surviving steel supports and ornate stone staircases which mark where the entrances were. And all around it, a large and beautiful park which is our destination for today.

We meet Cris at a nearby street to be picked up in his

oversized and very comfortable car which is practically a van. This drive takes us through some of the most exclusive areas of London and eventually - an hour and a half eventually, I had no idea it was so far away - to Crystal Palace where we meet Rob and Jade. This is a little of an emotional reunion for me as I last saw them around 18 months ago. We all used to work together on domestic scale building sites that Cris was in charge of with his own company. Rob and Jade are roofers and would do all the up high jobs and generally bring a great atmosphere to the workplace. I would be down in the dirt and mud labouring and sweating away and the two of them would be so wonderfully encouraging and welcoming. I came to regard them as friends and I would sometimes be invited to go up the ladder with them and hang out on the roof and get to survey the surroundings from a completely different perspective. Rob would also help me out a lot with his considerable construction experience, sometimes saying things like, 'Mark, you've done all you can on that job. Leave it now. It's fine.' Little things like that really helped to give me a lot more confidence around the sites. He also happens to be one of the brightest, most positive people I've ever worked with and this is a guy who's out in all weathers. Probably why him and Cris get on so well I suppose. He's turned up quite a lot on jobs I've done and he really does feel like Cris' most go-to guy.

I started working on these construction sites when I started getting so busy with bass gigs that I had to quit my evening bar job and go get something in the day so that I could be available for the relentless schedule of rehearsing and gigging with five different acts. One of these acts was the heavy metal band Wild Child, fronted by Cris. So the four of us know each other quite well. Now into this comes London newbie Maja who is warmly welcomed and embraced by Rob and Jade. Indeed, as the day progresses, I find myself more and more walking with Cris and Rob while the two girls walk together by themselves, engrossed in conversation like old friends.

We meet by a housing estate in our respective cars, and then drive onto the site of the crystal palace itself. As we start to walk through it I suddenly realise I am in serious memory lane territory. I had totally forgotten about this. I used to come here every week in a whole other life and it represents and brings back so much.

My second job in journalism was as the editor of an entertainment supplement called Leisuretime. This was a magazine type thing in the centre of a free broadsheet sized newspaper called The News Shopper. I know. Terrible name. But it had a big reach. Every week, this paper distributed 400,000 copies across 11 different London regions, each region receiving a slightly different edition, a concept which extended to my own Leisuretime. As well as being the editor, I also wrote most of the articles, many of which were generated by me being out and about on the nightlife scene all around south east London - one of those areas was Crystal Palace. Gigs, plays, comedy shows. Between free tickets and newspaper expense accounts, I never had to pay for anything and I got to know all the movers and shakers. As well as my role in the newspaper with Leisuretime, I was also kind of a floating reporter in the newsroom as I was expected to pitch in with news articles for the various regional newsdesks. Oh. Now I'm here, I'm going to go a bit further now. This is a perfect set up to write about all this. One of the movers and shakers I came into contact with was an international correspondent for a national newspaper. He kind of poached me to take over as the England correspondent for a weekly magazine in India, which was one of his freelance assignments that he wasn't able to do anymore. This is the weekly million selling publication I mentioned earlier on.

So now I was doing that job freelance, which mostly meant evenings and weekends, but sometimes secretly in my day job office when phone calls and emails absolutely had to be taken care of. Occasionally I would even receive an email from India saying a story was needed for that day and I would somehow have to find the time to write that - without anyone in my office knowing - while keeping up with the deadline demands of the day job. When I was headhunted to become the assistant editor of a very exciting new entertainment and lifestyle magazine based in central London, they insisted they needed me immediately, something my newspaper absolutely could not allow. This was an opportunity I was not prepared to let go and the magazine really, really wanted me. So my prospective publisher called my editor, and they negotiated a deal that would allow me to start on the magazine immediately, while also continuing to work for the newspaper for the first two weeks of my notice period. After that I would be free to leave and start on the magazine full time. Which meant I would go to the newspaper in the mornings - the editor made it a non negotiable part of the deal that I went to my 'real' job first - then travel to central London in the afternoons to take up my duties on the magazine which was in the frantic final period of putting together its upcoming issue. And yes, through all this I had to keep up my responsibilities to the magazine in India which I now came clean and told my current editor about. So this accounts for the first two weeks of my legally required four week notice period. The second two weeks would be accounted for by me having completed enough material in the first two weeks to cover those editions. Material which of course had to be relevant to the time periods in which they would be published. So, as well as working on the upcoming new magazine and the India magazine, I now also had to produce double the amount of normal material for the newspaper. And the newsdesks would also continue to require their own pieces of me.

Bear in mind the relentless, unforgiving nature of the newsroom and the general prolific nature of journalism when I tell you this. When my editor learned of my additional India commitment and took in what my schedule would be for the foreseeable, he went into full sympathetic mode. First, his head went into his hands. Then he looked up and said, 'Mark, you can't do this. This is not possible. This is just too much.' I might have nodded and agreed with him and yes I did have my moments of overwhelm over the next period which I have no idea how I got through. But get through it I did, and it all got done.

From that memory lane we return to my Crystal Palace memory lane. During my time on the newspaper, I was the goalkeeper of their five-a-side football team and we played in a league right here. As we walk across a high walkway, on our left we have the site of the football pitches I came to every week and I suddenly realise where I am. I stop, caught in feelings of totally unexpected nostalgia and remember those days, shuddering a little when I remember the time I just wrote about above. Everybody else stops too and we hang out here in the sun for a while. I stay, lost in my own thoughts, as the others go and fetch ice creams from a nearby shop, Maja bringing one back for me. Below us is an interesting sight and a cool addition to the day. Remote control car racing round a mini Formula 1 type track. It's clear these guys are serious and really know what they're doing, and their mini cars are fuelled by petrol and not electric, so they really can go. We watch this, enthralled, for something like half an hour, then we continue onwards.

Maja:

Jade has a little dog. It's a friendly little chihuahua, and I can't help being delighted about this. I've always loved animals, they make me feel better and it's like I can speak their language. I still have my little pup Tommy somewhere in Sweden. There isn't a day where I don't worry about him. Is he being taken care of properly? Is he eating alright? I mostly try to put those thoughts aside and focus on the moment. And this very moment I am with new friends, and there is a dog here. And as always, it's best to just let the people be and enjoy the dog. I do hope I get to pet it some more soon.

Mark:

After a while of walking through the grounds, at times in open, cultivated fields, at others through dense, enchanting forest, we come across a large open air street market. It has so many stalls selling food from all over the world and, as disparate as our group of five is, we're practically guaranteed to find exactly what each of us wants in a place like that. So we go in and go food hunting, arranging to meet up on a hill overlooking the whole place.

Fed, watered, and all content again, we set off on another meander and wander, this time heading towards and then through the ruins of the palace. Here, we can now truly see and appreciate the dimensions of what this absolutely enormous thing was. You kind of believe you're in a field, the size and perfect shape of dozens of football pitches. But take things in a bit more panoramically and you can tell that you're walking on the first floor of a huge, destroyed building which has partly been reclaimed by nature. Over there you can see old sections of the original wall that would have been the edge of the structure. At your feet, and as you look down the whole scene, you can make out markings where walls and other elements would have stood. And every now and again you can still see occasional snatches of skeletons of original architecture that have survived and now look like bizarre abstract sculptures.

It's a slow, summery, lazy walk and once through the grounds we make our way back to the cars to say goodbye and head on home. But Cris has one more thing on his mind as we set off. There's a route we can take that will see us go past the site where Marc Bolan was killed in a car crash. It has become a shrine to his memory, visited by people from all over the world. Now it is about to receive another international delegation from Italy, Sweden and England.

All through today, and over the weekend, we've had a voice message thing going back and forth between ourselves and Kylie, including during our little excursion today. Relations between us have never felt so good and it's really cool to be able to encourage her along in what she's doing, and to hear how she's getting on. Along with the bar decision, and us finally being able to get our freedom and time to do what we really should be doing and jumping into that, everything feels like it's really slotting into place after a very difficult and stressful period. Of course we don't expect the difficulties or stresses to stop, and other tests no doubt await us, but it truly truly feels like we've found some blue sky and green grass to rest and work in. And, with Kylie's love, support and hope, along with her beautiful chaos, we have constant inspiration and motivation.

Day 45
Monday April 5

Mark:

Late morning, early morning, we have no idea. We're back to cancelling time again. But somewhere in there we go out house shopping and buy a few bits and pieces that Kylie has really been wishing she had. Like a cool set of knives that the kitchen desperately needs, and all in their own knife block. We also buy household items like washing powder and cat food. We've really got into that; as we're paying no rent, only covering bills, we've been buying more and more things for the house to help out with this as much as we can. And we love buying things for Kylie, like these knives which we're thrilled to have found. We were hoping to get out and back before she returned, but she beats us to it. Just. We're about 10 minutes away when we get a lovely voice message with her saying that she's returned, had an amazing trip that she can't wait to tell us all about, and that she just loves the changes and improvements we've made to the apartment while she's been away. All the time we've been there we've been doing little things almost constantly, often with Kylie helping as well. But I guess when you've been away for a few days and it continues, those little changes being made each day add up and become even bigger, even more visible changes. And the most dramatic of any of the changes we've made is that the hallway is now almost a clear passage. It probably hadn't been for years, and now you don't even have to brush your way past that massive clothes rack anymore. Sometimes if you were carrying something, you would even have to walk sideways to get past that thing.

We enter the apartment, all proud with our purchases and eager to hear from Kylie and to show her the latest few goodies we've found. I go to the bedroom to get a few things put away and organised and Maja goes through to the kitchen. When I start leaving the bedroom to go and join them, I immediately sense that things are not right. No. Things are very wrong. There is no joyous laughter, only quiet protestations of innocence from Maja. What the hell is going on? I walk down the hallway and hear Kylie saying, 'I don't know. Maybe it's just me but I was brought up to not do things like this. It's just not something I would do. If you were brought up different, I'm sorry about that. I don't know. Maybe this thing just isn't supposed to work out. I don't know how you guys feel.' Maja looks down the hallway and catches my eye. She looks bewildered. I speed up my walk and get in there as quickly as I can to lend my support and find out just what this could possibly be about.

It's the rack of clothes that we went through, tidied and moved. For all the talk that this is our place and we can do what we want with it, to the point of Kylie becoming agitated a few times when I checked if we could do this or that, she is now furious that we took her at her word and went and did this thing unsolicited. Yes, right to the point where she says, yet again, that things might not be working out. What was all that about then in the message she sent us, just 10 minutes ago, when she said she loved the changes we'd made over the weekend? Here we go again.

Maja:

I am absolutely fuming. I'm so angry that I can't contain myself. This is all so very very fragile. Much too fragile. How can someone be so quick with changing everything she communicates with us. From being all flowers and rainbows saying you can feel free to do anything around the flat, it's your flat too, to this? Only a couple of days ago she was telling me that it was OK to remove the carpet in the bedroom and install flooring if we wanted to. Now I just got a long telling off because I sorted and moved a clothing rack. I mean, I didn't toss anything, I just hung the garments on their hangers, put them in a better order and moved the whole unit to the next room, to free the hallway. It's not a major change! It's not like I started huge renovations and ripped the carpet out. I just moved a bloody clothes rack!

This isn't feasible anymore. We can't stay here. This is crazy. Waaay too crazy. We need to get out of here. Sooner rather than later. Mark, come on. Let's go outside.

Where do we go from here?

Mark:

As soon as this conversation is over we leave the apartment for yet another panic walk. But there is something different about this one. Now we think we really should leave. In the past, especially in the early days of all this, we spoke about not letting Kylie down and so not taking off on our travels if we thought we were in a position to do so. There's no talk of letting her down anymore. If anything, we're feeling let down. Massively. Things are really starting to feel fragile, like they could totally burn at any moment, and we still really don't understand what we could have done wrong this time. We tidied something up. That's it. Nothing got thrown away or irredeemably changed. We're now talking about having to get ahead of the situation before it takes control and gets ahead of us.

Well, we were already thinking about going off and living somewhere abroad, although we had no idea where that would be. We decide the time has come to start doing something about that. Why leave here, go to another house in London, and plan to go abroad from there? Might as well just cut out the middleman and go for it. Not to mention the difficulty of even finding another place in London in the meantime.

My first thought, I tell Maja as we tramp these familiar

streets, is that we should call Rick. We might just be able to stay at his place in Madrid. It would only be a temporary solution, but it would be a significant move and, if he's up for it, we could do it almost immediately.

We get hold of him and he tells us the timing isn't great so no, that isn't an option. No problem at all. Oh well. He jumps straight into telling us about Thailand and how that could be something for us to think about. He knows people there on the music scene and is confident we would be able to hook up with them through knowing him. One of the guys was in an earlier, Thailand version of Drunken Monkees. So he would almost be a colleague. Rick is convinced he could make a call or two and find someone we could stay with while we got things organised. He also says we would have an almost instant musical network, or at least an opportunity to get in on the network straight away. We really get into the idea of this during the walk and call, both of which go on for well over an hour, possibly reaching two.

As soon as we get back to the apartment we're on it, looking very seriously at where we could move to. Less than five minutes after starting, Maja excitedly asks me to take a look at what she's found. A perfectly affordable hotel type setup with a pool right in the centre of Bangkok. Yes yes and yes. This could definitely be a place to land. It would give us a destination and from there we could start to look for something more settled. It's Monday now. We could get ourselves sorted here and be on our way by the weekend. She doesn't even hesitate and immediately starts to look at flights. We are really doing this. If she can buy flights now, she'll get onto the hotel online and book us in and that will be that. We're moving to Thailand this weekend. This is really happening. But we stop and check ourselves just a little, allowing for the reality that, with Covid still very much top of the agenda all over the world, these are not normal times and it's not so easy to just up and leave as it might have been four or five months ago. So, while she's planning the practicalities of the move, I'm looking at travel restrictions, both as far as the UK is concerned with being able to book foreign travel, and how policy currently is regarding Thailand.

Oh damn. Maja's face falls with mine as I start to discover restriction after restriction. First, the UK has banned all travel. We didn't know that. But then we look at Thailand and see they've banned travel from the UK. But we're already on this flow and we don't want to stop now. So we flip ourselves on the traditional dime and start to consider other countries, kind of dismissing thoughts of the UK travel ban for now. We'll deal with that when we come to it. Flights are still leaving so there has to be some way around it. Brexit is an issue for me regarding just moving to live somewhere in Europe, so we're only looking at countries outside of Europe. Central America, north America, Asia. We go and look at the official government websites of every country we think could work for us, and one by one they get crossed off our list of possibilities for the same reasons as Thailand. We're seeing now that this really is not an easy fix. More than that, we just can't see how it can be fixed at all.

We can't go anywhere in Europe. What we thought would be our international alternatives have all been smashed off the table. Maja's visa for the UK will run out at some point so she won't be able to stay here, and I won't be able to go to Sweden - because it's in Europe. And I think we can rule out help from Kylie's lawyer friend on any of this at this point; we've not even had an acknowledgement of the initial email she sent. More immediately, we were already looking for places in London before Kylie handed us the lifeline of this apartment, so we know how difficult to impossible that is. And moving back to the old place? Well that's a big no no no no. Yes, Maja kept the room on for just this type of scenario, but now it's come to it, we do not not not want to go back there.

We feel trapped. With that, we give up for the night. We're exhausted and very emotional. Despite the tiredness, sleep comes hard and is uneasy.

The knife block is still unopened in our room and unmentioned to Kylie. We'll be keeping this for ourselves. Where it will eventually be getting unpacked we have absolutely no idea. Has anyone seen that impossible list?

Day 46
Tuesday April 6

Mark:

We do not feel remotely like doing anything creative today. Even if we did, we just don't want to be around the apartment. Kylie seems to have forgotten all about yesterday and is being very jolly and loving towards us. Her attitude seems to be, 'I said my piece, it's all over and we're all good now.' Which is great and cool that things can be said and you move on. It really helps to keep the air clear and lets everyone know where they stand. Brilliant. But this schtick is really wearing about as thin as we can take it. It's constantly like, 'Ignore me, it's wonderful and I love you guys, it's all good,' followed by, 'It might not be working out,' followed by, 'Ignore me, it's wonderful and I love you guys, it's all good.' The feeling has just become, and has been for a while to be fair: When is the next one going to happen? After every crisis, we calm down and we're like, it's OK. We're good here. Everything's actually fine. And then we catch ourselves and say something like, 'Yes it is. Until the next time.' As we know by now, there will always be a next time. Until, and if, Kylie comes good on her initial promise of jetting around the world and leaving the place to us. But that promise seems to have just quietly and gradually slipped away. Unless things really do calm down and we all make it to May 1, which is when she's decided she's going to The Congo to do humanitarian work there. Great. And yeah. That's really going to happen. You're going to have to let me know. Does sarcasm come across very well in black and white? I'm really not sure. But yeah. Congo. You go for it.

So we're still a bit emotionally knocked out by yesterday and not at all feeling like doing anything creative so we push ourselves out of the place. I've got a little trip planned which I've been meaning to show Maja for a while and this is the perfect day to roll it out.

This trip is a particular walk I would recommend to anyone visiting London and, indeed, many people who live in London because the truth is, many people who live in London don't use London. But then, one can understand that when you see the prices for tourist attractions. So many of them are not priced for locals. They are priced for people who may be in London one time in their life and it's taken for granted that they have enough money to think, screw it, I'm here once, if it costs the better part of 30 quid to do that little thing, then fine. I've been on plenty of walks round London, seen something really interesting, thought it would make a wonderful addition to the day, then discovered it cost north of 50 quid. So no. London is not made for Londoners. But this walk of mine definitely is.

We just take a bus into the centre and first make our way to Tower Bridge which is a worldwide destination in itself. It also has the Tower of London on its north side, another great place to go and see. But we're really here today for the southside. Apart from offering views of the other side of the river and the spectacular city buildings all the way down, this route also takes you by City Hall, then immediately past HMS Belfast, an imposing battleship moored right at the dock. Further down and you meander through an outdoor bar and street restaurant scene and right past a spectacular replica of The Golden Hinde, Sir Francis Drake's 16th century flagship. A little further on and you're back in time again, this time to the 17th century for a walk past the reconstruction of Shakespeare's Globe theatre. Not far past that and you're at Millenium Bridge, a beautiful pedestrian bridge which takes you in the direction of St Paul's Cathedral which sits right at the end of it, creating a wonderful picture. We go a little further once we hit St Paul, then get a bus back home. However, when we get close to home, we realise we really don't want to go in. So, just like we did the other day, we set off on another walk, this time all the way to the end of Holloway. What we're practising now is home avoidance and we're almost limping by the time a bus just happens to stop next to us at a bus stop and we decide it really is time to go home.

Day 47
Wednesday April 7

Mark:

Somehow there's still very much a sense of fun in the apartment, although I'm starting to feel it's a bit strained.

An outside observer wouldn't have a clue though. All they'd see is Kylie and Maja being best friends, while I look on and see them merely playing at being best friends. There's a manic energy in the place as Kylie constantly performs her new song and dance routine. She also asks me again if I'll be ready to practise some bass with her later on. I say of course I will. I won't. Almost everyday for around a week she's been telling me we'll do a rehearsal. I've got myself all ready for it, made sure to get back in touch with the repertoire, then it's been cancelled, or simply just not happened. I've given up being prepared. The rehearsal, or whatever it was going to be, isn't mentioned again. Of course it isn't.

But anyway, who needs bass and vocal rehearsals when one of you could be dressing up as a giant chicken? Yep. Kylie's ordered a chicken costume. It arrives in the mail today and she can't wait to try it on. Cue more hysterical scenes of, 'We're all best friends here.' Then, costume on, she decides to go one stage further. She's going to go out to the shop. Dressed as a chicken. Of course she is. Folks, that's how wacky and zany we are round here.

Later in the evening, things have calmed down. The fun has slowly seeped out through the walls but we're still all friends here. No hard feelings and all that. Let's talk. Frankly.

We sit around on high stools in a triangle in the main room and it's quickly and quietly agreed that we should move on. As and when we want to of course. No pressure. But it's started to feel like it lately with Kylie regularly asking us when our big move is going to happen. This started out as friendly interest, or at least that's how I decided to see it, but it soon felt more like a hint. She wants her apartment back. Fair enough. It's hers and for her to do what she wants with. We tell her we've been looking at options and, although we could possibly just leave and go, it really doesn't look as viable as we thought it was going to be. We tell her we've looked at a lot of other countries and it all looks complicated due to Covid. 'Oh that's rubbish,' she barks back. 'Covid's a scam, it's a hoax.' You know, have that viewpoint if you want, but saying that won't help when a borderguard is telling you you're not coming into the country. No matter how much we try this argument, no ice gets cut with Kylie at all. 'If you want to go somewhere, just go,' she says, voice rising to shrill. 'Don't let Covid stop you. That's pathetic.' 'Yeah, but try telling that to someone when...' I give up. You can't argue with this.

One of the things we have decided on is to stay in the UK until the world is more ready for travel again. For a start, the UK's travel ban is set to be lifted on May 17, so in about six weeks. We could wait and see how the world's changed by then. We've been thinking we could stay here as long as we wanted, provided we had a plan to move on when it was possible. But without saying it out loud, it's quite clear Kylie is thinking of us being here for just another two weeks max. 'There's loads of places round here you could go,' she says breezily. Hint hint. Been there, done that. There isn't.

We finish the conversation very amiably with all best wishes raining down on us from Kylie, but we really do have to start thinking about moving on now. And very soon.

Maja:

I have had enough. Enough with her nonsense. Enough with the insanity. I mean come on. Nothing inside these four walls makes any sense anymore. I'd rather be at the Carrol getting despised by Jenn then here. I'm glad the room is still there and mine. We might just need it.

We go inside our room, sit on the bed and I start to think. Where can we go? We've already been over travel restrictions due to Covid as well as Brexit visa restrictions stopping any long term move. We've looked at visa application processes to many countries, but everything, which already seemed so complex in normal times, is now just impossible when you factor in the Covid travel bans everywhere you look. Mark has been talking a lot recently about Brexit and the implications of it, and that has triggered a thought in my head. How does it really work? I mean, you can travel freely in the UK without covid restrictions because it is the same country. And Northern Ireland shares a land border with Ireland. That border isn't a hard border, right? People cross it fairly often, right? I need to check this with Mark. Maybe, just maybe, I've stumbled upon a conclusion.

Mark:

We return to our room and have a chat about things for a while. One of the topics we touch on is Brexit with Maja having suddenly developed a new curiosity of how it works with the island of Ireland and the border between Northern Ireland and the Republic of Ireland. She starts to ask a few searching questions. 'The Republic of Ireland is in the EU, right?' Right. 'And Northern Ireland is the UK right?' Right. 'There's no hard border between them, and people from Northern Ireland can go to Ireland and live there?' Right. In fact, going between them is like going from one London borough to another and back again. Where's she going with this? 'Well, Northern Ireland is in the UK. So if people from Northern Ireland can live in the Republic of Ireland, can't anyone from the UK do the same?' Oh damn. Lightbulbs everywhere. Before I've fully realised what she's getting at she goes right for it. 'Couldn't we just move to Ireland?' I'm hit by the sudden realisation that she really might just be right.

OK. If you're from the UK or Ireland, or are familiar with either or both, you can probably skip this next bit or skim through it. But I know there will be readers for whom the issues and geographies of the UK and Ireland, not to mention Brexit, hold little significance, so I feel some kind of potted explanation here is necessary. To be fair, Maja is still coming to terms with the fact that there are four countries in this country - England, Scotland, Wales and Northern Ireland, all centrally governed from

London in the UK, but each with their own parliaments. The latter of these countries shares an island with The Republic of Ireland, from here on to be referred to as Ireland. Northern Ireland will be referred to as Northern Ireland.

Maja:

I must say that I don't agree. Four countries in one country? How can that be? Is England really its own country if the UK is one country? That doesn't make any sense! I don't like it. It's too… Confusing.

Mark:

When the UK left the European Union, for our purposes, we'll say for various political reasons, it was decided to keep the island of Ireland more or less as the one trading entity it had been. With that, it was also declared a common travel area - CTA. This meant that the peoples of the two countries - Northern Ireland and Ireland - could continue to come and go between their two countries without hindrance, the same as they had before. With Northern Ireland being in the UK, this CTA also extended to the rest of the UK; many Irish people live and work in the UK and vice versa. And of course, they speak English in Ireland. Ireland does actually have its own language as well, but it's not generally used, so if you go there and you speak English, you're fine.

We're starting to get a little excited now as this really begins to take shape in our minds, as I hope it is now starting to take shape in yours. We research a little deeper and come up with the answers we thought and hoped we would come up with. Maja is Swedish and so, European. Ireland is still in the European Union. Maja can live and work there. I'm English and although I have lost my previously easy European living and working rights, with the CTA, I can move to, and live and work in, Ireland. Maja looks up from her latest mini research project as she realises she's negotiated the last hurdle. 'This is it,' she says. 'We can move to Ireland.' Wow. For the first time, it feels like we might actually have reached a solution. We said quite a while ago we would not be prisoners to the visa situation. We now seem to have found a way to completely break free from it.

Maja:

We talk through the practicalities and political implications, and read up on the CTA which is a fairly new agreement made in 2019, after Brexit. As we're figuring out how all of this would affect us, I'm starting to calm down. My head, that's been spinning constantly for so long, trying to think of a way to get out of this mess, is starting to calm down. I can finally see a path forward. This can work. It's not going to be an easy task, but it can work. We can do it. Or most importantly. I can do it. I can get through this.

Day 48
Thursday April 8

Mark:

Kylie comes into our room this morning as we're waking up and all's nice and chilled with a lovely morning vibe. Almost like we've all got our apartment mojo back. Full of fun, she tells us a little story about herself. One of those little self deprecating tales of comical disaster. Towards the end of it, mid laugh, her face suddenly turns to stone. She looks at me and says, 'Stop thinking that.' What the hell am I supposed to say to that? 'I've got powers,' she says. 'I know what you're thinking and you can stop it right now.' Oh dear. This is not good. Yes ladies and gentlemen. We have reached that stage. The one where you don't even have to say anything anymore. We are now actually being accused of thinking the wrong things. It's kind of an irrelevance, but I really wasn't thinking anything. Just enjoying the story. I guess that's what you get these days if you happen to catch Kylie's eye the wrong way, kinda like Maja most likely did the other morning. If you're now being accused of committing thinking, and almost everything you say, no matter how positive, is being twisted into being something you didn't mean at all, with offence totally taken by the way, any kind of communication is impossible. All I can do now, as I lie in bed and she stands over us, is wait out this horrible misconceived, awkward misunderstanding and hope she eventually gives up and goes away.

That's it. That's finally done it. Camel's back broken. Straw all over the place. We realise now that this particular mindset just isn't going to stop. It had already started to become almost impossible to say anything to Kylie without it being taken the wrong way. Now it's even become impossible to not say anything as well. What can you do with that? After she's gone, me and Maja look at each other and quickly agree that we really do need to take control now and look for something else. The time for hoping this situation will stabilise and all will be OK has passed. It just won't. In the same breath, we agree that going back to the old place with the two of us living in that tiny room with Jenn living directly below just isn't an option. But the rent is still being paid so it still exists for us. But no. Just, no. But it still does exist. Just saying.

In any case, this apartment is no longer the place for us right now so once more we go out for no other reason than we have to get out. The difference this time is that we're totally cranking up the hunt for a new place. We're starting to reach desperate town. With what's just happened, it's time to just leave. We would still rather jump straight to another country and we've been speaking about that a lot, but at the same time, we just need another place. Now. And if that's to be somewhere in London again while we sort out the real move, fine.

We go up onto Hampstead Heath and I start to call friends to see if they have, or know of, any rooms going. This turns into quite a nice catchup with a lot of people as

I let them know a little of what's been going on - only the good stuff of course - and I get to hear how they've been doing. Some of these people I haven't seen or spoken to in well over a year. I'm turning nothing up though, although the word is getting out and people are saying they'll keep an ear and an eye open. But again, this is still pandemic, lockdown London. Not total total lockdown London, but there remains very little fluid movement of the kind that would normally see a room shake itself free sooner or later.

Then I call my producer friend Alex, who also works as executive chef at a pub in Angel. I played a few studio sessions with him last year as he was putting together his pop/electronica album. Like everyone else I've spoken to so far, he doesn't know of anything but he does tell me he's having a party at his place tomorrow night in his apartment above that pub. He says he was going to call me about this some time today anyway. A lot of people I know will be there and he's doubling it as a video shoot for one of the songs I played on. He asks me to bring my bass too as he might want me to film a scene with me. Cooler and cooler. We will be there. Me, Maja and bass.

I make some more calls for a while but still nothing concrete turns up. Oh well. We've got the word out there. Time to head back. It's now sometime between six and seven.

We get to the apartment and Maja decides she wants to keep walking for a while. No problem. So we continue, this time heading into residential London rather than the deep green of the wonderful Hampstead Heath. All the while of course, we're talking about our experiences with Kylie and our feelings about them. Then we start to talk about the day she came into our room and started filming. Then Maja says, 'I'm really glad she deleted that video.' Oh dear. It is true that we asked for that and that Kylie immediately agreed, but I think it's time the truth was told here. I take a deep breath and dive straight in. 'Maja, the video wasn't deleted. Kylie sent it to people and got a negative response back from it. I'm sorry I never told you but...,' I don't get any further. Maja has already started to react and it's stronger than anything I could have imagined. She's hyperventilating and nothing I can say is going to help right now. I guess I should have just told her at the time, but like I said then, I really didn't want things to blow up. Well, something had to give, and here we go. It's blowing up. There and then we turn around and head back to the apartment. This is happening. Now.

Maja:

Oh no, she did not? She did not delete that video?! So you're saying a video of me looking shocked and all other kinds of bad is just circling around Kylie's friends? And they are judging me badly for it, even though she said that she deleted it? She stood right in front of me, looked me in the eyes, soothing me saying that she had deleted that video and that was a pure lie! I can't believe this. That's it. I've had enough. I'm not staying in that place any more.

No way. We're leaving. Now.

Adrenaline pumps through my blood as I am completely engulfed by rage. We walk quickly to the flat to pick up the bare necessities, such as the duvet, pillows and computer. Who knows what will happen next? Let's just hope we manage to not confront her tonight.

As we open up the door to the hallway ready to leave, it's clear that we're not going to be that lucky.

Mark:

Oh yes. That confrontation. Neither of us is in the mood to speak to Kylie right now, and certainly not to have the moving out conversation. We plan to just go in, pick up some backpacks and leave with overnight stuff, come back tomorrow and have that chat then. We're in and out with backpacks all the time anyway so we figure it will be inconspicuous enough. But somehow Kylie is able to read the situation exactly for what it is and lets her deep offence known that we're trying to just secretly sneak off. We have to come back again over the next day or two anyway to clear out everything else and that certainly couldn't be done in secret so no-one's sneaking off anywhere. We just didn't want to have any kind of big deal thing going on tonight. Of course I don't get to say all that and of course it wouldn't cut any ice if I did. It really is best to just let Kylie say her thing and get out of here. But if there was ever any chance of us leaving on good terms, that's gone now.

But before any of that happens, and before we head back to the apartment to have that confrontation we were hoping to not have, I call Cris to tell him we're coming back. What I'm really thinking is that I can ask to see if he could help us move with his super huge seven seater car. But he has a bad reaction to the fact that we're moving back, saying this would not be good for Jenn. I tell him I totally agree and that we're really sorry about the situation, but it's happened and we really have nowhere else to go. I'm quick to tell him that we're planning on moving to Ireland soon so hopefully it's only going to be a temporary thing. He finally comes round to the idea and says, 'Yes, I understand. I see you have no choice.' Great. It's not like we needed his permission, but it would have been a bit wrong to have just turned up and moved back in without this conversation. But there's no way I can ask for car help now. Then, in all fairness, I have to call Jenn just to give her the heads up that we're moving back in. She's stunned, but ends up with some kind of resigned acceptance.

So, back to the old place it is. We enter quietly and reach the tiny room without encountering anyone. Straight away we start to look at apartments and rooms to try to get ourselves out of here as soon as possible. Nothing fits any kind of realistic budget. We talk it through and decide instead that we'll just try to get to Ireland as soon as possible. So let's lie low here. I'll work my notice at the bar and then we'll leave. Two weeks give or take, and we'll be on our way. At least, that's the plan.

MUSIC, LOVE AND IMPOSSIBILITIES

THE LONDON DIARY
THE LAST TWO WEEKS

Day 49
Friday April 9

Mark:

We're exactly where we didn't want to be. Living back in what we're now referring to as The Carrol, after the name of the street. It was my home for six years, I loved the place, and I didn't really see any circumstance in any kind of mid to even long term where I would have been thinking about leaving it. Well, I did leave it, accidentally and overnight, and now I'm accidentally and overnight back here again and it's the last place I want to be. Instinctively I don't even refer to it as home. It doesn't feel like home. Not anymore. It is just The Carrol. As you might remember, I didn't sleep in here before because the bed was too small so I continued sleeping in my own room downstairs. That's not an option anymore so we've opened up the single bed to make it into a double, which means it now covers the entire width of this tiny room. It literally touches both walls. So, as you enter the room, immediately on your right you have the wardrobe, in front of that and touching the bed is the cake trolley with a lamp on top of it. And to the left and up against the wall at the end of the bed you have our basses. All of which means the patch of floor we have available to us between the door and the bed is about the size of a large toilet mat. Not even luxury large. And of course, below all this is Jenn. Who is simply delighted that we've moved back in. Of course she isn't. Oh damn, we really need to be moving out of here again. And soon. Forget the fact that we have a plan to move to Ireland as soon as possible. This is going to be beyond awkward and beyond cramped. Right now, all we're thinking is to rest up and go to Alex's party, aiming to arrive around seven. Then tomorrow or maybe the next day, we can start to get our stuff out of Kylie's and move it into here, all the while trying to see what kind of other place to stay we can shake out of the trees.

I go outside and make a bunch of phone calls to friends to see if anyone has a heads up on anything, but the most we get is people saying they'll be on the lookout. I do get told of the possibility of a small apartment in Clapham, south London, for way over double our budget. When I say our budget is probably less than half of what's on offer, I get laughed off the phone. Fair enough. Yeah. I don't think we're going to turn up anything in London. And that's a shame too because, as much as I previously had no thoughts of moving out of this house, I had even fewer thoughts of ever leaving London. This is a city I'd wanted to return to for so long before the opportunity to do so came up.

As we talk more about this, we start to think that, rather than try to move somewhere else in London when we're ultimately looking at leaving the country anyway, maybe we should just stick it out here and make the big move when we're ready. With that, we agree that we should try to move to Ireland as soon as possible after I've completed the two weeks notice I've committed to at the bar. That will probably take at least around two weeks to plan and execute anyway. So why throw away all my goodwill and reputation, built up over three years, for the sake of leaving a few days earlier? After all, we still have a lot of research to do. All we know is, somewhere in Ireland. Beyond that, we have no house and no leads on one, and no car, and no leads on one. So no. Bar or no bar, this is not going to happen overnight. So yeah. I'll do the two weeks as planned while making a plan, and then, all things going well, soon after that we'll leave.

I phone Paul for a bit of a chat and an update, and a little about what we're thinking next. 'Bloody hell Mark,' he says. 'You two should be on Oprah.'

Yeah, there still seems to be a lot going on. I think we really want to forget about all this, just have a nice time at the party, and worry about tomorrow tomorrow.

Maja:

We're back at the Carrol. Living over Mark's, I guess I could call her ex. She avoids me at all costs and hates me being here.

Mark:

Fair enough to be honest.

Maja:

We can't live at Kylie's anymore, she hates me and doesn't want me around.

Mark:

Not massively fair enough but OK.

Maja:

I can't stand the thought of returning to Sweden, whenever I might do that. I know it's going to be a tough situation. And my visitor's visa is slowly but surely running out. I groan to myself and turn around in a bed that takes up almost the whole space of this tiny room. As I once more rest my eyes on the tree outside, I think to myself, 'It's time to start something new. It's time to leave.'

Mark:

Approaching 4pm we're just lying down taking it easy, not intending to move until we have to. Maybe a couple of hours of just total chill time. Sounds lovely. Doesn't happen. This plan lasts until 4:30pm when I get a voice message. It's from Kylie. With trepidation, I hit play and we listen to it together. Oh dear. She's telling us that if we haven't got our stuff out of the room today, it will be taken out. She says it will only be put into the hallway, but whatever, it doesn't sound good. We need to go. Now. But how? We have no car and I wouldn't feel comfortable asking Cris to help us out because he's not at all happy that we've come back and plonked ourselves right above Jenn again. Fair enough. Which is why I won't put him in the position of having to say no. Then I remember Rafael who was so put out when we didn't ask him to help us with the last move. If anything, I actually have an obligation to make this call. We'll be walking to and fro past his place, so if he was mildly offended last time, he'd be proper offended this time. It's worth a call, but I really have to ask him to meet us now now.

I put the call in. He's happy to help, but really not sure he can help now. Maybe tomorrow. No, I say. Really sorry, but tomorrow's no good. It's now or I'll say thankyou very much and we'll just do it ourselves. Oh damn this feels bad. He says he'll call back in a few minutes. This is a tense time. Nothing we can do between now and then. But he does call back in a few minutes and says he'll meet us there in ten but he'll only be able to help for an hour or so. Thankyou thankyou thankyou, but I have to tell him we'll be there in more like 15 because it will take at least that long to walk there, and that's if we leave this very instant, which we will pretty much do. Fine.

As we approach Kylie's we're keeping a curiously

nervous eye out to see if any of our stuff has been thrown out onto the street. Thankfully, it hasn't. But there's behind the apartments as well, with a whole garden area back there. I go round and have a look. OK. Nothing out here either. That's at least a little relief. Now to go and wait for Rafael. We really don't feel like encountering Kylie before we have to so we decide not to wait out front, preferring to go to the end of the street, on the corner with the main road. Every now and then, I walk out into the road to see if I can see him. After five minutes or so, here he comes. His van is painted in his company's colours and has a bit of a strange roof for carrying particular materials, so it's very distinctive. I thank him very much for coming. No problem. He goes and parks up outside the apartment and me and Maja go in.

We reach the front door and, although we have a key, I think it's only right to knock rather than just walk in. To be fair, Kylie is someone who, if she has an issue, says her piece and mentally moves on. So outwardly at least, she is friendly and welcoming, although she does make a point of sternly demanding we take the fridge as well because she doesn't want it. Fine. I walk in first. I don't see what looks the two girls exchange behind me.

Maja:

As I walk into the apartment, my whole self is filled with ice. I am in cold, focused panic mode. I look at Kylie. She looks at me. Our eyes are filled with mutual hate. For a moment we both stop there. Then I walk past her into the bedroom. It's time for action. This place, that felt like some kind of lovely home once, needs to be emptied. Immediately. The contents of the drawers get quickly thrown into the suitcase while everything else is hastily stuffed into black bin bags. It doesn't have to be perfect. It just has to be quick. In a matter of 30 minutes, everything is packed and ready to go. If anything is forgotten, it will just be left and never seen again. We are OK with that.

Mark:

We walk into what we'd started considering home until last night and thankfully, everything is as we left it. To make things a little easier on Maja, who really doesn't want to encounter Kylie too much, I opt for the heavy lifting and carrying everything downstairs. This means Maja can concentrate on packing. And out on the street, Rafael says I should just drop everything next to the van and let him pack it. We have a few backpacks and a whole bunch of shopping bags. Plus, there are quite a few things that can just be taken down whole, such as the two bass amps. We get started. It takes an hour or so and is done without incident or any kind of harsh words. Only best wishes from Kylie as we reach the end and give her her key back. The one bit that could have been sticky and that I was most concerned about is getting the fridge out of there. But those things are a lot lighter and easier to move about than you'd think, even down stairs. Van all packed and we give our eternal thanks once more to Rafael and we're off. Once at The Carrol, the job does take on a bit of a seemingly never ending quality as we first empty the van, which is parked about 40 yards from the house, and then get everything downstairs and back into the room, which Maja is organising. This sees us both carry everything from the van to the house, piling up the front garden and then the street, and then I start to take everything downstairs, bit by tiny bit. Yes, including the fridge, which means we now totally have our own fridge and freezer in the house which is quite handy.

Unbelievably, from receiving the scary message at 4:30, by 7:50pm we're on the bus to Angel. It was horrible having to do everything like that, and in the mad dash way in which we did, but now we can go to the party with the whole move behind us and tomorrow is completely clear.

And this party will be Maja's first indoor London social where she will meet what I consider to be my central London crowd made up of some of the coolest and best bar staff and bar managers in London. Basically people I met while me and Dan were playing the scene as pop cover duo The Insiders. And yep, when we arrive, there they all are. Not quite everyone, but a really good representation. Kristoff, Alex, Tom, Jess, Shane, Molly, Jess, and a few other people. We're here considerably later than we meant to be and the place is deep in party territory. So we don't get around to any of the recording I might have been part of. That's OK. We just get stuck in. Oh, these guys love Maja and she's instantly the centre of attention and having a great time. So the pubs aren't open yet, Maja's never been to a London pub, and now here she is at a party above one. And yes, we're going to stay the night. Of course, it turns into a very late one.

Maja:

The context switch is enormous. From feeling hated by everyone, I'm being totally included and loved in a group. It's amazing. And I feel so good having closed the Kylie chapter in my life. I'm done with it, thank you for the adventure, but that's way too much drama for me. I don't think I ever want to do that again. Maybe one of our notepads got left behind in the rush, but that is a loss we have to take.

Cheers to us! And yes, I'd love another glass of wine.

Day 50
Saturday April 10

Mark:

Alex's apartment sometime late morning. A few guys have hung around and we have a wonderfully relaxed and fun morning. That includes a full English breakfast, cooked by Alex, an executive chef no less, and playing Uno until we decide it's time to leave around 3pm. We're very close to the financial district and one of the best preserved sections of the original London Roman wall. This once encircled the whole of London when it was very much smaller than it is now, and I suggest we take a walk to see it. This is a very strange archaeological site - and sight - of Roman ruins right in among the super modern London banking buildings. It's the perfect setting to round off a very eventful few days as we enter the ruins and meander through the rough, broken stone and haphazardly kept vegetation between it all, trying very hard to picture a London that began and ended within these ancient walls.

Maja:

I love to look out of Alex's window and see the people walking towards us. It's central London, in one of the cosiest places I can imagine. I'm looking right down a lovely alley with stores and restaurants left and right. Nothing is open yet of course, but there is still a good amount of people I can stare at while they're walking by. And there's a lot of people around here in the apartment right now too, all sitting down drinking Lucozade and nursing their hangovers.

I can't remember even once waking up in such lovely company and I'm completely basking in the moment. I mean, I've done a lot in my life, but this kind of situation, not so much. And Alex cooks us all a lovely breakfast with all the English things, like eggs and beans. I also try the Lucozade, but I don't like it very much. Weird drink. Just tastes strange to me.

When it's time to leave, Mark puts the basscase on his

back and we walk downtown. I look at him every once in a while. That bass on his back really suits him. We find our way to the London Roman walls and I am fascinated by the absolute contrast between old and new in a city like this. I've been in old cities, and new ones too, but the mix of the two here is quite unique and spectacular. And we have it all to ourselves.

Yes, there might have been a couple of skips down the road holding hands. OK. Yes. You're right. We totally skipped down the road holding hands.

Day 51
Sunday April 11

Mark:

Wow, I have been in and out of furlough for a long time. This whole saga, as far as I'm concerned, began almost a year ago on March 23, 2020 when the bars first closed. They reopened on June 23. On November 5, with Covid on the rise again, a second lockdown was announced so the bars closed again and into furlough I went again. Then we went into farce territory with bars opening again on December 2 with the government desperate to 'save Christmas,' only for them to close again on December 21. Me and Maja then spoke for the first time on the phone on December 26.

Now we're opening again again tomorrow, although one caveat of bars reopening is that they can only serve outside and everything has to be table service so this will be fun. It also means that bars with not enough viable outdoor space will not be able to reopen, so only a partial return to form anyway. As for the Palmerston, well that has six tables out front and a whole massive garden out back, a long way away from the front garden. So while we do have plenty of capacity, it will just be a bit of a stretch keeping everyone happy as we carry out the compulsory table service for those two wide apart areas.

Today we have a staff meeting at the bar where I announce to everyone that I'm leaving in two weeks. This is of course met with shock, and a why and a what the hell, and then quite a bit of happiness and congratulations as I tell a short version of the story. Next, the important bit. Who can take shifts off me? The big problem is that a few people who went home to their native countries haven't come back so we don't have a full complement of staff. I'm very disappointed that I only manage to get two days taken off me at this first time of asking. Oh well. OK. I start tomorrow.

Back to tell Maja the news and she's equally disappointed, but I make it clear that, as the days go on, I may well be able to arrange cover for more shifts. But really, it's no big deal. I can just do these two weeks, cover what I cover, work what I don't, and then we're back as we were.

With the bars opening up tomorrow, that means no more lockdown London and Maja wants one last look at the epic emptiness of it, so we take a trip out. First to

Kings Cross from where I suggest an overground train. I have a very good reason for this as there's something I've wanted to show Maja for a while. This train goes to Blackfriars station which is quite possibly one of the most stunning train platforms in the world. The whole platform is a bridge across the River Thames, quite close to St Paul's Cathedral, so offers incredible views all across the city centre on both sides. Of course, by default, it also takes us into the city, so this is where we get off for one last walk through empty lockdown London. Maja's London. There is a real feeling of loosening in the air so it's not quite as iconic as it has been, but still. These streets are definitely not bustling. And there's a moment on the way back, as we approach Farringdon in zone one, that we're able to look all ways on a crossroads and not see a single person. So yes, we did get what we came for. We end up walking all the way back to King's Cross where we started and get a bus back from there. Which is weird, as it means I'm back on the old and familiar 214 bus to The Carrol.

Maja:

Lockdown London. Maja's London. All I've ever known of London. A London void of people and life. It's been fitting. It's been a great time for a wreck like me to arrive in, when everything in life was wrong. But this is the last of it. It ends tomorrow. And I don't feel ready for that yet. I need more time. It's been fitting to have the whole world stop when my world stopped. But the world has now decided it's time to move on. Maybe I have to as well.

Day 52
Monday April 12

Maja:

Mark's first day at the bar since I've been in London. Once he's left I feel empty. What am I supposed to do now? Nothing seems fun, nothing seems interesting as I am alone. I'm not ready to be alone. I sleep a little bit and then search for rental properties and cars, as we'll also need a car for the move. And to be able to get by in Ireland, because our house budget means we're probably going to be living somewhere quite isolated with not too many shops nearby.

Later on I take the short walk up to Mark's pub, enjoying the early spring day and the sunshine. On the way there I sit down on a low brick wall and just observe the environment around me. The air is crisp. It's a beautiful early spring day. Cold but sunny. As the clock ticks closer and closer to 5pm, I am feeling how I get happier and happier. I make sure to be there by five and shyly look in through one of the many windows. I can't immediately find Mark, so I stand out of view so no-one speaks to me by mistake. Then I take out my phone and call. 'I'm here, can you come meet me up?' He lets me know he's just finishing one last thing and will be done and out in a minute.

I'm feeling very shy and nervous.

Mark:

Oh wow. I really did not see this coming. The bar is traumatically busy. Just non non non stop. And it's only me and the boss, Moni. It really is one of the busiest days ever. Not in terms of the number of customers, but in terms of the total non-stopness of the day and the speed at which we have to move and juggle so many things happening at the same time. All. The. Time. It's going to continue to be like this for the foreseeable. Which, at least for me, is only two weeks. I've never seen anything like it. Not as a customer or a worker. Not even on the busiest of Sundays, or Christmas Days, or anything. Even Moni has a moment where she just leans back, half sitting against a wall, and says, 'This is just too much.' I've never seen anything remotely like this reaction from her.

With everything having been closed for almost four months, I can totally understand the feeding frenzy which means that you can't just walk in here and claim an outdoor table. Anyone who's been remotely clued up has seen this coming and has booked. You can see the bookings on the system and again, I've never seen anything like it. It's already booked exactly like this everyday for the next ten days. You just know that the days and weeks after that will end up being the same. And like I said yesterday, a lot of our staff haven't returned so we've got a stretched rota. Oh, the relief me and Moni have when Kitty comes in to start sometime mid afternoon. But then the absolute opposite experience poor Kitty has as she starts to realise what she's walked into. But with three of us on now, it does feel somewhat easier.

I finish at five and Maja comes by as planned. The gardens are all full so we do what customers can't and go upstairs to the function room where we share a burger and chips. We could get a beer and actually be inside a pub with one when no-one else is allowed to, but we decide to go home and get some stuff done instead. I like this idea because all day at the pub I've been wanting to get home and research what it could take to live in Ireland. We think about how to get stuff there and I suggest we hire a van we can leave in Ireland. Maja jumps in with, no. We buy a van as we need one anyway.

So the plan now is to find a detached house in the countryside of Ireland. Just Ireland. We don't care where. In that house we will set up a studio, write songs and rehearse to develop our sound and act, then tour the country and beyond from there. The detached thing is so that we can make noise anytime we want, night or day, while we're targeting the countryside because properties in general will be cheaper.

With this decided, Maja immediately starts looking at vans for sale. The idea is to buy an actual van rather than a camper van, and adapt it for living, to make it viable for touring. Unfortunately we won't be able to share the driving as I can't drive which is a little harsh and yes, I know, a pretty fundamental life skill to be missing.

As the plan starts to take shape, Maja reveals she's long had the idea for an adapted van but didn't know what she really wanted to do with it. I now say that I've long had the idea to tour in this kind of way but didn't know how it could really happen. Where we are now is that Maja had the how, I had the what, but neither of us knew the where or when. Now the whole thing has come together. We just have to make it happen.

We're planning all this upstairs in our room. Well, Maja's in the room, sitting on the bed. Outside the bedroom door is the hallway with a railing above the stairs and immediately opposite the door is the toilet. I'm sitting next to the toilet with my back against the railings. Yep. We have basically annexed part of the hallway to our room.

Day 53
Tuesday April 13

Mark:

April 13 - the last 13th, we almost killed a cat. I wonder what will happen on this one.

I'm in the bar sometime early afternoon, and finishing around nine, so Maja can come by and have her first drink and hangout in a bar in London. Or at least her first drink outside in a bar in London. But her very first visit is to go there for a coffee as I have the idea to call regular and friend Ricky to see if he could meet me around noon. I've never suggested meeting him in the daytime before and he's quite intrigued. He goes to Ireland quite regularly, so I think he will be a good person for a preliminary chat. It will also be fun to tell him about what's happening.

Once we've settled down and we've told him of our plans, what he comes back with surprises the hell out of both of us. He starts talking about the three bedroom house in Donegal he's been taking care of and is trying to sell, something we've spoken about before. He now says he might be able to offer that to us for almost no rent. He says if it was up to him, he would just let us have it for free, but apparently there are other people to consider, so some rent would have to be charged. Totally no problem with that. He asks how we'd feel about £300 a month. Damn. You can't get a room in Ktown for anything like that, no matter how small. You're talking almost twice that just to begin. And there'd be no deposit on this place either. Damn again. Just a pretty much token rent. For a three bedroom place. He says he'll have to make a call or two, but he really expects we'll be able to do this. So just like that, we're touching distance from having our starter home in Ireland.

But it will have to be just a starter home because he now says that there is one little issue. It could be sold at any minute and if that happens, we might have to vacate the place with very little notice. However, he adds that it's been on the market for so long that he really doesn't expect it to shift anytime soon. We tell him we're all good with that. Just the thought of now having somewhere to land, and at such an amazing price, is a fantastic development. At the very least, this is a great possible fall-back option; given the whole being sold thing, even if we do end up there, we'd be well advised to be out of there again as soon as possible.

Oh, the Donegal and far up north thing. I should explain as not everyone's going to know this. Although Northern Ireland is, well, in the north, the border doesn't cut fully across the island. So the Republic of Ireland continues running up the island to the west of Northern Ireland, going all the way to the top. The result is that the far north of Ireland, which would be the far north of Donegal, is further north than the far north of Northern Ireland. Interesting fact I discovered while checking this out. The most northern island of Northern Ireland is Rathlin Island. However, the Republic of Ireland's most northern island is Inishtrahull, part of Donegal, and this is more northern than Rathlin Island. So even with Ireland's islands taken into consideration, the northernmost point of The Republic of Ireland is still more northern than the northernmost point of Northern Ireland.

Now Maja goes home and I go in for my Tuesday, which is every bit as busy as yesterday, but at least I know what I'm walking into this time. When I've finished, Maja arrives and we have drinks outside. Ricky's returned for the evening as well, and a few other off duty staff members join us. This is where the rule about only being able to drink outside hits its first real snag. It's April, so the evenings can still get a bit chilly. To sit out there and drink cold beer doesn't really work so well. And this is the south east of the UK. This outside thing is going to bite a lot more up north, and let's not even start on what it could be like in Scotland. We have a couple of drinks and realise that to stay for anymore would be to endure rather than enjoy. We've enjoyed this little tickle, but it's time to get off now. But it's been lovely for people to meet Maja in this way, and for us to tell them our plans.

Maja:

After leaving Mark at the pub for his shift, I walk down to Kentish Town and have a look at all the pubs that are opening up. You can really feel how the joy is returning to the streets now, when all the people that have been going through lockdown and isolation for ages are finally able to go out and meet people again. Every little shop now has a couple of chairs and tables outside it in the street, it looks so lovely. I can't wait for my turn, I think as I go home for the day.

When it is finally evening time, I eagerly hurry to The Lord Palmerston where I'm meeting Mark. As I come to the corner of the building, I don't dare to go in even though I was here yesterday. I haven't really gotten introduced to anyone yet and I am feeling a bit embarrassed. So, just like I did yesterday, I call Mark. 'Hey, I'm here now, can you come out?'

I'm feeling shy, I'm about to meet these other people around him for the first time. And I don't have much experience going to bars, it's never really been a thing I've done. Yeah, of course I've been to some bars with friends in Sweden, but then you're with friends. You never have to worry about talking to anyone out of your group. Here it's more common. I think. I don't know. I'm just going to allow Mark to take lead on it and enjoy the situation.

Which turns out to be really lovely. Not long after Mark finishes his shift, we're sitting outside and chatting with some of the regulars. Just some English banter I assume. It's lovely and I feel my shyness slowly evaporate into silliness. We stick around for quite a long time and I get to discover that I really like a beer called Neck oil which is an English IPA. I also discover I don't like espresso martini. At all.

As the night gets later and colder, it's not really comfortable staying out much longer. Cue the usual, me and Mark go skipping down the road. All smiles and laughter, and we start walking after a while. As we're getting close to the end of the road, Mark signals to me that he wants to cross to the otherside of the street. Yeah, sure, and I take a step to the side to start to cross the road.

It's dark.

I must have screamed.

I am in the middle of the road and I don't know how I got here. The asphalt is cold on my cheek. I can feel the small holes in between the grains of the relatively newly laid asphalt and I smell it. I'm not used to smelling asphalt, it smells a little bit like fresh tarmac. I'm holding my foot, I'm in a foetal position.

There is no way I am moving.

And now the pain really hits me.

Mark:

It's a ten minute walk home. Half of that walk is downhill, all the way to a crossroads pretty much where Kentish Town, Highgate, Gospel Oak and Tufnell Park all meet. At that crossroads it's a left turn and then just five minutes more of a walk to the house.

We're approaching it on the right hand side, hand in hand, walking at a pretty decent pace down the hill, me on the inside. I give Maja a little indicative shove, signalling that we should start crossing the road at a diagonal angle, to take in the corner as well, walking all the way across the road to be on the pavement on the far side, which will put us on the same side as the house. Maja responds and steps off the kerb. She goes down immediately with a scream. I react, trying to pull her hand up to stop her from falling but nothing can be done. She goes all the way to the floor, landing very heavily on her knee and just stays there, head down, not quite screaming, but scarily loud all the same. The speed of the fall has taken her deep into the road but she is making no moves at all to get out of the way of any cars that could be coming. But it's very quiet right now and no cars are coming. I have no idea what to do. I go and crouch down with Maja to see what's going on, but she isn't responding at all. It's just very clear something has gone very wrong. She's sobbing quietly now but still no acknowledgement of any awareness of her surroundings, or the fact that I'm even there. I have no idea how long we stay like this, but eventually she at least manages to get up and allow herself to be dragged somewhat to the kerb and somewhere a little more safe. I then ask if she can get up and walk. She slowly gets up. But walk? That's another thing altogether. I support most of her weight, or as much as I can, and she hobbles very very carefully to the end of the street. There are no thoughts now of trying to cross the whole thing in one go. Instead, we stay at this side, intending to walk a little further down, then cross just where the estate starts, about 40 yards away from here at a zebra crossing where we'll have right of way and will be able to take our time. This walk is clearly going to take a whole lot longer than five minutes.

A car stops. The guy asks if we need help getting

anywhere. Yes. Yes please, we do. Except I don't say that right away. Instead, I first want to reassure him that we really don't have far to go, that we just live a little way past that bridge over there. Before I can say anything else, he says, OK, no problem, and drives off. Noooooo. Come back. That's not what I meant. Damn. We carry on the very slow, hobbly walk home. My first indication that this is bad comes when we're just 10 yards or so away from the house. Practically outside next door. Maja goes down again and says she simply can't go any further. She takes a break for a while and we go again, pushing it for the last 10 yards. But then of course, when we reach our upside-down house, there are a whole bunch of stairs to negotiate downwards to reach the bedroom.

We reach the room and have by now decided that this might just be a hospital call. Maybe a really bad twist. I call 111, the non emergency number and we get given an A&E (ER) appointment for 11am the next morning. Then we try to sleep, but for Maja, this is far from a comfortable night. I do what I can, but really, there isn't much I can do.

Day 54
Wednesday April 14

Maja:

My ankle is broken. In two places. The tendons on each side of the ankle, the two little bits that stick out, were pulled so hard and fast that pieces of bone were pulled out of both of them.

Mark:

When I hear that, a shiver goes through my whole body. And at the same time we realise we won't be going to Ireland anytime soon. There's no way Maja will be able to drive in any near future. And I can't drive anyway. That two weeks is not going to be two weeks anymore.

But anyway, the hospital visit goes like this.

We take a taxi and as soon as we arrive realise we will need a wheelchair. I leave Maja by the entrance to go in and see what I can do. I speak to someone on reception and they tell me wheelchairs aren't given out. You just have to walk around and try and find one another patient has vacated and left lying around. So that's what I do for the next five or ten minutes or so. I'm almost giving up until I realise that's not an option. I don't want Maja waiting too long wondering where the hell I've got to, especially not in the distressed state she must be in, so I make my way back to the entrance just to let her know I've not found anything yet but am still looking. On the way I walk past the ambulance bay. And there, right in front of one of the ambulances, is a wheelchair. Wonderful. Job done. But it's not one of those large wheeled things. No, this only has little wheels, meaning the person sitting in it can't get around by themselves. Totally takes away any independence. But when I think about it, it totally makes sense. I think. I may be wrong, but I kinda guess they don't want drunken people, or non drunken people for that matter, finding wheelchairs and deciding to have races down the corridors Hollywood style. Little wheels with no volition it is. Sorry Maja. I'm in control now.

Back home and I leave Maja in bed and go off to the shop across the road. I get there and before I even start to have a look around, the manager asks me to wait a second because he has something for me. What could he possibly be talking about? He disappears out back, and comes back carrying a bass. Yep. He disappears out back, and comes back carrying a bass.

'This was left here by someone about a month ago,' he says. We kept it to see if anyone would come back and claim it but no-one did. I've seen you in here with that bass case on your back, and decided that if it was still here after a month, I would give it to you. Wow. Just wow. So this is what apparently happens now when I pop out to get milk. I also see immediately that it's tuned B E A D. Very cool. You could say Maja's a bit surprised when I arrive back at the room with a, 'Guess what I got from the shop.' Just for the record, it's a light brown Satellite so not particularly vintage or noteworthy, but it's still a free bass. Oh, and we plug it in and it really is super quiet, but we're confident this is something that can be fixed. Probably just a loose connection somewhere.

Although she's gone to the hospital and been well looked after, Maja is continuing to be in some discomfort and, at times, pain. Luckily I wasn't rota'd on at the bar for today, but I am supposed to be in tomorrow. I decide I won't be and, if it comes to it, I will just refuse. But I make my calls and give the situation a little while to see if I can be covered, hoping it won't come to me having to make a flat out refusal. I'm also hoping to get Friday and Saturday covered as well. Tomorrow does get sorted, but there's nothing to be done for Friday and Saturday. I even check with Moni to see what can be done, but she says we're currently operating with such a tiny staff and Duran, the assistant manager, is also working at another pub while continuing to work with us. It really is a stretch to get any days covered at all. OK. Fair enough and thankyou. Let's deal with this.

Today, as the shock subsides and reality settles, we realise Maja won't be able to drive for seven or eight weeks, which puts Ireland off for some time. A driver needs to at least be able to do an emergency stop comfortably, meaning you really have to be able to slam down on the brake, so just being able to soft pedal the thing is no good. But even without that to consider, it's going to be a long and unpredictable drive. At least from here to Liverpool for the ferry to Belfast, then from there to where, we have no idea. This would be a tough drive at the best of times. With a recovering broken ankle? Forget about it.

Day 56
Friday April 16

Maja:

The good thing with having a broken ankle and being left alone is, well not much. But at least I'm sleepy. You need to sleep a lot when you're injured, the body needs the sleep to heal. At least Mark is looking after me before and after work. And I get to eat all the treats I want.

Outside my window there is a lovely tree, in full bloom with spring flowers. Spring flowers and a bright blue sky. It is beautiful.

Mark:

I'm in from 1pm till 8:30. Maja can't begin to think about stairs, and our bedroom is on the mid level, with the front door upstairs and the kitchen downstairs. At least the toilet, like we established a few days ago, is directly opposite the bedroom so that's an easy reach. But the kitchen is a no no. So before I leave, I have to make sure Maja has enough food and drink to get her through the amount of time I'll be out. It's a very unhappy Maja that I say goodbye to shortly before 1pm as I leave for the bar.

During the day, I tell Moni how things are and ask if she could at least get me out sometime early tomorrow.

Day 57
Saturday April 17

Mark:

Moni comes through for me and goes above what I asked for. Way above.

I'm due in today from 10am till 5pm. At 8:30am she texts me to say that tomorrow and Tuesday are now covered. That is just amazing news. The way the rota has worked out, this means that after today, I only have two days left to work before I'm all done, and that will be Friday and Saturday.

When I get in today, it gets even better as Moni tells me I can finish at two today instead of five. Result. She then adds that she has 15 applicants for my job, so if she gets to interviews this week, maybe even Friday and Saturday will go. Damn that all happened quick. I'm almost done, and could yet be totally done by two today. Thankyou very much Moni.

During the day I tell one of our regulars I'm quitting the bar job. He naturally asks for the why and I tell him some of our story. As I get deeper and deeper into it, he collapses more and more in laughter at the continuing absurdity, not least the fact that right now this very moment, my girlfriend, who I met online and who came from Sweden to stay in lockdown London seeking temporary respite when her world fell apart, is lying in our bed, right above the room I used to share with my former girlfriend, who is still living there by the way, and is there as we speak. It takes him a while to grasp the fact that we are all actually living in the same house. And that I'm about to move to Ireland with this girl who I met less than two months ago and with whom I've already moved house twice, the second one back to where we started as we fled the crazy naked communal, musical living situation we'd walked into which just happened to come with an offer of a free apartment which never fully materialised. That's all before you consider the fact that me and Maja became an item on the way from the airport to my house during what was supposed to be a friendly visit, and were talking about having kids together less than a week later, shortly after, deciding to get married and tour the world playing songs we haven't written yet with Maja having never played a single live show in her life. We were planning on leaving for Ireland next week to get started, but a few days ago she broke her ankle walking back from the bar.

This guy is a head cameraman who works on top Hollywood productions. As I'm talking, he stops me and says, 'You do realise this thing is just too implausible for a movie?' I nod. I know. 'But you're telling me all this actually happened?' Yep. He shakes his head in disbelief and acceptance. 'If it's a true story, that's totally different as far as a movie's concerned,' he says. 'What I'm really reminded of is Catch Me If You Can. They would never have been able to get away with that, except it was all true.' This is a Steven Spielberg movie starring Leonardo DiCaprio. Then my friend says, 'You also realise that there's too much here for a movie? It would have to be a TV series.' Took the words right out of my mouth. That's exactly where we think this is ultimately all going. We very much agree with him on the implausibility factor as well.

Maja:

I remember when we walked down the streets of Camden, joyfully giggling and shouting at times: 'We need to fire our script writer, this is all too crazy!' Just too many things that have been happening lately that it stopped making sense ages ago. One enormous development after the next, and I, for the life of me, would never have been able to foresee what would happen next. When Mark comes home and tells me about his conversation today, I feel oddly validated. Yes, it's not only me. This really is a bit over the top.

Mark:

Just as we start to think we're going to be OK with this, Maja says her foot is numb. Not good, so we call 111 who say we need to go to A&E immediately. Damn. Fine. We get a taxi and when we arrive, I'm told I can't go in because of the Covid thing. OK but not OK. It is pretty cold and I'm not dressed for a long wait outside. I get it, but Maja is not independent at all right now and no-one had a problem with me being in with her the last time we were here. That's not cutting any ice. At all. So I wait outside for the hour and a half it takes for this to be sorted. There really isn't much to do so I content myself with sending silly messages to Maja.

Maja:

Come on Mark! Stop it! Seriously, I can't stop myself from laughing!

Day 58
Sunday April 18

Mark:

We have a first rehearsal at the house today, just chucking some songwriting ideas back and forth with the guitar. Getting the musical feeling back really. I also hit the bass with pretty much the same attitude. Just getting back into it. What's really nice is that I wake up just needing to play so I do.

Then, once we're up and about, we're in the garden for the first time since we got back. It really is nice to be outside and relaxed like this, and it's here, reclining in deckchairs in the sun, that Maja first has the idea of maybe travelling about with a car and a tent. This could be an effective touring strategy - turning up at venues in which we could stay the night after a show, but demonstrating that we're self sufficient at the same time. We kinda think that in touring, we could also stay at the houses of audience members if we're lucky, but we still like the idea of having a tent handy, kind of in the spirit of, people help people who help themselves. All in all, we're just putting detail on the bones of how a life of musical touring could be possible.

Day 59
Monday April 19

Maja:

The weather is nice so we go on a walk around the block, making our way to the outdoor coffee shop where we have a nice coffee and chat with the locals. We meet a friend of Mark's, also called Mark, by the coffee shop and he sits down with us to have a chat. I'm resting my superboot on a chair, so it's only natural that he sits with us. He tells us about his filming project going on a motorcycle all around the island of England to interview locals, and I misinterpret it as a filming project about him travelling all around Ireland to interview locals. I really think it's fun that he is looking at travelling to Ireland as well. Mark explains my misunderstanding to me as we walk back home at a super slow pace. He was actually talking about going round the UK, referring to it as The Island.

I haven't been out and about in about a week, so this little outing has been exhausting so I go to sleep for a while. Around 8ish, we're awake, hungry and annoyed about not being as productive as we'd like to have been. And we haven't even played any bass today, or worked on any songs. At all. We eat something small, and I decide that we'll do a bass session. Mark wants to do some music writing, but we start off with bass. It's another one hour session entirely on right hand plucking technique. I start to somewhat get a hang on how to pluck more fluently. My plucking technique is now better than it has ever been before, and I am now using the same technique that Mark uses - free strokes. I've always used rest strokes before. After finishing a session on bass, we continue to finally get some original music writing done. Mark's a brilliant songwriter. I'm not sure if that was clearly written enough in his own Mark's Diaries, but he really knows what he is doing. So finally, after everything we've been through these couple of months, after everyone we've told about our project, we are finally in a mentally calm enough space to be able to even start to consider writing music. Even if writing music has been our top priority, even if it has become our self chosen duty to actually write music, every disturbance that has come along has just put our heads further and further away from actually doing it. We'd prepared a couple of documents with lyrics ideas in advance. So we take a look through them and start with the one that is most ready. And here the magic happens. Mark just does, well how to say it, his magic. I've never worked with a true professional like this before, and it is clear as day that he knows exactly what he is doing. Line after line just comes out, accompanied by his bass playing.

I struggle to sing along and be helpful. It's quite fun, but compared to him, I have no idea of what I am doing. I get one melodic idea during the session, to do with one of the lines, but he has so many. It's truly wonderful to be able to work with him. Amazing really. I don't feel pressured to perform any good in this situation, I know that it'll come around when I'm more used to it. He has had a lifetime in music, and now he has decided that he wants to invest that in someone like me. I am truly flattered. I know that eventually, I am going to have more to give in the creative aspects, but for now, I'm going with the flow. Watching. Learning. Using what I have to do what I can. For me, it's like I am a student, working with a colleague that is a star.

Mark:

What can I say? All the above is true. But seriously, sometimes ideas and melodies come, sometimes they don't. Today they just happen to be exploding in me. But also, Maja really has woken the dormant songwriter in me and it's so cool to be thinking about original music again. That's something I've not really had an interest in for around eight years, despite, for a long time, songwriting being all I wanted to do. I just hit a point when I realised so many of the impossibilities of making a living as a songwriter who wasn't in a band and who couldn't sing well enough to do it solo. That thing of writing songs for other people as a profession, which is what I really, truly wanted to do, or thought I did. For a start, it took a long time to learn this, but I discovered that to really make it work I had to be able to make full radio ready demos. Basically demos that would already sound pretty much like what the finished product would sound like; it wasn't enough to think you had a great song recorded with just guitar and (not particularly good) vocal that you could play to people and they would then imagine how it might sound blown up to a full production and say, oh yes please. We would like to have that song. No. You had to make that full production. Leave nothing to the imagination. I subsequently learned that some very successful songwriters, before sending a song for consideration for a particular star, had someone singing on the demo who sounded like that star, or they would even mimic the voice and potential performance themselves. I just straight down didn't have enough of the skills required to do any of that. Couldn't sing, not to any level anyway although I could at least hold a tune and get my ideas across. Couldn't play all the instruments, couldn't produce. Nothing. I could get on a guitar and write a song and present it kind of OK, and that was it. After a particularly chastening experience I realised I'd hit a hard wall of reality where I knew that what I had just wasn't enough. I knew people who could do the other stuff but I was barely earning enough money to support myself, never mind even think about paying people to work with me, and I did want to be able to pay them if I was going to ask them to work on a project that wasn't in their own interests. Which meant to help me make a great sounding song for my own purposes rather than us being in a band or studio project together. I did speak to the relevant people I knew, all of whom were friends of mine, and all of whom were prepared to do what I wanted them to do to help me put some of my songs together. So far so good. But I could never get them all in the same room at the same time which is what I felt I needed to do.

As for that chastening experience, I think we should revisit that. It was something that began as a dream, oh-my-I-can't-believe-this-is-happening, opportunity. One day in Madrid, by pure chance and in a bar, I happened to meet someone who said he was a successful businessman who was thinking of going into music. He was an English guy in the city just on a weekend away and our paths happened to cross. We hit it off, and it came up that I was a songwriter, or at least that I was someone who could write songs. It just so happened that he was looking to become what he called an executive producer. I understand this as being the person who isn't actually creating but who puts the right people together to make creation happen, and also works on opportunities on the other end so that there are people to get those creations to. The very mechanics of what it takes to write songs for other people. I would liken this concept to the movie producer who gets the script, hires the director and so on. That person maybe doesn't do anything to actually make the movie, but does bring all the components together, including finance, so that the movie can get made. That's my layman's understanding of that process and what I understand where this guy was coming from.

This meeting somehow eventually led to me being flown to New York, all expenses paid, to meet a producer with the idea being that we would work together. Before that happened, we were put together on the phone and exchanged songwriting ideas over a period of a week or something, and I got the impression he was really into what I was doing. See what I mean about that I can't believe this is happening thing? It was a whole go to New York for the weekend - yes, from Madrid - and just hang out at various live music venues, and see if we got on and then see how we were going to work together. Me and the producer really hit it off on a personal level but I'm still not entirely sure if he knew why we had been introduced. At some point one night, the subject of us working together came up in earnest and damn, he could not have been less interested. It didn't get ugly as such, but I was stunned and hugely disappointed. To put it mildly. This was supposed to be the big opportunity and it was smashed out. Just like that. On a New York side street. It got worse when Mr Executive producer went on a full U-turn of his own. Now I just wasn't good enough and had wasted everyone's time and money. Well, excuse me, but this whole thing really hadn't been my idea. I was asked to come, remember? He took me out for a coffee the next day and I thought this was where we were going to have a rethink. Instead, he went straight to the point and said, you're just not good enough and this is not going to happen. To go to what he actually said, it was, 'You're not a Paul Simon or a Paul McCartney or a John Lennon.' Never said I was. 'If you were, someone would have picked you up by now.' Even if that was all true, is the requirement of this job to be among the best of all time? Sure it helps, but if you're holding them up as the best, you're saying that if you're not as good as them then you're not good enough. Sorry, but you can be a successful or even famous sports person without being among the best of all time. The same as a songwriter, or anything to do with music. I never heard a story that went, the guy wasn't as good as The Beatles so we had to pass. Or imagine a football manager saying to a trialist, I'm sorry but you're just not as good as Lionel Messi. This whole professional football thing isn't going to work out for you. But this is exactly what I was being told. Apart from anything else, what I was hearing Mr Executive producer saying was, 'I'm not going to take a chance on you because no-one else has.' What kind of vision is that? That's the whole point of taking a chance on someone. It's not like you get the chance to do it when someone else already has. What? When everyone else has said, oh yes, we think this person is the next Roger Federer and we're going to make it happen, you think you're going to say, oh yes, I'll jump in and have a piece of that please. No. The opportunity has gone. For you Mr Executive Producer that is.

But despite all this, and despite me feeling like the entire bottom had dropped out of my world, I was left with something to cling to. For a start, there had been something invested in me and Mr Producer was willing to give it one last spin, saying the exact words, 'You'd better (sweary word) deliver.' I was told that I had one chance to come up with the killer song. But that I would have to do it all under my own steam once back in Madrid.

This is where that episode began where I was trying to get the right people in the room to make it happen. And it was during the New York adventure that I was told that to present a song, it had to be the radio ready finished article. So this was now what I had to do.

With this in mind, once back in Madrid, I put up an advert saying I was a songwriter with an opportunity looking to partner up with a producer. An enthusiastic young guy replied who had a studio in his home about an hour away from me. I went there and we got on fantastically. We immediately began to work on songwriting and recording. I came up with a load of songs including one we both agreed was absolute killer. We got the thing written and recorded in some kind of demo fashion and were really excited about it. It was then about getting the right people to sing and play on it to make it as good as it could be. This was where it started to unravel and the whole thing dragged on and became massively frustrating. I felt the right opportunity had come, and I had written the right song to make it happen. But to do so, there were simply too many moving parts. I was having to try to involve too many people. People I couldn't afford to pay and people I could have absolutely no ill will towards for not being available in the time and manner in which I needed them to be available; they owed me nothing, graciously said they would work with me on this project I had, but we just couldn't get enough diaries to match at the right times or places to make it work.

So much so that one day I sadly and silently called time on the whole thing. I realised this just wasn't going to work. With that I made a complete turn and said to myself, I'm not doing the songwriter thing anymore. I decided there and then to become a professional bass player. A sideman for hire. My theory was that if and when the opportunity came, I would only have myself to rely on to make it work. I totally dedicated myself to bass playing, reinventing myself as a bass player and musician in the process. I got down to work and studied bass playing and theory like I never had before. It was in this process that I discovered and signed up to scottsbasslessons.com - SBL. Using that incredible resource and Scott's own amazing lessons, I hammered myself into real professional bass playing shape from a pretty good raw material starting point. Once that process started, I lost all interest in playing any type of original music and would turn down all offers to join original bands, and I got a lot of offers. So, unless it was a jam session, with very few exceptions, I wouldn't play live unless it was a professional gig. Which mostly meant playing covers. Fine. I'll play covers.

This was around 2013, and in 2014 I took off on the adventure that would become Mark's Diaries. Which ended about two months ago when Mark's Diaries crazily collided with Maja's Diaries and became The Diaries.

Going way way back in time, I've been the primary songwriter in almost every band I've been in, which included writing about 80 per cent of Drunken Monkees' self titled album in 2010. This is the one that saw us take off to Hamburg to try to be rockstars. Going further back, I've run songwriter nights, most notably the legendary regular Tuesday night at Fred Zeppelins in Cork city, Ireland. I can claim absolutely no credit for its legendariness. That kudos all goes to Ronan Leonard, a fantastic songwriter and musician, and just a general make things happen kind of guy, who ran it before me and then handed me the reins. That, for me, felt like the moment I'd arrived in Cork as part of that incredible musical city. At the time I was a journalist on the Evening Echo, the city's daily newspaper. I had this job for four years, at some point kind of morphing into the paper's de facto music writer. From day one in Cork I became totally immersed in all things musical in the city, so that just naturally became a big part of my job.

As well as writing about all the original bands of the time, I was also playing in a whole bunch of them - ten at the same time at my absolute peak - including my own, Fly On The Wall, which played mostly my songs. If you're thinking conflict of interest by now with me also being a Cork music journalist, I won't argue with you. I'm just telling you how it was. This might not cut ice with everyone crying conflict of interest, but I think I played fair.

This all continued until I had to leave journalism and

also stop playing music in the illness/ fibromyalgia episode that lasted around five years until I had my breakthrough and moved to Madrid. During that five year period I couldn't see myself doing any conventional nine to five or whatever work again. So I had the idea that I might, might, might just be able to become a songwriter and have my songs placed with other people. I called a mildly successful producer who knew me as a songwriter and musician, and he was like, yeah, that could work. He asked me to send him a whole bunch of what I already had, and then to keep the process going. So I got to writing as much as I could and regularly sent him new songs. Sometimes he would even call and request a particular type of song for an artist he was working with. One time he called me and asked if I could just write and send him ten choruses. But nothing came of any of these songs, or choruses.

Day 60
Tuesday April 20

Mark:

Maja sits down to properly budget today to see how much time we can last on the money that's available. Into this go a few things we can't quite know such as the car we need to buy and how much rent we'll have to pay for whatever we find in Ireland, including deposit. But we put figures here on the highest amounts we want to spend, and factor that into the equations. What comes up is that if no more money comes in at all, we have enough to last six months give or take.

Maja:

I like doing budgets and planning, especially when it's regarding things I want to accomplish. Going over what we have available at the moment, a little cash injection certainly wouldn't hurt. There are going to be a lot of outgoings, such as rent, buying a car and living expenses in Ireland. And buying things to set us up as we begin. It's not like I can just bring all the home comforts I own in Sweden over to the next place that easily, so in many regards we need to start from scratch with that as well. It feels exciting and very real to look at the completed budget. Yeah, we can do this. Maybe just for a fewf months, but it is doable.

Mark:

A little cash injection would definitely help and I think it's now time to make a suggestion I've been thinking about recently which could help us to pull in a chunk more before we set off. If it works and really comes through it could add four or five months to our viability. It might sound scary, but the answer is this. Medical trials. But really, not as scary or outlandish as you might think. I'm not coming at this blind. I've done two of them at the same facility in north London and the place in question was considered so safe that even the nurses working there would take out holiday time and join a trial. Kinda like the workers in a sausage factory happily eating their own sausages or bar staff eating the food from the bar's kitchen. Adds a layer or two of consumer confidence. It also helps that on my two trials I would get to know and speak to people with a lot of experience of doing them, and it was often a topic of conversation between people that you could listen in on as well. Without exception, they said that this was the best place to do them. Some even did them as their main source of income, and others saw them as a very powerful financial supplement to their self employed endeavours. The only financial restriction is that you can't take a trial within three months of finishing one so you can't just hop immediately from one to another. But even so, it is still possible to do three or four a year if the jigsaw of schedules falls right. And if you get on the right ones, you really can make a liveable wage. I have a look and there are a couple starting soon that don't take too long to complete and pay £3000 per person, so £6000 to add to our battle kitty should we both get on. Perfect if we could do that, especially as we have an enforced longer period in London now we have to wait for Maja's ankle to heal. It would also get us away from the house for a week or so. From what, I'm sure you can imagine, isn't always the most comfortable of atmospheres. We decide to have a look at it just a little more, sleep on it, and if we still feel good about this tomorrow I'll make the call.

I also start to think further forwards and research, digging up and starting to remember contacts of mine from my time in Ireland. As do, I begin to feel like I've spent my whole life preparing for this. A few bullet points.

As covered pretty well in here, I've been involved in live music performance at many different levels for most of my life. Bass mostly of course, but a decent enough amount of experience on guitar, at the very least at a basic rhythm level, perfectly adequate for accompanying purposes.

I was a journalist for 10 years, covering a lot of different topics but I mostly gravitated towards music. There, I very deliberately researched that industry on so many different levels.

Four years of this journalistic experience was in Ireland where I built up contacts and knowledge of the country and its music industry.

I already have a lot of songs which we can look at and use as a foundation. Or at the very least, all that songwriting gives me a very solid basis of experience.

Now let's have a look at Maja.

She's a singer, or at least has already embarked on the journey of becoming one, along with already having embraced the possibility of fronting a band.

She drives.

She also has songwriting and music experience and is very keen to develop all of that.

She has the very highest level of computer and internet skills, a vital component in any business that wants to make a real impact whatever the industry.

And for both of us

We share the same drive, ambition, work ethic and intensity.

Here's something we could both say: I've always had this intensity. I now feel there are two of me.

It's a cliche that any multiple of people can be greater than the sum of its parts, but we're feeling even greater than a sum. Instead, we more have a feeling of things multiplying.

So basically, on a broad level, we very much share the same skillset, and have the same ambitions and directions in which we want to take that skillset. But we also both have things the other doesn't and this complements and fills gaps in the others' spectrum. As we contemplate all this we have a realisation. We are going to be famous. This is said as matter of factly as if we were saying we were going to pop out and buy some bread. It just feels like a totally unassailable, unstoppable truth.

Maja:

We are going to do this. There is no doubt in my mind.

Day 61
Wednesday April 21

Mark:

I get on the medical trial trail and speak to a person called Hannah who is very happy to hear from us and says that there's no reason we can't get the ball rolling. During these phone calls we discover that Maja weighs just a little bit too much to participate right now, so she decides to go on a strict diet until the trial. Maja is also told she has to register with a GP but we are already looking at this so that's handy. That happens today at our local practice in Kentish town where I also take the opportunity to get the relevant medical records I need for the hospital.

We really start to dig deep today, looking at the modern music industry and how we can use it to actually make this thing work. It helps if you can break these things down into actual workable, tangible, realistic projects. With that, we realise we have our first goal: get a place in Ireland and organise the means to get there. Which means finding a house in a country we're currently not even in, and buying a car so that we can drive to wherever that ends up being. We also talk about what kind of music we're going to write and play. We conclude that it will be cute and poppy, maybe with a touch of attitude. We're on our way. Kinda.

I call my friend Per to say hi and then get round to what's happening here. Kinda. He's a friend from my Madrid days who now lives in London a little way up north. Not long after I'd first started talking to Maja on the phone, I went to visit him and one of the things we did was listen to some songs from Maja's band that she'd sent me to critique. Me and Per did that together then sent voice messages with our opinions as we were doing so. We were generally positive about what we were hearing, thinking it had a kind of Nirvana/ grungey vibe.

Now I say to him, 'Remember that girl whose music we listened to and critiqued on the phone to her a few weeks back?' 'The Swedish one?' 'Yeah.' 'Well she's living with me now and we're an item.' I might as well have just told him I'd built a rocket in my back garden, was setting off for the moon today and did he fancy coming along. He reacts like it's obviously a joke and not even a very funny one. 'Yeah yeah. Of course she is.' 'No, really, she's here now. Upstairs in the house and asleep right now.' This actually goes back and forth a bit - more than would look good on the printed page - until finally something breaks. His voice suddenly changes tone and he says, 'You're actually not joking are you? What the hell's going on? What happened?' When I'm finally able to get clear sky to fill him in, and to tell him about the plans to move to Ireland, he couldn't be happier. For me, for us, for himself for simply hearing this kind of story happening in reality to a friend of his. 'You think things like this can't happen mate,' he says. 'To meet a girl who's on the same page as you as much as this on the things you both want to do. And that you're really making a plan to go off and do all that together. That's just the best thing I've heard in years.' Then, when I tell him about the ankle break and what that's done to our plans, he goes slightly into overdrive. 'That's too much now,' he says. 'You know this is a movie right?' Yeah, I've been hearing that a lot.

Day 62
Thursday April 22

Maja:

Neither of us sleep very well, possibly with minds racing that this has all suddenly become very real and very doable.

Not sleeping would normally be OK and we'd just sleep more in the morning, but not today. I have to be at the hospital by 9am for an ankle appointment. We both go, and the prognosis after it's had this bit of time to settle is promising. It's apparently healing exceptionally quickly. I ask when I'll be able to drive again and I'm told in a week or two. This is great to hear, and may make our Ireland move possible at an earlier stage now.

Mark:

Maja comes out all positive and almost ready to leave for Ireland this week. I put the brakes on just a little bit, saying, 'When the doctor says you're OK to drive, he's probably thinking about a trip to the shops or something. Not a road trip of four or five hundred miles.' A slightly sheepish OK comes back.

Maja:

I can walk a lot better now and sometimes I don't even need the moonboot. So we take a gentle walk to Hampstead Heath and sit on a bench just looking out over London. I am particularly affected by lack of sleep in general. Mark seems completely fine. The diet I started yesterday is also affecting me. I am hungry all the time and feel very dull, and the lack of sleep is multiplying my anxiety.

Mark:

Ambjorn, a friend I haven't seen for over 20 years, gets in touch online today wanting to make a donation to the Diary. He says he's read the whole thing, absolutely loves it and feels he really should pay something. Wow. I never even knew him that well. He was more a friend of friend, but yeah, you do the hang out thing and get on and all that, and now, here he is. The timing is perfect. His reachout makes it feel a bit like day one of the project, as an actual person has got in touch and wants to make a payment into it. That's real.

Per is delighted today when I call back and tell him I have someone here I would like him to meet. With that we're on a three way call as Maja says hi. Before I know it, they're chatting like old friends and then they start speaking together in a language that isn't English. I interject to say I had no idea that either Maja spoke Norwegian or Per spoke Swedish. They both laugh and say that their languages are so close they're able to speak Norwegian and Swedish respectively and be understood. That's my thing learned for the day. As we chat, Per says they're having a barbeque at his place this Saturday and would we like to come? Absolutely. Sounds wonderful. Thankyou very much. Here, I tell him that that's my last day at the bar and I'm doing the early shift so I'll be done by five. Perfect, he says. I guess I'll be seeing you guys around seven then. You most certainly will. So that's my last day at the bar party planned.

Day 63
Friday April 23

Maja:

Finally we get some great sleep in. Mark had set the alarm for 7am to get some writing done before going to the bar. I'm taking the opportunity to sleep some more. The good news regarding my foot has removed some worries and I enjoy feeling a little bit more relaxed as I allow myself to continue to slumber.

Mark:

Which means I'm doing the day shift, which means I've done my last evening, although I am in tomorrow day; Saturday days are a bit like weekday evenings.

And going to the bar. I've never called it going to work or being at work, as in, 'I've got to go to work now, or, I was in work when…' I've always, always said, 'to the bar, or at the bar,' as just part of what I do, with music and writing being the other parts. So, am I also not at work when I'm doing them? Do I say I was at work when talking about something that happened during a gig? Or a time a phone rang while I was writing? No. The other significant reason for me is that calling it work would make it seem permanent. Which would by definition imply that the other things I do would then fall into hobby. I wouldn't even be different about it if I got quite high in the barworld tree, and yes, I've had plenty of opportunities to climb that which I've turned down. Because, well, that's not what I do. It's not my work. I'd much rather be somewhere on the rock'n'roll tree.

Maja:

Mark gently wakes me and asks if I'd like to have a coffee or if I'd like to go back to sleep. I look at him and say, 'What have you done to me?' He stares at me with big eyes. He has no idea what I'm talking about.'Well I want to have tea,' I say softly. 'I mean, you've made me coffee these last couple of days, but it doesn't taste as good anymore,' Mark starts to laugh and so do I. 'You've made me a tea drinker!' We can't stop laughing about it. I can't believe it. Mark has transformed me into a proper British person. I drink tea now. Yorkshire tea. Or as I always used to say, that boring English breakfast tea that I could never understand why anyone would want to drink.

Tea made, and we're up and about starting our next writing session. We take a look at the funding pool on paypal that I started yesterday for Mark's diaries. And yes, the promised payment is there. So now we've made the first money on our writing projects. This is amazing, and is an important milestone in making them self-sufficient.

Mark is editing my diaries, since we need to get them properly edited before putting them on a public forum. In the meantime, I am updating our shared diaries, the words you're reading right now.

THE DIARIES

Day 64
Saturday April 24

Mark:

My last day at the bar. My last actual day at the bar. And it's right up there with some of the busiest I've ever seen, including some of the deepest days of Christmas. Certainly one of the most booked bars I've ever seen as we're fully booked right up until 8pm and will probably be booked for the rest of the evening before eight O'Clock comes. I'll be gone by the time it calms down as I'm set to finish at five, although I don't really think it is going to calm down until the tills are closed for the night. What really doesn't help is that one of our most on the ball members of staff, Kitty, comes in with a bad foot. I immediately tell her she can just stay on the bar as much as possible, which leaves me having to run all over the place as I'm now fully in charge of three, maybe even four sections with not a great deal of help. These sections are the front and back gardens which, as we established earlier, really are quite far apart, the restaurant area, and the bar area. On really busy days, of which this is definitely one, the bar area alone is split into two sections with one person responsible for each. Did I say Saturday days can be a bit like weekday nights? This one is busier than most Saturday nights. Yes, this is a big one to go out on.

In a rare lull, Kitty asks how I'm feeling about my last

day and how I'm feeling about going out and doing our music thing full time in Ireland. I know she wants to hear a lot of adjectives in the ballpark of excited, but I really don't know how to answer. Is it just too much to think about? Has the reality not sunk in yet? Or is it just that it's more natural than anything else, just the next thing I'm doing and I'm thinking why not? Of course, there's also a hell of a lot of uncertainty. The true reality is that all we're doing is giving ourselves a chance. We don't yet have any real prospects of making this thing work financially beyond belief, work ethic and hopefully a little talent and hard won and hard practised ability. But I don't want to say any of those things either. I mumble something a little underwhelming while still thinking how to answer the question, then duty literally calls both of us as things kick off again. Saved by the kitchen bell.

But this has got me thinking. I really do not know how to feel about any of this. The thing is, it really does feel natural, which is just the most unnatural thing I can think of, and it didn't quite feel right to say that out loud. So Kitty, if you're reading this, there's your answer.

The place is still busy when I finish at 5pm so there are no big goodbyes. I just finish the last thing I was doing and I'm out the door. Back home and I talk to Maja about my inner reaction to being asked about all this. She says she feels exactly the same - doesn't know how to feel, and also that that natural feeling is the most surreal thing of all.

All I want to do after this frantic last day at the bar is

to flop on the bed but there's no time for that. Instead, we're up and out again straight away. Off to Per's for a Filipino barbecue, and where he will meet Maja for the first time.

We arrive and are joyfully greeted by him and his family, and then joyfully taken out to the back garden to join in with the generally eating and drinking thing, the centrepiece being a spectacular spread of fish, shellfish and squid. While we're taking all this in and everyone's getting to know Maja, Per says we can stay in the caravan in the garden tonight if we want. Brilliant. That's made that simple. And in this warm environment as I sit, drink in hand, for the first time I'm finally able to take in the fact that barworld really has ended for me. Who knows what may yet transpire, but for now, I really am done with it and facing a new future with Maja somewhere in Ireland.

The caravan we're to spend the night in is pretty much as big as a conventional caravan can be, and has been converted into a wonderful entertaining space complete with Per's signature karaoke system. And in the front is a large double bedroom where we will sleep.

As festivities die down in the main garden, the three of us retire here for beer, whiskey and karaoke until Per leaves us to it deep in the early hours.

Maja:

I love asian food, and a homemade Filipino spread like this is about as good as you can get. The food is flavourful and made with love. Absolutely astonishing. Delicious. I've never had this type of food before. Everything is fresh, the shellfish still smelling of the sea. I can taste the sea in every bite. This is by far the best meal I've had in a long time. And in great company.

Day 65
Sunday April 25

Mark:

We don't emerge from the caravan until 1pm.

As soon as we do, we're presented with an amazing Filipino breakfast of pork, veg and noodles and take it in the garden in the April sun while we talk about our plans that we're about to get onto tackling today. We say goodbye to Per and our hosts in mid afternoon and, on the bus, we're online to look at cars. We find a great looking one being advertised in the West End, which is what the main central part of London is known as. Cool. We start a text conversation with the seller and all's going well and we're starting to make plans to go, have a look and maybe pick it up. All that's left is to ask him exactly where he is. Just outside Bainbridge comes the answer. That's strange in itself because, once in the West End, you never refer to yourself as being just outside somewhere. Intrigued, I look it up. Bainbridge. Glasgow. It's in the west end of Glasgow. Over 400 miles away. I get back to the guy to tell him of the misunderstanding. I think, even from that distance, we can almost hear each other laughing as we sign off and wish the other well.

Once we're settled back home, for the first time we begin to look at houses in Ireland to see what's available and what kind of budget we could be looking at. As you know, we're looking at countryside Ireland. Oh, and that Donegal place Ricky told us about? Yeah. It's been sold. Oh well. We knew it was only a possible fall-back, most likely tenuous and temporary at best, and that we would have to get on this anyway. So let's get on it.

The first one that really looks viable is 20 minutes outside the town of Ennis, standing almost on its own. A three bedroom house for €470 a month in Frure, Lisseycassey. Which is around £410 at the time of writing. You couldn't even get a room for that in Ktown, no matter how small. To recap, the tiny, just-about-fits-us-both room we're currently in costs £490 a month - €570 - and pre Covid it was £550, putting it at around €640. The house we're looking at is slap bang in the middle of nowhere but by now we've decided that if someone offered us an affordable and viable house in Ireland we'd take it without asking where it was.

So if we think of our house as being in the ballpark of €5-600 a month, and budget around €2500 for a car, the medical trial alone that we're thinking of doing would cover a house for six months, a car, and leave around three months living expenses. And that's before we begin on the budget we were already looking at. This plan really is starting to come together and to look realistic.

It's now that I have a sudden realisation. 'Maja, you know we're talking about songwriting yeah?' 'Yeah.' 'Well, I might just have a whole bunch of songs sitting on a computer under the bed downstairs. The computer's broken, but the hard drive might just be retrievable.' Maja sits up with a start. 'And you're only mentioning this to me now?' 'Er, yeah.' She laughs in disbelief and says, 'OK. First thing tomorrow, we're going into town and seeing if we can get that sorted out.' If we could, that really would give us a hyperboost. I have no idea how many songs are on there but it's a lot. We could use them whole, we could adapt them, we could take lyrics from them, we could use the musical ideas with lyrics we've written since we've been together. And that's a lot of lyrics. Incidentally, this is the computer that I actually discovered was broken while chatting to Maja one time. She asked me if I could give her some files, probably for my bass website that she was building, and I said they were on my other computer, so give me a moment while I turn it on. That was the moment I discovered it wouldn't turn on, and it hasn't since.

Maja:
I can't believe you have songs that you've just let go to waste by keeping them on a computer so old it breaks. I mean, a usb stick isn't even expensive and would definitely do the job in keeping a little backup.

I make a playful frown and tap Mark on his shoulder with my hand. 'Bad! Bad boy!' I say very playfully. 'Bad boy let his songs rot away on an old computer'. I tap him again as I try to keep a stern face but end up laughing so hard I have to bend over. 'Tomorrow we'll go into town and try to recover the files'.

Day 66
Monday April 26

Maja:

Mid morning we travel down to London town to visit a little computer shop I found good reviews for online. I hand over the broken computer and ask if they think they'll be able to recover all the files on the hard drive. They say they'll have a go and quote me a price for the service. I also have to buy a harddrive for them to put it all on should it be recoverable. All very fine and as expected. Now we just have to hope that they are able to salvage anything. After exiting the store we find ourselves in the middle of Oxford street without any other plans for the day. That means I can now go have a look at Primark. It's a huge store and almost completely empty of people. I get to have it almost entirely to myself and I browse through the clothes enjoying the eerily quiet environment. As I fully enjoy budget shopping without the stress, I realise there's no way this four storey superstore would ever normally be as quiet as it is today.

Day 68
Wednesday April 28

A call to the computer shop and we discover that the guys have been able to rescue the computer files. They're still in the process of it though, so we won't be able to pick them up until tomorrow. That's absolutely fine. And wonderful news.

Day 69
Thursday April 29

Today we can pick up the rescued disc containing the songs. This will be a fun project to get on and listen to when we get back.

Before heading out, we receive a call from the hospital to tell us we've been confirmed for screening for the trial. This is where they check to see if you're healthy enough. We're seeing that as a formality so while we're out we go shopping for toiletries and other supplies to see us through the two weeks of the trial.

Day 70
Friday April 30

Mark:

The hospital thing for the trial screening is a bit of a trek, being in the middle of industrial far north London, up past Wembley stadium and a little way off any bus routes, but I've done this many times before and so am familiar with how to get there; as well as having come here for the two previous trials, and the screening processes, both trials also included a number of follow-up visits after completion of the actual in-patient part. You don't get paid until you've completed all follow-up visits, and one of my trials had 10 of the things. The beauty of this new trial is that there is only one follow-up visit, so it's two weeks and a bit, then one follow-up a week or so later, then all done. Money in your bank a week or two after that.

We get there and meet our friendly contact Hannah who is delighted to see we've made it, then it's onto the formalities of the checks. For a start, by definition, I've already been through this process twice, and Maja's been able to answer yes to all the questions. They just have to confirm it all scientifically then we're on our way. They split us up into two rooms and we go through the tests. Heart rate, blood pressure, blood samples and a bunch of other stuff. Then I'm told Maja's all done but that I have to wait a while. I wait. A long while. As does Maja. After about half an hour I'm told I'm allowed to go and visit her and let her know I have some kind of hold up. What it is, we have no idea. So I go back and wait in my little medical booth. I'm a little alarmed when a doctor, different to the one who's been checking me out, comes in and she looks a little serious. She informs me they've found some kind of heart defect in my results and I won't be able to take part in the trial. What now? She pulls out the charts and goes through them with me. Apparently some electrical charge, or period between electrical charges in my heart are too close together. She says that in some people, this can actually be part of their normal heart function and nothing to worry about, but if it's a new development it could be an issue. Something like that. She says she suspects it is part of my normal make-up but they can't be entirely sure and, until they are, I can't proceed any further. That's a bit of a balls. This puts a stop to the whole thing because we've already decided it's both of us or neither of us. They show us some other trials we could do if we miss out on this one, but we explain that we're kinda on a deadline here as we're moving to Ireland soon. Also, none of the others coming up pay anything like this one, and they're also spread out over a much longer time frame with their follow-up schedules, which would put our plans off even more. No. This is the only one that suits. We talk about this on the way home and while there is the possibility that we could also wait for the next consort group of this particular trial as it moves to its next stage, that's simply too far off for us to wait around for so that doesn't work either.

Maja:

I passed the weight check, I've done the health screening, had my reflexes checked, and I am now lying on a bed connected to all kinds of wires to check my heart rate. I am supposed to lie down calmly so they can get accurate readings. Everything seems fine until all of a sudden Mark barges in with a nurse. We can leave now. I'm not eligible so there's no point in you continuing the testing. You can literally see my heartrate suddenly rise in shock on the monitor.

I'm surprised. Suddenly the nurse is helping to disconnect me while explaining that I can still do the trial as she tries to persuade us to keep me on. Sorry, but it's an all or nothing kinda deal. We decided that before we came in, we explain as we pack up and leave the hospital. I guess we're moving to Ireland early.

Mark:

Bars and restaurants are of course open again and I'm no longer working in one, so we have our evenings clear again now. With that we head out on what we realise is going to be our first actual date. We're going to Rosella's, an Italian restaurant right across the road, run by my good friend Luca. Cheers.

If you ever find yourself in London, or in the vicinity of Kentish Town in general and Italian's even remotely your thing, pop in. It really is among the very best in north London. And if you're lucky enough to meet Luca as well, please tell him Mark and Maja sent you.

Now, at the end of this entry, I'm going to say all is good with the heart/electrical anomaly thing. I don't think it would be appropriate to treat such a potentially serious situation as cliffhanger material so I'll just say here that over the next few days I do get it checked out and it comes back that this is indeed normal for me, so not something to worry about. However, totally understandably, after a few back and forth emails, the hospital says that, with apologies, although they were happy to take me before, they've decided they still can't take me on this one as the side effects of the drug to be trialled are unknown and they are reluctant to take on someone with any kind of discrepancy like this. Fair enough and nothing to be done. But that is a massive chunk of money we're having to say goodbye to.

Day 71
Saturday May 1

Mark:

I've known this for a while but it only really hits me today when I get up sometime before 6am already itching to write. As I start to get down to it, I suddenly realise I potentially have the best job in the world and am setting out to do everything I ever wanted to do. Well really, I'm already doing it and am doing it right now. When I was a journalist, my main strength, the thing I loved doing most and the thing I was quite fortunate to do a fair amount of, was what I called experience writing. That is to go out, experience something and write about it. Beyond and above that, my biggest thing is music. But then, as this whole Diary thing attests, I love to take my musical inspired events and write about them. Today, to fill in a few details from the beginning that I didn't realise at the time were important, I'm suddenly looking back over what has and is turning out to be the best experience of my life and I'm getting to relive it all again as I write about it. I'm almost jumping about in the kitchen too much to actually be able to sit down and put words on the page. Excuse me. It's time to get up and go have another jump.

Maja:

It fills me with joy to see Mark's joy. Excuse me. It's time to go join him in the jumps.

Day 72
Sunday May 2

Mark:

Wow. Just wow. Today for the first time we have a look at what the rescued hard drive has to give to us. I had an idea of what was there, but the sheer scope is taking even me by surprise. And Maja is ready to do all kinds of bad things to me for almost letting this just slip away. I'd told her I might just have a few songs lying about. What we discover here is something approaching a hundred songs and too many sets of lyrics to count. But then as we look further into it, there's more. Files within files within files, each one giving up more songs, or more ideas. Choruses, concepts, more ideas, sketches of songs. One file is an actual book I'd kinda forgotten I'd written, or at least forgotten I still had. This is a book of poetry, each piece inspired by a particular painting of a notable artist. The idea was to have it published as what he called a coffee table book. Big, glossy, fully colour and probably quite expensive. Each spread was to have a poem on one page, probably the left page, and the corresponding painting on the other. He and I managed to get a book deal for this thing but then the publisher went under. Both me and the artist moved onto other projects while we were waiting for this to get picked up by someone else and the whole idea of it just disappeared. Well now we have it as raw material for songwriting and it's just one piece of treasure among all that we've unearthed in this huge and unexpected cave.

We get down to listening and identify at least 16 songs that could be goers, but by the time we even make it there, there's still so much more to go through. While Maja is delighted with it, the happier she gets with the discovery, the less happy she gets with me that the whole thing came so close to being simply forgotten about and lost. Oh no. She is not happy about that at all.

Maja:

We put the recovered songs in a playlist and listen through the speaker, both of us sitting on the bed that fills the whole room across, wall to wall. As I lean back on a pillow against one of the walls, I gaze at the beautiful spring tree that was filled with blossom until just a couple of days ago. How fast time goes, I think to myself, pondering over the fallen flower petals as I get myself ready to listen to the playlist. Here goes. Mark's forgotten collection of songs that we are now free to use for ourselves. I wonder what is in here.

Mark:

I've got to say that I'm very much wondering the same. I'm aware of what I consider a few highlights or whatever you might call them, but I'm also aware that there's so much I'm no longer aware of.

Maja:

I listen to the songs, and am really feeling some of them. There's some great songs or song concepts in here. Many are naked. Just guitar and Mark's often questionable vocals with zero production added. And there hardly any other instruments or extra musical parts. But the melodies are catchy. They are masterpieces forgotten to the world. Or never even introduced to the world.

I am furious. 'Mark! How could you have been so stupid to let these rot?' I rightfully shout at him. He looks embarrassedly down at his feet. Thinking back at this, I think he was secretly happy to be scolded about it.

Day 74
Tuesday May 4

Maja:

Just a wonderful wander around central London today and back by 8pm, going through the old songs again. Beer, chill, and a wonderful steak dinner at 11pm. And yes, I love hearing these songs, time and time again.

Day 75
Wednesday May 5

Maja:

Finally it feels like my broken ankle is starting to heal. I'm trying it out in the hallway holding the bannister like a ballerina supporting herself on the barre preparing herself for a new pirouette. I'm putting weight on it, yes, that seems fine. Then I carefully try to move it left and right. Ouch, I can't move it too well, but. I seem to be able to put proper weight on it. And I can manage a slight sideways movement without too much pain. Yes. I think I'll be able to do this. That big, long, drive to Ireland and to wherever we might end up. Yes. I think I'll be able to do this.

Mark:

Maja says she's feeling good about her healing broken ankle and it seems we're starting to look at the final strait in London, or at least we think we can start to think about the next step. We then have a hit of reality with something we haven't mentioned in here up to now. Probably because so much else has been going on, not least the whole ankle thing. But Maja now faces up to the wrist surgery she needs on the ganglion that's been bothering her for so long. Physio hasn't been helping, it's only getting more painful, and surgery in Ireland won't be an option. Not without paying for it. Which won't be an option. Like so many other things we've had to deal with since February, we have no idea how this circle is going to be squared.

Day 78
Saturday May 8

Mark:

This house searching isn't exactly going as we expected either. We've called and emailed about quite a few houses all over the country. Because we're not there and can't see the places or meet the landlords, we've been offering a deposit and two to three months' rent straight up to take a place sight unseen. No dice. I even have a phone call or two where people are downright confrontational when I try to up the offer to three, then four months. One of them responds saying, 'You won't be getting round me like that now,' like this is some kind of adversarial competition between me and him. I don't even reply, instead hanging up immediately when he says that. I then turn to Maja saying, 'I don't care. I will not deal with a guy like that. No way is someone like that going to be our landlord.' I do manage to get one person to give me some time beyond business and he explains to me that demand for houses in Ireland is far outstripping availability, especially in the countryside areas which is where we're looking. He wishes us luck but warns me that there are so many people in the running for every rental that it's tough enough if you're there. To try to do this remotely like we are? He doesn't hesitate. Impossible. Add that to the impossible list. With that, we have a little talk before the next call and decide to up our game. I make the call and offer a deposit and six months rent right now. Even then they refuse, and say they would have to meet us first. Oh dear. We really thought we could do a deal on the phone, get a house sorted, then move there as soon as we were ready. But no. This really isn't going to be as straightforward as we thought.

Day 79
Sunday May 9

Mark:

A wonderful late Sunday morning on Hampstead Heath,

and for the first time I actually stop and watch a cricket match. On walks around when I've seen games happening, I have sometimes stopped and watched from the path for a little while. But this is the first time I've ever come in and really taken in a game. Maja's transfixed by this mad looking game played by men all in white. We've just bought ice creams and it seems just too perfect to be able to enjoy them in the sun while taking in this perfect scene of Sundayness. The ground is just off the main walking path a little beyond our entrance to the heath. It's also behind a line of trees so this enormous playing area is almost completely concealed from the main thoroughfare. We find a free spot on the grass next to the boundary and settle down in the sun as gentle battle commences in front of us. As for telling Maja the rules, I just answer questions as they come up from the action in front of us. How do they score? The two men in the middle run from that end to the other end, and back again if they can, and again if they really think they can. Why aren't they running now? Because he hit the ball all the way off the field so that automatically gives them a score of four. If he manages that without the ball bouncing he scores six. And so on. As when introducing anyone to cricket, it is fun when I tell her there's a version of this sport that can go on for five days. This little fact almost always solicits an incomprehensive look of wonderment. A truly wonderfully lazy activity for a Sunday. We stay for about an hour and a half until Maja's decided she's seen this thing now and we carry on with our walk.

Maja:

Cricket. Oh Cricket. The sport known to me as nothing more than the crazy sport Englishmen play. Finally I get to see what it is all about. I sit down on the grass, ice cream in hand, looking at all the players. And I point with my whole arm, smiling from ear to ear asking all the same questions a toddler would ask. 'Mark! Why are they dressed in white? Mark! Why are they over there? Mark! What is that stick? Mark! Mark! He is throwing a ball!!! Did you see that?!? Mark! He hit the ball with his bat?! What does that mean? Why are they hitting the ball? Mark! There's a new player coming in to hit the ball, why? Mark! Mark! .. Mark!'

And yes, I am enjoying being childish asking all these questions. But I am also genuinely fascinated by the sport and am having a great time seeing it like this, sitting in the sun on the spring grass. Feeling myself overjoyed with love and excitement.

Mark:

Back home and we resume our attempt to find a new one. In another country. And in the country. We're thinking about budget and the fact that we really do need a house, not an apartment but a house. And a detached one at that. There's no way our budget would allow for one in a city centre; most of the ones we've called about weren't even near any towns. That's fine. We're thinking of a small, out of the way place. Maybe with at least one or two local shops so that we don't have to drive everytime we need a pint of milk. You get the idea. We're not expecting to be anywhere near anything that might resemble even a small town. Something with a near enough convenience store would be just fine.

We've found a place we really like in Mayo on the north western coast. It's a big three bedroom place, but because of its isolated location, it is well within our budget. Although we've not had much luck with progress, we really can't believe the sizes of the places we might end up living in, for how little they cost. I guess that's what happens when you move from central London to, well, almost anywhere. I make the call, have a chat with the landlady, and she says, 'Yes, we can hold it for you.' Wow. Great. Finally. A breakthrough. Before I can continue with the next part of the discussion/ negotiation, she adds, 'But if someone comes in the meantime we may have to let them have it.' What? That's not holding it. What if we offer to pay right now? 'Why would you want to do that?' she asks. What do you care? I think. You're being offered money right now to give us the place. Six months up front. If anything, this only makes her more suspicious. 'And you're in London now?' Yes. 'And you want to take it and pay for it now?' Yes. 'And what would you be doing that for? Sure you'd have to see the place first.' Oh here we go again. It's like she's trying to persuade us not to give her any money. Surely that's our decision. I patiently explain that this would mean that we had a place to go to, so we could leave whenever we were ready and just move in comfortably. 'But in the meantime you'd be paying rent for a place you weren't living in?' Yes. 'What would you be doing that for now?' Oh, I can't get through here. 'We'd have to meet you first, you know,' she says. Oh dear. This really isn't going anywhere. 'But we're in England and are trying to secure a place in Ireland so that we can move there.' 'Well maybe you could come and see it before you decide,' she says. 'There are a lot of people interested. It isn't only you.' What happened to the, 'yes we'll hold it for you,' thing? We've really moved a long way from that haven't we? This just isn't working. She then says she's looking after it for her daughter. So negotiations are going on at a remove here. Never a good way to go. I feel we're in the middle of a circular conversation so I thank her for her time, say that we may be in touch again and we hang up.

We realise this just isn't going to happen. We're just going to have to go. People want to do the whole face to face thing rather than do a let on the phone. Fair enough. I do get that. So that's what we decide to do. Forget about all this doing it from here stuff. Drive there and just turn up. Get ourselves in situ and take it from there. I call the lady back, say that OK, we'll come and meet. She agrees that if we get there and meet her, we might be able to do something.

This is our first solid lead, but given her total refusal to commit, we accept there's a possibility the house may no longer be available when we arrive. If that's the case, we decide we'll simply make a plan and get something else. What that plan could be we have no idea, but surely we'll be able to come up with something.

So this is it. We're going to start tomorrow by beginning the search for a car. Once we have that, it's just a case of loading it up and leaving. Next stop, our possible house in Ireland. Mayo?

Casting its shadow over all this is Maja's upcoming but yet to be booked surgery. We've been toying with the idea of her going to Sweden for it, then coming back here, then we go to Ireland. We really don't like the sound of that, so we come up with this wonderful plan. She books the surgery for something like in three or four weeks. In that time, we move to Ireland - to a house we don't have yet - get settled, then we both go to Sweden for Maja's surgery in the knowledge that we have the place in Ireland to come back to. If, if, if we can get a car tomorrow, we think we can make the move this Tuesday. It's Sunday now.

Maja:

It is all feeling quite hopeless. I've been looking for place after place in Ireland, but no one wants to commit to anything. I guess we just have to go. Go there, cash in hand, see a place and say, 'We'll take it!' and move in there and then. That seems to be the only way to get a place to live in Ireland. So I guess we just have to do it.

And I really need to get to Sweden to do the wrist surgery and to finish up the business with my divorce and my flat. Also I've never had surgery before, and I wouldn't like to try it during the best of times. Ugh, I really don't want to go and do all of this, but I need to. I just need to.

And if something goes wrong along the way, I don't know what I'll do about it. Cry. Buy a tent and live in that until we get a place sorted. I mean there's no hotels because of covid, so what are the options really? We just have to do this.

I am terrified.

Mark

Plan made, if you can call it that, we go out to The Camden Head in Islington where we hang out with Alex and his friend, Raul. We're outside in the beer garden and we also chat with the bar staff as they pass by when they get a moment or two. Prominent among them are Tom and Molly. I've known Tom for years, mainly from Kristoff's bar The White Hart, but also from The Marquis. And Molly we met at that party here a few weeks ago. When they're finished, they come and join us. We then tell everyone our wonderful, foolproof plan. We're moving to Ireland. On Tuesday. In a car we don't have to a house we don't have on a ferry we haven't booked. They all fall about in hysterics and the sheer audacity and adventure of it. Brilliant, they agree. Right? What could possibly go wrong?

Day 80
Monday May 10

Mark:

I'm up at 6am today. No idea why, just felt like it. So there I am at the kitchen table looking at what cars are on the market. Cris, who leaves for work early every morning, comes down and is surprised to see me already there as he prepares to have breakfast. 'What are you doing up this early?' he asks. 'Looking at what cars we could buy,' I reply. 'You want to buy a car?' He sounds shocked although I remind him, 'Yeah, we're hoping to move to Ireland tomorrow.' He kind of knew this, but is a bit shocked to hear it put into actual words. 'I've been thinking of selling my car,' he says. Now it's my turn to be shocked. 'Would you be interested?' Hell yes. I know his car very well. Me and Maja were both in it when we went on that trip to Crystal Palace a few weeks ago. And I've been in it with Cris many other times. It's huge. A Mazda Sport 5. A seven seater in which all the back seats can be laid totally flat. Essentially a minivan and way bigger than anything we thought would be within reach. I'm almost scared to ask how much and can't believe it when he tells me. Well within budget. Ridiculously within budget. Oh wow. I'll have to check with Maja of course, but yes. Just yes. This is the car we decided we couldn't ask to use to move all our stuff out of Kylie's to here. Now we could be looking at owning it and then using it to move everything we have from here to Ireland. In a bit of a state of disbelief, I go outside just to have a look at it again from a totally different perspective. This could be ours. Really ours. While I'm out there I see Luca, who's also having an early start preparing his restaurant for the day. He comes and says hello and we have a chat about the car and our imminent move to Ireland. 'Oh,' he says. 'So there's a room coming up in your house?' Yep. One of the small upstairs ones. Luca knows the house. He's taken rooms in it before for workers at his restaurant. He says he's now looking for a room again for a returning worker. A guy called Mike who we know well. He's lived with us before, was a great housemate and friend, and is apparently now thinking of coming back to work in the restaurant again. And just as Luca is thinking where he could house him, along comes a room in the very same house. This would work out very well for us; we've been very uncertain about timeframes so haven't given any notice to the landlord here, so we're not going to be leaving with the requisite month's notice. This means the rent really should be paid for this coming month even though we won't be there. We have every intention of honouring this, but if we're able to replace ourselves in the room almost immediately, this empty expense disappears. It's not even 7am and it looks like I've solved two of our big issues - a car we can afford which is big enough to move in, and a new tenant to take over from us which would save us from having to pay next month's rent.

I go back inside and ask Cris if I can borrow the car

key for a few moments. No problem. With that, I go upstairs and into the room where Maja is sleeping. I gently wake her up and wave the key and fob in her face. She shakes the blurriness from her eyes and a car key comes into focus. 'What the hell is that?' she asks. 'That's not a car key?' 'Yep, but not any car key. This is Cris' car key. He's said we can have it for a ridiculous price.' Maja shoots up in disbelief and takes the key in her hand, regarding it in wonder like a precious, fragile treasure. She looks up at me again in something like shock. 'And there's more,' I say. 'Looks like we've got the room sorted as well.'

She says I should go downstairs right now and confirm the sale of the car with Cris. With that I say, 'We've started the move haven't we?'

'Yes.'

Maja:

I can't believe the key that's in my hand. It's heavy and shiny. I stare at it in amazement, feeling the weight of what it really means. This is going to be our little home for the time being. This is going to take us to where we don't know. We're going to lose everything we have right now, and step into the unknown at any second now. And this will be our little stable point that will be with us doing that journey.

I let my fingers close around the key, and I close my eyes. This is it now. This is it. I just need to make a phone call to get that surgery booked.

Mark:

Maja makes the call as soon as she can and the appointment gets booked for June 3. Three weeks and three days from today. This means that we now have to be in Sweden a few days before that, so three weeks from today. Which means we definitely have to have a house in Ireland sorted by then and already be moved in so that we can book a return flight to Sweden from Ireland. Oh this would normally be a huge ask, and it really is a huge ask, but mentally, and in terms of actual preparation and general focus and alertness, we are already very much on it.

There's a formality for the car before it can be sold, which is that Cris has to take it for an MOT. He says he can organise this for tomorrow, adding, 'My worst fear is that I sell you this car without checking and it breaks down on you on the motorway. No way. No way. My reputation is to do things in the right way and of course I want to do that for you.' This all means that we probably won't be able to leave until Wednesday now, but yes, he's obviously right. So now we almost have a car, which means we can make a solid(ish) plan to leave. Just to remind you, it is now Monday. Have I mentioned we still don't have a house to move to?

Day 81
Tuesday May 11

Mark:

Insurance. Damn. I'd totally forgotten about the need to insure a car before you can do anything with it. With things developing until close of office hours yesterday, this morning is the first chance we get to have a look at this. Maja begins the process and all of a sudden a few issues arise. Before long it starts to look quite unrealistic to think we could be leaving tomorrow.

Maja:

Why does everything have to be so complicated? All the time. I can't solve one problem without the next one emerging, can I? We really need me to buy this car. That goes without saying, so that means I also need to get insurance. Which needs to be valid in the EU as well the UK. I contact a lot of companies and start to feel devastated about all the complexities, mainly because of Brexit. After a couple of hours of reading fine print, I finally find a company that'll work. Expensive, but they can make everything happen. The biggest plus for this company is that I discover they can help with getting a green card, a part of the process we hadn't been aware of at all when we first started. A green card in this context is proof that the car is insured internationally, so you need to have one if you want to cross any international borders.

All so far so good, but then a new problem arises when I am told it will take three days to be issued. You see what I mean? It just doesn't stop.

We don't have three days. Maybe I can pay a little more to get it issued on some kind of fast track? I don't know. I just have to make a decision. And apparently it can't be fast tracked. You just have to wait.

My decision is that I will not worry about it.

It might solve itself. Hopefully. We have about one and a half days for that to happen before we reach Ireland, so it should be OK. Probably not, but we'll have to cross that bridge when we come to it.

Mark:

It's around now that I go into total denial of all possibilities of failure or setback and get on with the business of packing. It's a bit of a fraught day as Maja goes through the contortions of trying to secure insurance while Cris is off having the car checked out. Somehow, semi miraculously really, by 5pm, the MOT and insurance stars have aligned and we have a car ready to go and legal for Maja to drive in Ireland. We're not covered in the UK for any pickup or roadside assistance, but we'll only have it in the UK for the drive to Liverpool for the ferry to Ireland, so what's the point?

With all that sorted, we're truly on it now as Maja goes ahead and books the ferry from Liverpool to Belfast for

10pm tomorrow. She says she's going to book a cabin so that we'll at least be able to have a shower on the boat. Afterall, once we're into unknown territory in Ireland there's no telling when we'll be able to have a shower again. Or a comfortable bed. We really are throwing ourselves out to the wind here.

Now I have to get on with trying to make sure that this doesn't go as wild and feral as it could. I call the people with the house in Mayo to tell them we'll be there Thursday morning. So with that commitment to being there, could they please hold it for us now? I speak to the owner's father this time who tells me it's gone. Balls. So now we really are going to Ireland with nowhere even remotely possible to live and absolutely no destination. We think about getting a tent and just camping where we can, and looking at houses that way. We discuss not getting a house at all this side of Sweden and just camping until then, and then resuming the search when we get back. We really don't know. This is starting to look like a real adventure with so many unknowns as we prepare to step into it.

Cris used his car for his construction company and it's a bit of a state, so it needs a proper clean. No problem, we told him we'd sort that. But before we do, Maja insists I call the Mayo house people again, this time trying to speak to the lady who seems to know a bit more about what's going on. Maja suspects the husband just told me it was gone out of assumption. And yep. She was right. I speak to the lady again who says it is still available but that a lot of people are seeing it, but yeah, if we can get there on Thursday we can throw our hats in. So much for her initial claim of holding it. This really is starting to feel like a lottery.

We did have a kind airy dreamy delusional not-really-thought-it-through thought of arriving in Ireland on Thursday and then doing nothing but sleeping for two days. But the more likely reality is we'll arrive on Thursday morning, rush to see the house sometime early afternoon, then have to wait a few days to see if we have it. In the meantime we have no idea what we're going to do. Buy a tent on the way maybe and find somewhere to pitch it? Or a B&B. Oh. Did I mention? Ireland's still in Covid induced semi lockdown mode so no hope of getting a B&B there. Probably a tent somewhere then. Or, if the initial house attempt isn't successful, we could drive back to Northern Ireland, book into some kind of cheap hotel there and use that as a base from which to go into Ireland during the days to look at places that we've secured a viewing for. Oh, there's seat of the pants, and there's…this. As you can see, we're making it all up as we go and we really have no idea. Absolutely none at all. And the clock's ticking. Our ferry to nowhere leaves in less than 24 hours.

Maja:

It's become a bit of a habit by now, but before bed I once more look through my phone looking for any good looking properties in Ireland in our budget. Oh, how about this one? I think to myself and send away our email template once again. It looks bad, dark and probably filled with mould. Oh well. I have nothing to lose by sending an email. I mean, we have nowhere to go as it looks right now anyway.

Day 82
Wednesday May 12

Mark:

Right. Moving day. Before we get onto that, incase it was so long ago we were writing about this that you've forgotten, we're moving to Ireland because it really is the only place in the world where me and Maja can legally live together. Her visa for the UK is only valid for six months - doesn't have to be six months all in one go, but it is valid for only six months. Bottom line and thanks to Brexit, she can't legally settle here. Again thanks to Brexit, I can't go and settle anywhere else in Europe either. We examined other countries around the world and discovered a lot of barriers everywhere we looked, this time thanks to Covid. This is May 2021 and Covid restrictions are still in place in varying degrees all over the world. But travel and relocating is still OK between the UK and the Republic of Ireland, and citizens of both are allowed to live in each others' countries. And of course, citizens of Europe are allowed to live in the Republic of Ireland. Because it's Europe. So Maja can live there. So can I. Problem solved.

As long as we can get ourselves around all the other problems of getting there from London. Including finding a house, which we still haven't managed to do.

Here we go.

6:45am: We wake and see we have an email from an agent we've contacted who is up for the six month rent up front thing. Finally, someone has said yes. But we really don't like the look of the house he's proposing for us. After discussing this, Maja tells me that, on a whim, she sent an email about a house she saw and is only mentioning to me now. No problem. She shows me the pictures and it really doesn't look good. She actually apologises for having contacted about such a dingy looking place. But really, no problem. Making the contact doesn't hurt. We dismiss it and think no more of it until I decide to check out the location. It's bang in the middle of the country. Maybe we should just remain open on this. Later we get an email from a guy called Adrian replying to Maja's email. He seems quite downbeat and says the location isn't good at all for two musicians thinking of moving to Ireland from London. He suggests we try somewhere like Galway instead. Well, thanks for the heads up. We're really not thinking that hard about this place anyway. But there is still that thing that it's bang in the middle of the country.

7am: Maja and Cris have completed the paperwork. We now have a car and it is enormous. While they're doing that, I'm checking out new houses that have popped up. I email them now and will follow them up later.

Maja:

All the paperwork is finally done, and the car is ours! Or mine, legally. The sense of relief of owning something this significant is huge. Somewhere along my spine I start to feel a little sliver of stress releasing, telling me repeatedly 'at least you have the car'. That is good. But the short relief keeps on getting eaten up by fear of the unknown.

Mark:

9am: The proof of insurance needs to be printed before we leave. I go over to the restaurant to ask Luca if I can use his office to print it. No problem, he says. We get on that straight away.

9.30am: I'm walking across the carpark back to our house when I see a traffic warden three cars away from the car that is now our responsibility. And it has no permit. Cris would sometimes chance his arm with parking it here, but more often than not would keep it somewhere else. Today, because we had to clean it yesterday, it is not at that somewhere else.

I run into the house and into our room. After completing the paperwork, Maja went back to bed and is now fast asleep. I wake her up without hesitation. 'You need to get up right now,' I say. 'A traffic warden is about to ticket the car. We rush out, Maja wearing slippers because they were faster to put on than shoes. The traffic warden is inspecting the car next to ours as we jump in and drive off. Maja's first drive of the car and it's a getaway drive.

Me: 'Are we ever going to have something happen that isn't dramatic?'

Maja: 'No.'

But the getaway isn't at all smooth. She's never driven a car this big before, and when she searches for the biting point in the clutch to go to first gear, the revs suddenly go mad and the car makes a huge noise. But she gathers herself, finds the right balance and we ease out of the parking spot and away from the inquisitive warden who's now standing right next to us. Kind of like the Millennium Falcon escaping being eaten by the giant space monster at the last second but a bit slower.

Out in the small streets and we just can't believe the sheer dimensions of this thing. It seems to be far too big for the roads we're driving on right now. Maja drives it a few streets away from the house and then we stop and take in exactly what we have here. We can even sleep in it, and we do exactly that for a 15 or so minute nap. Wow. We have this as a sleeping option now. But at the same time as we realise that, we remember it will also have all our stuff in it when we get to Ireland, so maybe not the accommodation fix it appears to be.

Maja:

This car is huge! I am used to driving a little Toyota, and this is anything but that. I've run straight from bed to the car in my jammies and slippers, turning the car on for the first time. As I watch the warden get closer and closer I try to get the car moving. It's like nothing I've ever driven before. It's almost impossible to find the biting point and the engine screams as I give it too much gas to make it move. It then suddenly moves with a jump which feels way too quick. My brain goes into some kind of panic concentration mode where I suddenly get hit with a million impressions all at once. The pavement is too close, adapt. How can we be that close to the big road already? Adapt. My mind screams as I hit the brakes. The car stops with an engine stop so I have to restart. I put the blinkers on, mount the curb then bump off it, then we're on the big road. Finally. That's safe enough. I drive to the nearest small road, turn off and find a parking space where I can finally stop. Car off and I take a deep breath. One more problem solved. Well done Maja.

But seriously. What's up with this clutch? Why is it so incredibly hard to drive this car slowly?

Mark:

11am: We get back and Maja does some more cleaning on the car while I get onto house calls. I won't detail them. It doesn't go well.

3pm: We've finished packing and the car is loaded to the roof. Damn, we had no idea that we actually needed something this big. We say our goodbyes and we're on the road and away. The move is officially on. We still have no final destination. All through the small, slow, winding streets of north London, Maja is learning the car and having trouble with the clutch. She assumes this is just because it's such a big car and so has a different make-up to the smaller cars she's used to.

Maja:

I really would have liked to have been be out a bit earlier than this, but practically speaking, we'll still make it. We just don't have time to drive leisurely or stop for a relaxed lunch while taking in the scenery. No. We're on the clock from the get go.

Mark:

5:30pm: On the motorway and we suddenly feel something bang under the car. We catch a glimpse of whatever it is as it bounces away and we think it's a shoe.

6pm: We have to follow a diversion away from the motorway for a little while which means slowing down and picking up speed at a few junctions and roundabouts. Which means Maja has to use the difficult clutch quite a lot. At a particularly tricky roundabout the rev counter suddenly goes crazy, the engine roars, and the car is filled with a horrible burning smell. Soon after this it starts to lose power. Fortunately we're soon back on the motorway and Maja is able to keep it going. Just. I can tell she's using all the concentration of a racing driver and is in hyper focus mode. We need to get this looked at. Now. So while she's doing that I'm trying to find a garage that we could possibly go to. But it's late. The only one I manage to get on the phone says they're closing soon so we won't be able to make it in time from where we are. He says all others will say the same thing. Thankyou very much. We're on our own.

Maja:

This is so hard. Mark is holding a phone with GPS that guides me where I'm going. And he says that I'm supposed to leave the motorway. All of a sudden we find ourselves approaching a huge roundabout. That's normally not an issue, but the car has just gotten increasingly harder to control for every mile I've been driving. I've just about been holding on on the motorway, and now as I come to the roundabout I have to change gears. Oh no, oh no, oh no. Come on. The engine roars again and I can't get the gear in. The cabin fills with a burning smell. It can't be true. I finally manage to get the gear in and we make it round the roundabout and onto motorway again. If I can just hold out a little longer, we can make it to the ferry, and then we can take the problems with the repairs later, when we're at the destination. Right?

I'm focusing with my whole might. Just two more hours. We'll be fine. We'll be fine.

Mark:

6.50pm: With the possibility of finding a mechanic gone, Maja declares that she's going to try to make a run all the way to the ferry which, if we can keep this speed up, is just under two hours away. With that she gives me a navigating job to do. Keep us on motorways. No junctions, no roundabouts. Nothing that could remotely necessitate a stop or even a slow down. As long as she can keep us moving with minimal use of the clutch we might just make it. She doesn't care how far I have to detour us if that's what it takes. Just keep us on uninterrupted fast roads. The plan is just to get this thing on the other side of the water and have it looked at then. The ferry leaves at 10pm and we have to be there for 9. By now I'm watching every mile of the GPS tick off and am watching every minute of the clock tick by. After an hour or so of this, Maja asks, 'Are you bored?' 'I wish I was,' I reply, and in the middle of this madly dramatic second by second drive we fall into hysterical laughter. I don't think I've ever been less bored by watching miles or minutes go by one at a time. Each time a minute ticks off, or a mile drops by one less, it feels like a little victory. I'm in hyper focus mode too. I'm starting to think that if we can just keep this up, one minute at a time, one mile at a time, we might just get there. Looking at Maja now, I realise I have never seen anyone operating at this level of focus. We have a horrible moment when we have to stop at a toll booth and the car absolutely crawls away, accelerating at a tortuously slow rate. Enough to have cars behind us beeping in frustration. Oh, they have no idea. And their angry horns do nothing to improve the dark mood in our little world right now. We get to some kind of speed, but it's clear things are very very weak. As we head round a downhill motorway bend we pick up some encouraging speed, but it's an illusion. If anything, it only increases the knowledge that we're doing little more than freewheeling.

8.30pm: We're 10 minutes away from the ferry. A little more than 10 miles away and we're starting to allow ourselves to believe we might just make it. But then all of a sudden the car just starts to slow down. No matter how much Maja pumps on the accelerator, nothing happens. We're going slower and slower. Soon the decrease starts to increase as Maja reluctantly pulls onto the hard shoulder. Down down goes the speed as though the brake is being applied. Then we stop. Maja looks at me in resignation, then a little hope as she charges the car again, gets some revs going and we start to pull away. But it's only a tease. We get a hundred metres or so, never managing more than walking pace, and then that's it. The car, which passed an MOT yesterday, really has gone. This is as far as we're going to get. It's dark, it's raining. We're on a lonely road. We're slowly accepting we're getting any ferry tonight but that's not even our biggest problem right now. We have no breakdown cover. We're totally alone, abandoned on the side of a road somewhere in the north west of England.

Maja:

The last half hour has been absolute agony. I've been, and continue to be, driving in the same gear with my foot pressed totally to the floor, pain shooting through my not quite mended bones, and we're just losing speed. Sixty miles an hour is now fifty, and then fourty only to be thirty. And then I have to put the warning lights on and go and drive on the side of the road. We're almost there now. Come on. Just a little more. Thirty turns to twenty and my heart drops even further. It's fifteen now, but we're almost there. Only a few miles to go to the ferry. Come on. Ten. Eight. This isn't much faster than a stroll. I don't want to look at Mark. Come on. You can do it. Five. Four. Three. Two. One. And then the car comes to a halt. Out of desperation I try again, turning the ignition to try to restart the car. Almost out of sheer will I manage to make it start and go a little further. But then it dies again and won't go any further. This is it. We've stopped now. Ten minutes from the ferry. It's raining. I don't know where I am. I have no one to call. I don't know what to do. I look at Mark.

Mark:

Maja looks at me with empty eyes. She's stunned, mentally exhausted, and almost emotionally broken. And lost. Both geographically and for any idea of what to do next. We've been together less than three months and have already been through quite a few crises. But this feels like by far the biggest. I saw an emergency phone a little way back and I'm going to walk to it and, I bet you're wondering this too, see what happens. We normally have pens and notebooks to hand all the time but we've somehow managed to neglect that on this drive. All I can find is a pencil and a single piece of paper, which is a till receipt from something or other, and frankly, I feel lucky to have found those. Unfortunately, the only thing the pathetically hopeful burst of walking pace driving has achieved is to take us further away from the roadside phone. Worse news comes as I open the door and a blast of cold rain is blown in on a harsh, icy wind, instantly destroying what has been a lovely and warm, if quite stressful, place until now. Moving day could not be further from fun right now. I jump out into the unforgiving weather and begin the dark, lonely walk back down the wrong direction on the motorway to the phone, wondering what's going to happen when I pick up and if I'll actually be able to talk to someone. I am, but it's not an encouraging conversation. The lady on the other end is sympathetic, but all she can do, she says, is give the numbers of some breakdown companies for me to call round myself. I don't really know what you were expecting, but I certainly wasn't expecting just this. Reluctantly, I retrieve the paper and pencil from my pocket and do my best to write down the five or six names and numbers she gives me. But the flimsy till paper is slowly going soggy while also blowing about carelessly as I try to write on it. With a small blunt pencil. As soon as I hang up, I get to work, calling the numbers as I walk back to the car, buffeted all the way by wind and rain. And it's a slightly stumbly walk as well because this patch of ground I'm on has not been cultivated for strolling on. It resembles some craggy, alien landscape complete with deep grooves and gashes you could break an ankle in. I go back and forth between a few breakdown companies, comparing prices and offers. This process of finding and comparing service providers can be challenging and frustrating enough when sat at a warm kitchen table with a laptop, pen and notebook and with a lovely hot cup of tea steaming away next to you. I can tell you that it's a little more challenging and frustrating right now. And I'm nowhere near a kettle.

I've spoken to almost every company on the list and am getting ready to make another call when my phone rings. It's a guy called Craig and he introduces himself as being from the RAC. It just so happens that I'd quite liked their offer compared to the others. What makes them the most attractive, apart from the name recognition, is that they offer the furthest towing distance from the scene. I have no idea where we have to get to, so the bigger margin for error we can have, the better. Having Craig on the phone also represents a bird in the hand as opposed to the other companies yet in the bush so I decide we're going with him. I also had the awareness to write down the serial number of the standing roadside phone I used, so Craig now knows exactly where we are. He also has a reassuring phone presence. He sounds decisive, professional and eager to get on with the job. Before he hangs up, he tells me that we are not to stay with the car. He must have a layout of the area in front of him because he seems to know that there's no crash barrier where the car is. It ends about 50 metres back towards the phone. He says we have to walk back to where that barrier begins and wait behind it. Will do. I feel as safe and confident in his hands as it's possible to feel in a situation like this. Totally independently, I take the decision to agree that all payments will be met and conditions agreed to. By the time I return to Maja in the car, I'm delighted to tell her we have the beginning of a solution, but not so delighted to tell her that she has to leave the warmth of the car.

This means walking back over that pitted moonscape which Maja, with her newly, well, barely healed ankle, is not happy about at all. Once we've reached the relative safety of the barrier, all we can do is wait in the dark, cold rain. In the time before Craig comes, we still somehow manage to have a few really big laughs, although I can't remember at what. But I think it's pretty cool that, even as we're going through this horribleness, we can have a laugh about it. In another attempt at positivity as our spirits start to drop again, I say, 'You just never know. Something might just happen out of this that wouldn't have happened without it.'

While we're waiting, we make the call to the ferry company to tell them what's happened and to book ourselves on the ferry for tomorrow night. They happily transfer us onto tomorrow's crossing with just a small admin charge, but unfortunately we no longer have a cabin. Not ideal but, given the circumstances, at least we're starting to get the dots joined again. However, as we're waiting here, one thing dawns on us. We told the guys in Mayo we'd be there tomorrow. Now we won't be and we know they're showing it to other people. Oh well, that house has really gone now.

The plan, as much as we can make it now, is to see if Craig can fix the car here, but we know he probably won't. We've missed the ferry anyway so that part is irrelevant. At best we're going to hope he can get us into a garage and they can fix it tomorrow. In the meantime, we'll be booking ourselves into a hotel somewhere in Liverpool tonight.

9.20pm: Craig arrives. As I suspected by dealing with him on the phone he's professional, friendly and quite brilliant really. He can't tow the car as it's too heavily loaded, so he says he'll winch it onto the back of his truck. Only then is he going to summon us to come and join him in the front cab. He confirms that the callout includes a lift within a 50 mile radius. He's already called a garage and says we're going to drive there, leave the car there, then he's going to drive us to whatever hotel we're able to book ourselves into.

9.30pm: While Craig is sorting out the car at the side of the road and we know we're rescued, I call Cris and tell him what's happened. He point blank refuses to believe this isn't a wind up, even when I send him a picture of Craig with the car against the flashing blue lights. It's only our increasingly desperate tone that finally convinces him, at which point he has something of an emotional breakdown and can't say sorry enough. He really thought the car had been checked enough to be totally solid but something has clearly gone wrong.

10.20pm: Craig is done and he gestures to us to come and join him in the cab. Finally we're getting out of the weather and into a vehicle again. Our feet are almost numb. We've been standing here in the cold, wind and rain for almost two hours. He tells us the clutch has burnt out and that only a garage job will do.

10.30pm: A short drive during which he asks about our story and soon can't believe what he's hearing. Then we're at the garage where he gets out and prepares to leave the car to be picked up in the morning. While he's doing that we call hotels. The first one is full. Oh dear. Not good. The second asks why we want a hotel because we're still in Covid times and you can't just go and book a hotel apparently. It has to be some kind of emergency. I tell them what's happened as briefly as I can and they relent. Yes of course we can have a room for the night. Oh wow. Now I call Paul who lives in Warrington, just a short drive from Liverpool. I tell him our story to stunned silence and then see if he fancies coming to meet us somewhere tomorrow, and in doing so, meet Maja properly for the first time. He's well up for that, although he does sound a note of caution that we shouldn't expect the car to be fixed tomorrow. Not really what I want to hear because we kind of need it tomorrow, but he does have a hell of a lot more experience of cars and repairs and garages than I do. I decide to re-engage the denial dial and concentrate on the real outcome of this call which is that bizarrely, we now have plans in Liverpool for tomorrow. I finish that call as Craig comes back and we're able to tell him we have a hotel to go to. Before setting off to drive us there he gives us the number of the garage he's just dropped the car off at and tells us to call the mechanic at 8:30 in the morning. Then it's off to the hotel where we gratefully check in. Despite the uncertainty still ahead of us, we're extremely relieved to be in a warm safe place with clean dry sheets and a shower. Will the car even be fixed tomorrow? We have no idea. We have no idea about anything. But somehow, feeling calm and even joyful - how? - we settle in for the most wonderful night's sleep.

Maja:

Of course we have to change the room once because the water doesn't heat up, but this is the most lovely hotel stay of my whole life. Nothing in this trip has turned out OK up to now, so a little inconvenience like that is even easily forgettable. I want nothing more than to rest. I am worried and scared about what is going to happen in the future. We have nowhere to go, but we're desperate to get there. As we manage to settle in and finish our showers, I'm just so happy to be warm and cosy under the white fluffy hotel duvet. I feel proud that we managed to get here. I've done everything I can. Let's just hope things get figured out tomorrow. Good night.

Day 83
Thursday May 13

Maja:

I'm waking up in the lovely white sheets of a hotel room. The bed is soft and warm and the adventures of yesterday seem unbelievably far away. I don't wanna wake up. I sneak my hand out from under the covers to grab my phone and check my emails to see if there's any news from yesterday. Maybe someone's gotten back to us regarding a house or something. Who knows? No. No house stuff. But the green card email is there. I must have gotten it in record time because I see now that they managed to deliver it to me by half three yesterday. That's speedy. Now we can ask the hotel reception to print it and that's out of the way. Look at that. One problem solved before even leaving the comfort of this lovely, temporary bed.

Mark:

On our first 13th of the month together, which was March, we almost killed a cat. On the 13th of the next month Maja broke her ankle, throwing all our plans into chaos. I wonder what will happen on this one. Surely we're due a good one, if for no other reason than to balance out yesterday which damn well felt like a 13th.

We're up at 8am and at 8:30, just like Craig said, we call the mechanic. He goes against all Paul's pessimism and promises they will have the car ready today. We'll see, but right now I'm happy to take his word for it. We chill around for a bit, call a few house prospects but get either no answer or no luck, then at 12 we have to check out. In the meantime I call Paul and he says he'll be here sometime around 4pm.

So at 12, all packed, we leave the hotel and find ourselves out on the street. We're in a pleasant enough seaside area called New Brighton but today is not a day for outings in the sun. It's raining and a little bit chilly. And we're out in this and homeless. And with Covid restrictions still in place, we can't even go inside anywhere to warm up. Not a library, not a cafe, not even a bar. Bars are open, but for outside table service only. So we do the only thing one can do in such a situation. We go to the seaside promenade shops and get donuts. The kind that are made right there as you order them and then covered in sugar. They really are quite wonderful and we go and find a bench on a covered bandstand and settle down with our hot sugary paper bag.

Maja:

'You know what Mark? It feels a little bit easier now.' I say biting into a doughnut, enjoying the sugar around my lips, the slight heat of the dough and the salty wind in my hair. 'Why?' He asks. 'Well, we're on our way now. We've started.'

Mark:

After this we call Cris. Last night, once he'd decided to believe us, and once he'd got over the shock, he offered to pay for the repair of the clutch. We don't mention the cost of the call-out, or the cost of the hotel. It's a well meaning, genuine gesture and I know he's horrified and thought he'd done everything he could to prevent anything bad happening. A clutch repair is no small financial thing so yes, we'll be grateful to accept a reimbursement for that alone.

Well, we're on the seaside, so we might as well go for a seaside walk. There is an interesting looking fort type building and we think we might go and have a look at that, but it's closed. Of course it is. So we take a casual walk along the seaside edge and pretend it's not raining. During this we try a few more house calls. Nope. Nothing.

We reach the end of the promenade and we've come to one of those newly built shopping arcade areas. The ones with a cinema and bowling and stuff. My phone rings. It's Adrian, the guy who has the house Maja emailed about late Tuesday night. The one she apologised to me about yesterday morning because we thought it looked really bad. He says he's had a few viewings but he likes the short story we presented of ourselves in our email to him. We now get into a bit of a chat as I tell him a little of what's happened, and a few encouragingly sympathetic sounds and words come back. This is a rare phone call in this whole house saga where I'm actually getting into an amiable conversation. I go for it now and say that our ferry leaves at 10 tonight. We'll be in Northern Ireland around six tomorrow morning and can be at the house sometime late morning. Basically, however long it takes to drive there. I promise we will absolutely be there. Is he willing to give us a guarantee right now that the house is ours if we turn up as promised? He mulls this over and I almost break the phone from holding onto it so tightly in suspense. Maja can't hear the other side of the conversation, but she definitely has the gist of it. She's also looking at me in the highest of anticipations. Could this really be it? The silence seems to go on forever and I don't want to break it and break this guy's thoughts. I just have to wait to see what comes back. His thinking done and he replies. Yes. Yes I can do that. See you at 12 more or less. Oh thankyou thankyou. Thankyou very very much. I hang up and me and Maja hug tightly but not yet in full celebration. But finally, finally, we actually have a destination. And hope. Realistic hope.

Almost as soon as I hang up, Paul calls. He couldn't have timed it more perfectly. He's ten minutes away so we leave now to the pub where we said we'd meet; on our little walk around earlier we checked out the bars in the area so have our location all staked out. We tell him what it is and make our way there.

The three of us all arrive at pretty much the same time and just manage to get the last table under the awning. Yep, it's still raining. Him and Maja have a big hello then we sit down and have lunch while Paul hears a little more about how we got here, and the big news hot off the press of our last phone call just a few minutes ago, not that anyone's completely relaxing just yet.

Maja:

I am very glad to get to meet Paul in real life for the first time. He is one of Mark's dearest friends, and it joys me to the core to be introduced as his girlfriend. Well we spoke a little on the phone before, but you catch my drift, right? Paul is quite tall, with a good sense of fashion and I'd describe him as charming. He definitely knows have to lead a conversation, and he makes both me and Mark feel a little bit better, a day like today. I'm glad he could make it here today, and I relax into listening to the boys' banter about everything. It feels safer having someone we know around, if only for a little while.

Mark:

While we're here, we have a look at the map and think about where we want to cross into the Republic from Northern Ireland. There's no hard border but we still want to avoid any stops from anyone. We just don't want to flaunt that we're trying to move there, especially given the fact we don't have an actual address to give, which we know is one of the requirements when entering a country during these Covid times. Despite the promising phone call, we are still homeless. So we don't want to cross the border at the first opportunity, instead we plot a route across Northern Ireland, planning to plunge south deeper into the country.

Final leg planned and we continue our joyous hang and catchup until we become aware it's painfully close to 5pm. That's what time the garage closes and they still haven't called. I have been in touch sporadically but no real news. Then at 4.30 my phone rings and it's the mechanic. The car is ready. Wow. Guys, we have to leave. Like, right now. We hastily finish our teas and cokes and Paul drives us to the garage where the mechanics lead us to the newly repaired car. As we're doing this, one of them comes out with the broken clutch that was the cause of all our problems yesterday. 'How far did you say you got on this?'

he asks. 'A hundred and fifty miles give or take. About two and a half hours.' Small gasps of wonder and appreciation break out from the mechanics all around us. I'm almost surprised they don't break out in applause for Maja's feat of determination and concentration. 'It doesn't seem possible,' one of them says. Yes, we had a massive rev count somewhere in the detour that started all this, but they are emphatic in pointing out that this clutch was already worn out to oblivion. 'No way this happened in one incident,' one of them says. 'This is clear wear over a long period of time. Basically, you guys had no chance.' Wow. We also now discover that even if we'd made it to the ferry, the car would have just broken down right there in the queue with all the stopping and starting required. We were never going to get on that ferry. So really, just as well it stopped when it did is their conclusion.

We get in the car now and Maja has a quick go at driving it. She's almost overcome with joy at how different the clutch feels. 'It's like driving a brand new car,' she declares. 'Thankyou thankyou thankyou.' While she's speaking to the guys and they're still in wonder at her incredible feat of driving, the payment gets processed and we're ready to be on our way with one last thankyou. As our two car procession leaves the forecourt, they close and lock the gates behind us, while happily waving us off, their day having ended on such a positive note. Wow. We really did just make it in time. There's still another few hours till we have to be at the dock, so we stop off for another cup of tea or two at a lovely countryside looking bar with a decent sized garden.

About 7pm we say our goodbyes to Paul and head off to the dock.

Maja:

'This car really does feel like a new car.' I say again as I start it up. We then wave bye to Paul as I drive down the road. Once we're in the car queue to the ferry I realise something quite big. Even if we'd somehow made it all the way here yesterday, it would have been impossible to get through this part with the broken clutch. All that stopping and starting as a queue inches forward. Simply wouldn't have been able to do it at all. So as it is, we really lucked out having it properly break before reaching the ferry.

As I'm thinking all this, I engage the clutch again as our turn arrives to enter the ship. We're really leaving England now. We're not going back. Not really. This is it. I have no idea where we're going but we're going now.

Mark:

Once on board, Maja takes charge of finding us a spot for the night and settles on a lovely sofa type thing against a wall facing the front. This is as good as it gets, she says. Yep. It's very comfortable and will definitely do.

On February 26, day seven, we each made a list of the things we would have to accomplish just in order to be able to be together: 'As an entire list, it's impossible. Just impossible,' I wrote at the time. 'There's no other word for it. We are totally deluding ourselves if we think we're going to get that lot ticked off and somehow sail into the sunset.'

And now, here we are on day 83, Thursday May 13, 2021.

It's still daylight when we find our little area and settle down with something of a spark of hope. That hope, of actually having a house to go to, of having a home to go to, lies with a man we have never met, and with whom we have no written agreement. We are leaping into the wide blue yonder with nothing to land our feet on. But when we get to where we're going, we believe we'll find something there. When we do get to that house, and if Adrian does keep his word to us, it will mean that after everything we've faced up to, including last night's actual breakdown, we will have ticked off all the impossibles on the impossible list that were needed to get to where we're headed right now.

With rising feelings of almost overwhelming relief, tinged with a bit of realistic caution, we settle down on our sofa and gaze out of the window at the slowly moving city skyline. As the ship leaves the dock, we are literally sailing into the sunset.

MUSIC, LOVE AND IMPOSSIBILITIES